Early praise for *Programming WebRTC*

Programming WebRTC is an exceptional book that teaches WebRTC theory through practical application of the specification. Through an iterative approach to implementing a WebRTC application, *Programming WebRTC* somehow makes an extremely difficult and nuanced topic approachable and easy to understand. It is a must-read book on the topic.

➤ **Stephen Watzman**
Software Engineer

Karl has a passion for WebRTC that shows in this book, and combining that with his experience as an educator and a technologist, he's crafted a book that is very accessible and informative. WebRTC development has a lot of nuances, but Karl approaches the topic in a way that is both reader-friendly and technically comprehensive. I highly recommend it to anyone new to WebRTC!

➤ **Arin Sime**
CEO/Founder, WebRTC.ventures

Dr. Karl Stolley, a developer, technical author, and prominent WebRTC expert, has consistently addressed the field's challenges and advancements in conferences, including the IIT RTC, and other academic settings. His insights highlight the dynamic nature of WebRTC implementations, yet underscore their current robustness through practical examples often employed in his teaching.

➤ **Alberto Gonzalez Trastoy**
Software Consultant and CTO, WebRTC.ventures

This book expertly blends technical depth with humor, making WebRTC accessible. Even complex topics like signaling channels are tackled with wit, reminding us that a well-designed interface beats the "Imagine this doesn't look like garbage" approach any day.

➤ **Paul Freiberger**
co-author, *Fire in the Valley*

Programming WebRTC

Build Real-Time Streaming Applications for the Web

Karl Stolley

The Pragmatic Bookshelf

Dallas, Texas

For our complete catalog of hands-on, practical, and Pragmatic content for software developers, please visit *https://pragprog.com*.

Contact *support@pragprog.com* for sales, volume licensing, and support.

For international rights, please contact *rights@pragprog.com*.

The team that produced this book includes:

Publisher:	Dave Thomas
COO:	Janet Furlow
Executive Editor:	Susannah Davidson
Development Editor:	Michael Swaine
Copy Editor:	Vanya Wryter
Indexing:	Potomac Indexing, LLC
Layout:	Gilson Graphics

ISBN-13: 978-1-68050-903-8
Book version: P1.0—July 2024

Contents

Acknowledgments

I wrote this book over the span of two very different careers and three jobs, with a global pandemic thrown in for good measure. Screenshots found throughout the book document my various hair lengths and unkempt beard for posterity.

Thank you to my past and current employers, supervisors, and coworkers who in ways big and small graciously accommodated and supported my work on this: Ray Trygstad, Nina Kuruvilla & Kwindla Kramer, and Alya Abbott & Tim Abbott.

Thank you to the students in my WebRTC classes who read and worked through the earliest iterations of this book, providing useful feedback that shaped what this work would ultimately become: Hareem Akram, Jon Andoni Baranda, Yelitza Castro, Chia-Chi Chang, Julaam J. Diop, Michael P. Kaczowka, David Singer, Rida Tariq, and Naveed Zahid.

Thank you to my professional colleagues and friends who offered encouragement, interest, and support for this project: Nancy DeJoy, Molly Holzschlag, Carrie Malone, Jayne Mast, Kate McLaughlin, Adria Neapolitan, Brian Okken, Arin Sime, Alberto Gonzalez Trastoy, and Brian Watts.

Thank you to my technical reviewers: Martin Deen, Tsahi Levent-Levi, and Kimberlee Johnson. Additional thanks to Dasha Day Hisholer for also reviewing this work while it was struggling to become a proposal. Special thanks to Aman Agrawal for his careful review of the completed book. I am solely to blame for any errors and shortcomings that remain.

Thank you to the team at or closely orbiting Pragmatic Programmers: Tammy Coron, Tim Mitra, Erica Sadun, and especially Margaret Eldridge who, among other things, shepherded this work in its proposal form to a head-spinningly quick acceptance.

A special thank you to my editor, Michael Swaine, for his encouragement, bone-dry wit, and saint-like patience in helping me see this book through to completion. Working with him was the best writing experience of my career.

And the deepest thank you to my family: to my dog, Hank, for his countless hours of unflagging dog assistance and posing for screenshots in front of a laptop. And to Amy, my incredible wife of almost 20 years, for her patience, support, and boundless love: you are the very best one.

Preface

WebRTC—or Web Real-Time Communication—is a standardized API exposed in all modern web browsers. The World Wide Web Consortium accepted the WebRTC specification as a full recommendation after a long decade of development.[1] Couple a complete, stable specification with browser support for WebRTC ranging from rock-solid to serviceable, and you find yourself in a perfect environment for developing and deploying real-time web applications in the browser.

Like any Web API, WebRTC doesn't enjoy a perfectly spec-aligned implementation in any browser. But this book will start you on your journey to developing real-time streaming applications, all according to the certainty of a stable specification. You'll also learn to write elegant, backward-compatible code to get your WebRTC apps working across the widest possible range of recent and modern browsers. Desktop and mobile devices, too. Support for WebRTC is everywhere.

Your WebRTC Journey

You'll start your journey by getting straight to work on building a basic WebRTC application to support peer-to-peer video calling. Chapter by chapter, you'll refine that app and its core logic to then spin up additional WebRTC-powered apps that will have your users sharing all manner of data with one another, all in real time.

This book treats WebRTC as a part of the Web Platform. No third-party libraries or heavy downloads are required for you to make your way through this book, or for your users to use the WebRTC apps you build: you'll be writing and strengthening your knowledge of modern HTML, CSS, and JavaScript to get the most out of browser-native WebRTC APIs.

---

1. https://www.w3.org/TR/webrtc/

From the outside, WebRTC is pretty daunting. Okay, really daunting. I'm proud of you just for peeking inside this book. But don't put it down just because WebRTC will challenge you and twist your brain around in some profound ways. That's both expected and totally okay. It means you're on the path. We'll walk it together. Things look better and more manageable from the inside.

This book will get you on the path to where you want to go with WebRTC right away. You won't find any throwaway code or opaque, puzzling examples here. We're going to be developing real WebRTC applications together from the outset. And it will be from those real, functioning applications that we will tease out how WebRTC works. By the end of your journey, you will have all the foundational skills and knowledge you need to build your own wildly imaginative real-time applications. And because work on the WebRTC specification continues, you will also learn how to stay on top of the latest changes and discussions.

Who Should Read This Book?

This book is aimed at intermediate and advanced web designers and developers looking to explore and implement real-time communication features in new or existing web applications.

Whether you consider yourself a designer or a developer, WebRTC is one of those rare Web APIs where design and development converge head on: not just conceptually, but in the actual code you'll be writing. WebRTC is a front-end technology that requires only the teeniest, tiniest server-side component, which I have provided for you in the codebase that accompanies this book. Almost all of your work will be run and rendered directly in the browser.

You should have at least some knowledge of JavaScript, along with HTML and CSS. I'll do my best to fill in any gaps that might arise for you and point out additional books and resources that you might find useful. You'll find yourself working with other Web APIs in this book—not just WebRTC. Many of those will equip you with added knowledge to enhance your work on all kinds of web applications, whether or not they include a real-time component.

What's Covered (And What's Not)

This book covers WebRTC's APIs as natively implemented in recent and modern web browsers. You'll be working with those APIs directly in vanilla JavaScript to build your knowledge and command of WebRTC independent of any third-party libraries. The promise of WebRTC has always been to provide real-time communication right in the browser without requiring users to download special plugins or add-ons. Your users' browsers already have everything needed to power your real-time app. All you have to do is build it!

But to build a stunningly accessible and usable real-time application requires more than just a strong JavaScript foundation. It is an all-too-common mistake to think of WebRTC as just another conduit for media streams and application data. Because of its real-time component, WebRTC knits together two or more remote interfaces where real, live users are interacting and cooperating with one another. Building a WebRTC app without thinking carefully about the user interface would be like building a bicycle without the seat and handlebars. Ouch, right? So don't be surprised to spend some time—perhaps more than you'd expect—working with HTML and CSS, too.

You will be doing WebRTC development within the friendly confines of your local network for most of the book, but a chapter at the end will walk you through the necessary requirements and steps for deploying your real-time applications to the web, and testing them out.

So what's not covered? In a phrase, this book does not cover issues of scale or millisecond-obsessed WebRTC optimization. While there are a growing number of server-, platform-, and system-based implementations of WebRTC, as well as numerous WebRTC-based communication platforms as a service (CPaaS), those are all beyond the scope of this book. That means you won't find coverage here of scaling apps up to handle dozens or thousands of concurrent users supported by server-side technologies like selective forwarding units (SFUs) or multi-conference units (MCUs). Although you will work with a small server that provides a signaling channel, that is the extent of the server-side content in this book.

And while you'll learn about some fundamentals of streaming-media CODECs and optimization, this book does not go deep on those topics. Nor does it encourage session description protocol (SDP) "munging" to coerce browsers to use a particular CODEC, or fiddling with RTCRtpTransceiver objects. Native browser code for those matters is better tuned and tested than app-based adjustments likely ever will be.

However, the core principles of WebRTC that we'll look at in depth—working with a signaling channel, establishing peer connections, adding and managing media streams and data channels—will have you well prepared to tackle WebRTC implementations and third-party services wherever you might encounter them.

How This Book Is Organized

This book is organized in a set of sequential chapters. It's meant to be read more or less front to back. If that feels overly prescriptive and stifling, or if you've just got a rebellious streak that you like to take out on tech books, try anyway to make it through at least the first four chapters before you jump around to the later ones whose topics most interest you.

In Chapter 1, you'll learn how to set up a development environment that will play nicely with WebRTC. You'll also learn how to get the most out of the starter and example code that accompanies the book.

With your development environment set up and tested out, Chapter 2 dives right into the only necessary server component of WebRTC apps: a signaling channel. As part of working with the signaling channel, you'll start to build the basic interface of your first WebRTC app, which provides peer-to-peer video calls.

Chapter 3 is where you'll really hit your stride working directly with WebRTC's APIs, all of which orbit around the RTCPeerConnection interface. By the end of this chapter, you'll be streaming video between two connected peers which—to start—will be two browser windows on your desktop.

Streaming real-time user video and audio is WebRTC's most famous feature. But that's not its only feature. Over the course of Chapter 4 and Chapter 5, you'll go from streaming basic data to streaming more complex data— including JSON as well as images and other binary files. WebRTC provides a powerful and flexible low-level interface for streaming arbitrary application data between two peers, all in real time. You'll learn to command that interface, and abstract away subtle differences found in browsers with incomplete WebRTC implementations. You'll even bring what you learn full circle by safely implementing user audio to complete the silent streaming video you'll work with at first.

Buckle your seatbelt when you get to Chapter 6. Connecting two peers is one thing. But how about connecting three or more peers? Chapter 6 will have you establishing WebRTC calls using a mesh-network topography to enable multiple peers to join the same call simultaneously. You'll also experience the theoretical and practical upper limits on the number of peers who can join a call on a mesh network, depending on what your app does and the amount of bandwidth and processing power it consumes.

In Chapter 7, you'll work more in depth with the MediaDevices interface on the Media Capture and Streams API to do things like help users determine what mics and cameras they have available, and handle edge cases in your logic when either there are no devices available, or users deny permission to access them. You'll learn to do some minor media-stream optimization, too, with the aid of the built-in, real-time statistics that WebRTC implementations provide in the browser.

Closing out the body of the book, in Chapter 8, you'll learn how to deploy WebRTC applications to production. You'll find a concrete deployment example, but you'll also learn how to adjust that example to suit your own needs and preferences.

And finally, you will find an appendix at the end of the book that will show you the necessary fixes for making your WebRTC applications work with legacy browsers that don't support the WebRTC APIs necessary for perfect negotiation.

Online Resources

You can download the source code for studying and working alongside the examples in the book from pragprog.com.[2] If you spot an error or even just come across something that is blocking your path forward in the book, consider this my personal invitation to you to join and post to the book's forum on DevTalk.[3]

If you would like to contact me directly, I am available on Mastodon at @stolley@hachyderm.io.[4] I also blog about WebRTC and other web topics at https://stolley.dev/

All right. Enough with the formalities that we classy preface readers enjoy while thoughtfully adjusting our monocles from the comfort of a high-back leather chair. Let's pop out the monocle, pull open a laptop, and get down to it: it's time to set up a development environment that will be your trusty companion on your exciting, monocle-free journey with WebRTC.

---

2. https://pragprog.com/titles/ksrtc/
3. https://devtalk.com/books/programming-webrtc/errata
4. https://hachyderm.io/@stolley

CHAPTER 1

Preparing a WebRTC Development Environment

Exciting new technologies often require developers to level up the sophistication of their development environments. WebRTC is no exception. Almost everything you'll be doing with WebRTC happens in and between browsers. While you'll be writing HTML, CSS, and JavaScript just as you would for any other web application, there are some important things to set up to smooth your way through the rest of the book and your work building real-time web applications.

In this chapter, you'll install Node.js if you haven't already. You'll also learn where to get yourself a copy of the code that accompanies this book, and you'll take a brief tour of the code's organization so you can find what you need, when you need it. You'll then generate and make use of your own self-signed certificates for serving HTTPS in development. HTTPS is necessary to fully and reliably access many newfangled, highfalutin Web APIs—including WebRTC, even in development.

You'll choose a WebRTC-ready development browser (spoiler: Chrome or Firefox), fire up the server that's packed in with the book's code to serve your in-progress work or the completed examples, and heroically machete your way through the dire security warnings that your browser will throw at you over your self-signed certificates.

It'll be a little bit of work, but once you've set this all up for yourself, you shouldn't have to think about any of it again.

All of the setup here should work without much fuss or drama on Unix-like operating systems, including macOS.

Install Windows Subsystem for Linux

 If you're developing on Windows, you'll need to install and use Windows Subsystem for Linux.[1]

Installing Node.js

The small server I've written to support your local WebRTC development relies on Node.js, a wildly popular JavaScript runtime that you might already be familiar with and have installed. Let's figure out if you've got a copy of Node.js already, and install one if you don't.

If you're not sure if you have Node.js, run which node on your command line. You'll see output showing the path to your Node.js installation, if you have one (now might be a good time to update it, if you haven't in a while).

If you see no output or know for a fact you aren't running Node.js yet, no problem: there are a few different ways to install it. You can find, download, and run a Node.js installer for your operating system of choice from nodejs.org.[2] Alternatively, if your operating system has a package manager available, such Homebrew for MacOS[3] or your native package manager for Linux, you can install Node.js that way.

However you opt to install Node.js, it's generally a good idea to be running the latest LTS version.[4]

As a sanity check, once you've installed Node.js, you can run which node and which npm on your command line, which should report the locations where Node.js and its own package manager, npm, were installed. That's simply confirmation that you've successfully installed Node.js, and also that your command line knows where to find it.

Downloading the Supporting Code and Installing Dependencies

Once you've set up Node.js, you should download the code for this book from pragprog.com.[5] Once you've downloaded and decompressed the ZIP file,[6] move

---

1.   https://learn.microsoft.com/en-us/windows/wsl/install
2.   https://nodejs.org/en/download/
3.   https://brew.sh/
4.   https://nodejs.org/en/about/previous-releases
5.   https://pragprog.com/titles/ksrtc/programming-webrtc/
6.   https://media.pragprog.com/titles/ksrtc/code/ksrtc-code.zip

the unzipped code/ directory somewhere you can conveniently access from the command line. You might also want to rename the directory to something more recognizable than code/.

Having done that, use your command line to navigate to the directory you've set up. Once you're there, you need to install the dependencies for the server that you'll rely on as you work through the book. Run this command:

```
$ npm install
```

A bunch of output will fill the terminal screen, but installation should only take a few minutes at most. Probably less.

If you see warnings about deprecated packages, you can try running npm audit fix or the more aggressive npm audit fix --force to try and resolve matters. But for doing WebRTC development, it's okay to ignore such warnings altogether.

Finding Your Way Around the Code Directory

I've prepared the book's accompanying code to include the examples that I've written and a separate starter directory for you to follow along in the book and experiment on your own.

Here is a brief look at what you'll find in the code directory and where:

- The book's completed examples are each in their own subdirectory under demos/. You'll see references to those files throughout the book.

- There is a www/ directory for you to work in as you make your journey through the book. If you get stuck, you can always compare your work against the files in the demos/ directory. Don't forget to mutter and curse about me under your breath, which you'll find therapeutic.

As you work through the book, you'll often find yourself in those two directories. But the accompanying code includes some additional files and directories that you might be curious about:

- The deploy/ directory contains a standalone WebRTC app that you'll use in Chapter 8, Deploying WebRTC Apps to Production, on page 197.

- The server.js file contains a basic web server using the ExpressJS framework. This file includes the basic signaling channels that are discussed later in the book.

- The scripts/ directory contains a server startup script, start-server, which (surprise!) starts the server, but you can simply run npm start on your command line to fire up the server.

- For further study and your future experiments, you will find starter scripts for establishing peer connections in the _starter/ directory. p2p.js contains the logic necessary to establish a connection between two peers, and multi.js is enhanced with logic to establish a connection among three or more peers.

Serving HTTPS in Development

In order to develop WebRTC applications, it's necessary to configure your development environment to serve HTTPS. Browsers disallow access to a number of APIs, including those that grant access to your microphone and camera, unless you're serving HTTPS—even in development.

To serve HTTPS in development, you'll need to create and use your own self-signed certificates. It doesn't take too much work to generate self-signed certificates, but you can still impress your friends that you managed to serve HTTPS over localhost.

Although self-signed certificates are not suited for use on the open web, they are perfectly acceptable for testing within the familiar comfort of your local network. The browsers you test your work on will nevertheless protest mightily, and they'll do their best to scare you away from using self-signed certificates. And when that doesn't work, they'll try to make you feel bad about yourself. But don't worry, and don't feel bad: we'll diffuse their unwarranted scare-and-shame tactics at the end of this chapter.

Generating Self-Signed Certificates

You'll need access to openssl to generate your own certificate and key files on your operating system. MacOS and virtually all Unix-like operating systems and Linux distributions ship with openssl. If you're a Windows user, you might need to install openssl yourself. The OpenSSL wiki maintains a list of download-able binaries.[7] If you run Git Bash on Windows,[8] it already includes openssl.exe, which you can also use.

Before you generate the certificate files, you'll need to create an easy-to-remember place for them to live. I recommend creating a Certs directory in your home directory:

```
$ mkdir ~/Certs
```

---

7. https://wiki.openssl.org/index.php/Binaries
8. https://gitforwindows.org/

The book's supporting code you downloaded includes a script you can run to generate your certificate files. You'll need to change into the directory where you're storing the book's code in order to do this. The base command is npm run ssl-keys, and it needs two arguments: the path to the directory you created (keydir) and the number of days before your self-signed certificates expire (numdays).

For example, to create self-signed certificate files in ~/Certs that won't expire for about five years (1825 days), you'd run this command in the book's code directory:

```
$ npm run ssl-keys --keydir="$HOME/Certs" --numdays=1825
```

Whatever values you choose, use the $HOME variable instead of the tilde, ~, and ensure there are no spaces around your equals signs.

If you're the suspicious type, you can examine the ssl-keys script in the package.json file before you run it. It's based on a command suggested by Let's Encrypt,[9] which is ordinarily in the business of offering free certificates that can be used on world-facing websites. If you'd prefer, you can head over to Let's Encrypt's original post[10] and copy from there into your command line instead of using the npm script. You'll need to change into your certificates directory before running the Let's Encrypt command to generate the certificate and key files. By default, openssl creates certificates that expire in one year. If you want to go longer than that without having to generate new ones, add -days followed by some number of days to the Let's Encrypt script, like -days 1825 to create five-year certificates.

However you generate your keys, once you hit Return, it will only take a moment to generate the key and certificate files in the directory you've chosen, like ~/Certs. Creating those files is an important first step to serving HTTPS. But you'll also need to make sure that any scripts and servers you run can find your certificate files with as little fuss as possible. Let's set that up next.

Storing the Certificate File Locations in Environment Variables

You'll need to export two environment variables from your command line's startup scripts. Those variables will point to the location of your self-signed certificate files. Your startup scripts will be in a file in your home directory called .bashrc or .bash_profile, if you're a bash user, .zshrc if you're a zsh user, or possibly even a file called .profile.

---

9.   https://letsencrypt.org/
10. https://letsencrypt.org/docs/certificates-for-localhost/

Whichever startup file your command line uses, open it in your favorite text editor, and add the following lines:

```
# SSL Keys
export LOCALHOST_SSL_CERT="$HOME/Certs/localhost.crt"
export LOCALHOST_SSL_KEY="$HOME/Certs/localhost.key"
```

Be sure not to put any spaces around the equals signs, =. And don't forget to adjust the path if you've saved your keys somewhere different from ~/Certs or named them something other than localhost.crt and localhost.key. Once you've saved your startup file, reload it in your terminal using the source command. You'll need to reference the name of the file your command line uses. In this example, the file is called .zshrc:

```
$ source ~/.zshrc
```

As a quick sanity check, you can confirm that your command line knows about these variables by using echo to output their values. To do this, prefix the variable names with a dollar sign:

```
$ echo $LOCALHOST_SSL_CERT
```

If everything has gone according to plan, you'll see the certificate location you specified output by your command-line shell for LOCALHOST_SSL_CERT. On MacOS, for example, that will look something like /Users/username/Certs/localhost.crt. You can check the LOCALHOST_SSL_KEY value the same way, if you'd like.

Choosing a Development Browser

You'll have the best possible development experience running the latest version of either Chrome or Firefox. I personally prefer Firefox Developer Edition,[11] but the choice is yours.

Whichever browser you choose, you'll need to open its developer console and disable caching, so you always load the latest version of your CSS and Java-Script as you work. Firefox and Chrome both have the Disable Cache option under the Network tab of the developer pane. If you're like me, you'll opt to pop the developer console into its own window to maximize your available screen space. You'll be building responsive interfaces that take advantage of the entire viewport. And you know the kinds of divas interfaces can be: steal their spotlight in any way and they'll make your life miserable and spread salacious rumors about you to their friends.

---

11. https://www.mozilla.org/en-US/firefox/developer/

What About Safari?

Safari has historically lagged in its WebRTC implementation, but as of April 2022's release of Safari 15.4, it is also up to snuff. If you opt to use Safari as your development browser, or if you want to test out your work on an iPhone or iPad, please be sure you're running at least Safari 15.4.

Incomplete WebRTC implementations in older versions of Safari and other browsers (Firefox prior to version 80, and Chrome prior to version 75) will give you a series of raging headaches. Consult Appendix 1, Connection Negotiation in Legacy Browsers, on page 225 to learn about the fallbacks you'll need to add to your code for the sake of older browsers, for as long as they remain in use (if history is a guide, that will be awhile).

Starting and Stopping the Server

I've tried to make it as painless as possible for you to serve both your own work and the completed demos over localhost. To serve your own files as you work on them, run npm run start or simply npm start on the command line. Your files are more important, so they get the more convenient commands.

Remember to Install Dependencies

 If you haven't yet run npm install, be sure to do so before starting the server, or if you encounter errors about missing modules.

To serve the book's completed examples, you'll need to run the slightly more verbose command npm run start:demos. No space on either side of the colon.

Whenever you start the server, you'll see output like this in your terminal window:

```
signaling-server:   ** Serving from the www/ directory. **
signaling-server:
signaling-server:   App available in your browser at:
signaling-server:
signaling-server:     -> https://127.0.0.1:3000/
signaling-server:     -> https://192.168.1.6:3000/
signaling-server:
signaling-server:   Hold CTRL + C to stop the server.
signaling-server:
signaling-server:   +0ms
```

Each time you start the server, it will tell you which directory you're currently serving from (again: www/ with your work, demos/ with the completed examples) and at least two addresses for reaching the server from your development browser of choice. Whenever you need to stop the server, hold down CTRL + C.

The first time you start the server, your operating system might notify you about a firewall restriction of some kind. Because you'll eventually be hitting this server from other devices connected to your local network, instruct your OS to allow incoming connections.

With the server still running, you can open your browser to https://localhost:3000/. Of course localhost is a shortcut for 127.0.0.1, which you can also use if you get a thrill out of typing numbers and dots: https://127.0.0.1:3000/. Don't worry for now about the second IP address you see. It will almost certainly be different from 192.168.1.6, but eventually you will be able to use whatever that second address is to test your app using other devices connected to your local network.

One big gotcha: you absolutely *must* type out the full https:// protocol portion of these URLs. If you leave the protocol off, your browser will try to establish a connection over http://. The server isn't actually listening for HTTP, but HTTPS. Your browser doesn't know that, though, so it'll dismissively inform you that it's unable to connect. And you'll lose a whole part of the day tracking down that missing s, which is made even more difficult to spot in browsers that hide the http:// protocol string on HTTP URLs.

Once you enter the exact HTTPS-serving address, you'll immediately hit a snag. Your browser, which demanded that you type out https:// in the address bar, now wants you to know that it has a big problem with your self-signed certificates. Instead of seeing the page the server is serving, you'll get a security warning.

Getting Past Browser Security Warnings

After you point your browser to any of the server's local https:// URLs, the browser viewport will fill with dire warnings, bad omens, and tales of an ancient curse. Firefox Developer Edition, for example, will present the screen on page 9.

On the open web, these security warnings are a good thing. But in development, they're just overly dramatic, pearl-clutching pains in the neck.

The good news is that you'll likely see this warning only the first time you hit your local address, and you will have to take these steps only once, too. To

get Firefox to chillax and let you get on with your work, click the Advanced… button, and then the Accept the Risk and Continue button in the box that appears. On Chrome, you'll likewise click Advanced and then the "Proceed to localhost (unsafe)" link.

Safari makes you jump through a different series of hoops to accept self-signed certificates: when confronted by Safari's warning screen, click on Show Details, then the "visit this website" hyperlink. That's all you have to do on iOS, thankfully. But on MacOS, you'll then be greeted by a popup asking, "Are you sure you want to visit this website on a connection that is not private?" Click "Visit Website" and then you'll see *another* popup: "You are making changes to your Certificate Trust Settings." Click Use Password… and then enter the password you use to log into your Mac.

Once you've gone through those steps, you'll see an overview page I've written for you. On the demos side, the page includes links to each of the demos. On the working side, from www/, you'll see some instructions and encouragement.

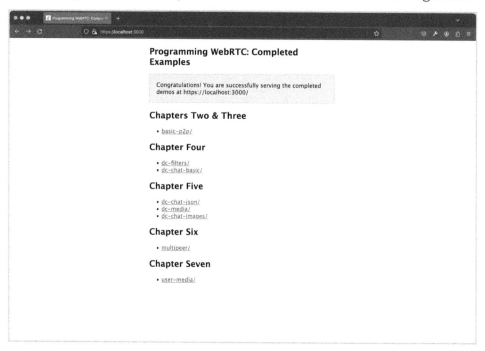

Next Steps

Excellent. Having viewed one or both of those pages over HTTPS in your development browser of choice, you can be confident that you've successfully prepared your WebRTC development environment. You've installed Node.js, and you've located, downloaded, and used the command line to find this book's accompanying source code and install its dependencies. You've also generated your own self-signed certificate files for serving HTTPS in development. And finally, you've convinced your browser, after some haggling over security, to accept your self-signed certificate.

In the next chapter, we're going to get right to work with the server you installed and fired up in this chapter. You'll be working with its signaling-channel component—which we haven't seen yet—while also constructing a user interface for your first WebRTC app. As we'll see, WebRTC meshes tightly with user interfaces. So we will want to make sure the code we write for the interface is as well crafted and expertly engineered as everything we'll be writing alongside WebRTC's browser APIs. Let's get going!

## CHAPTER 2

Working with a Signaling Channel

In this chapter, you're going to build the foundations of a video-calling app that will use WebRTC for connecting two peers who can stream video—and eventually also audio—to each other, in real time.

You'll start by building an interface using semantic HTML and CSS, including a little flexbox for layout. Some of that work will strike you as being very precise and detailed. But the goal is to build a lean, accessible interface that also displays responsively across all types of devices. With the interface built, you'll then do the necessary work to wire it up with JavaScript for handling routine events, like clicks, that happen in the browser. Those will eventually hook into the signaling channel and other WebRTC logic. So it's necessary to build the interface first.

With the interface built, we'll take a look at the peer-to-peer architecture of WebRTC and how it differs from the more familiar client-server web architecture of HTTP and HTTPS.

From there, we'll take a sightseeing tour of a crucial piece of technology for establishing peer connections over WebRTC: a signaling channel, which will take the form of a small server that you've already downloaded with the book's companion code. With a better understanding of the signaling channel in hand, you'll then write some skeletal, foundational code for simultaneously connecting multiple pairs of peers over your app.

Preparing a Basic Peer-to-Peer Interface

Let's begin with a basic process for building something new for the web: establishing a workable UI concept, structuring it in semantic HTML, and styling the HTML with just enough CSS to make it responsive across the full range of web-enabled devices. That will pave the way for much more graceful and efficient work with JavaScript for stitching the app together.

The UI work here is going to be pretty precise, probably way more than what you've come to expect from books on specialized topics in web development. The advantage to engaging at least some front-end design in your development work is that when you're selling some new API or idea to someone—a team lead, a manager, a client—you have something to show that actually looks good and helps to sell the idea a little more effectively than prefacing your work with "Imagine this doesn't look like garbage."

But it's also never too early to consider the obligations we as developers have to end users: front-end development involves precise work on interfaces that real users will have to interact with. Precise UI design is also the cornerstone of accessibility, which is as essential for real-time communication technologies as it is for anything else developed for the web. For that reason, it's nothing less than a professional obligation to keep users in mind when building something explicitly for them—no matter how deep down the rabbit hole the underlying API takes us. With WebRTC, that rabbit hole is deep.

And because the underlying WebRTC API is deep and complex, you'll also see that we're going to spend more than a little bit of time working through some core fundamentals of JavaScript, including code organization and the behavior of callback functions. The purpose of that work is twofold: first, as JavaScript continues to advance as a language, it can be harder to keep all developers on the same page with its newer features, especially as they relate to JavaScript's mainstay features. And second, because of the design of the WebRTC API, I think you'll find that you work more effectively within WebRTC's dizzying number of event-driven methods and callback functions if the connections between them and vanilla JavaScript are made more explicit. That will be especially true if your routine, day-to-day interactions with JavaScript are mediated through a JavaScript framework with a higher-level API than plain old vanilla JavaScript has to offer.

Designing Peer-to-Peer UI Patterns

Before you start to write a line of code for your video-call app, think for a moment about the kinds of interfaces that are common in peer-to-peer apps you've used. Their interfaces are generally modeled on one of two patterns—a caller pattern or a joiner pattern. A caller pattern is asymmetric: certain peer-to-peer apps, like FaceTime or Skype, and even the telephone, depend on one peer calling and the other answering. The FaceTime interface, for example, looks the same for two peers inside and outside of a call. But while a call is being placed, the interface is different for both the caller and answerer. The interfaces return to a symmetric state once the person being called decides either to answer, causing both interfaces to show the call, or to decline (or simply ignore), in which case both interfaces return to their states before the call was placed.

Other peer-to-peer apps, like Google Meet or Zoom, use a symmetric joiner pattern: instead of setting up a call between a caller and an answerer, symmetrically patterned apps treat a call as something that already exists for users to join whenever they're ready. The interface's state depends only on what any one user is doing: preparing to join a call, participating in a call after joining, or leaving the call.

WebRTC-backed interfaces can be constructed using either pattern, caller or joiner. But the joiner pattern simplifies the interface, because there's no need to create a screen to handle an incoming call, or wire up a bunch of buttons to answer or decline. Instead, one button is all that's needed—Join Call—and it's presented to each peer. In the joiner pattern, we don't even have to think in terms of someone calling someone else. From the perspective of the peers on the call, no one cares who joined first. As the designers of the app, we don't have to care, either.

Adding a Header and Button

With a joiner pattern in mind, you can start building the HTML and CSS to structure and style the app. No need to worry about special HTML, CSS, or JavaScript for a caller or an answerer: everyone on the call is a joiner, so everyone gets the same code.

Open the www/basic-p2p/ directory and find its index.html file, which already links to the CSS and JavaScript files you'll use. Start off by writing a basic header that has a first-level heading along with a button element for joining the call. You can write this inside the <main> element you'll find in the HTML file. The button will enable users to both join and leave the call, but you should set it up initially as a join button. When the app first loads, users will need to join the call:

```
demos/basic-p2p/index.html
<main id="interface">
  <header id="header" role="banner">
    <h1>Welcome</h1>
    <button class="join" type="button" id="call-button">Join Call</button>
  </header>
</main>
```

The `type="button"` attribute might look redundant, but it's good practice to include it for any button element without a browser-provided behavior: `<button>` defaults to `type="submit"` for submitting form data, in the absence of an explicit type attribute. But this button is not submitting a form.

The unique ID `call-button` is deliberately generic. It will save a lot of work we would otherwise have to do in JavaScript to swap separate join and leave buttons. The class `join` will work as a nice styling hook in CSS and, later, for JavaScript to determine the state of the button. The button's Join Call text should be an unambiguous cue to users. In a bit, a little JavaScript will change the button's class to `leave` and its text to Leave Call once the Join Call button has been clicked.

Adding Video Elements: Self and Peer

With a basic heading and button in place, the only other HTML this basic app needs is for handling video: one element for a user's own video stream, which we will refer to as *self*, and one element for the remote user's video stream, which we'll refer to as *peer*.

One of the many fun aspects of working with peer-to-peer streaming media is that you get to write some things in your markup that are usually big no-nos. One such thing is setting up multiple video elements to play simultaneously (one for self, one for the peer), with some attributes that might surprise you if you're familiar with the `<video>` element introduced in HTML5. If you're not familiar, that's okay, too. We'll walk through them.

Setting up the Self Video

This is how to set up the video element for the self video, which for convenience takes an ID of `self`:

```
demos/basic-p2p/index.html
<video id="self"
  autoplay
  muted
  playsinline
  poster="img/placeholder.png">
</video>
```

That `<video>` element sets a number of important attributes. Let's briefly explore each one's purpose in the context of live-streaming video.

The autoplay Attribute

Ordinarily the autoplay attribute is frowned upon. Users generally expect control over the playback of video and especially the accompanying audio. Browser makers have helped to enforce user control by disregarding the autoplay attribute until a user has interacted with a page in some way first. But for streaming video, autoplay is strictly necessary: without it, the browser will only show the very first frame of a streaming video. And because users will have to click the Join Call button you built above, they will have interacted with the page before any media begins to stream—all but guaranteeing that the browser will respect the autoplay attribute.

The muted Attribute

In the next chapter on page 37, for same-machine testing purposes, we'll exclude audio from the streaming tracks entirely. But to ensure that future audio-enabled streams don't cause hellacious feedback, the self video takes the muted attribute. That's different from muting your mic so no one else can hear you—a topic we will get to in a later chapter. All this attribute does is disable audio on the self video.

The playsinline Attribute

The final Boolean attribute to include is playsinline. This attribute instructs mobile devices in particular not to launch a full-screen presentation of the video once the stream starts, which is the default behavior in Safari on iOS and other mobile browsers. While full-screen video might sound desirable, it will obscure anything else on the page, including any user-interface components and the self video. With playsinline set, the peer video will play wherever on the page you place it with CSS.

The poster Attribute

And although not strictly necessary, a placeholder image can be referenced from the poster attribute. The image will display until the video stream starts, which is a graceful way to prepare users to expect to see video streams on the page. It's helpful for testing purposes too: without a poster or some explicit dimensions and colors set in CSS, video streams would appear out of apparent nothingness—or not appear at all—if there's something wrong with media permissions or the peer connection that you'll set up in Setting Up the Peer Connection, on page 42.

Setting up the Peer Video

The markup for the peer video is almost identical to the self video, except that it takes an ID of peer and omits the muted attribute:

demos/basic-p2p/index.html

```
<video id="peer"
  autoplay
  playsinline
  poster="img/placeholder.png">
</video>
```

You might have noticed that there is neither an src attribute nor any inner <source> elements for either video. Their omission is intentional. There's no file involved in streaming video. In the next chapter, you'll use JavaScript to set up the streaming source for each video element, using the srcObject property, in the displayStream() function on page 41.

Finally, let's wrap both <video> elements in an <article> element with an id of videos. It should open with a second-level heading to label the streaming videos for accessibility purposes. We'll give the heading a class of preserve-access that we can refer to from the CSS in a moment. Putting it all together, your HTML file should look something like this:

demos/basic-p2p/index.html

```
<main id="interface">
  <header id="header" role="banner">
    <h1>Welcome</h1>
    <button class="join" type="button" id="call-button">Join Call</button>
  </header>
➤  <article id="videos">
➤    <h2 class="preserve-access">Streaming Videos</h2>
    <video id="self"
      autoplay
      muted
      playsinline
      poster="img/placeholder.png">
    </video>
    <video id="peer"
      autoplay
      playsinline
      poster="img/placeholder.png">
    </video>
➤  </article>
</main>
```

That's it: a heading, a button, and two video elements—all wrapped up in a neat package of semantic sectioning elements. Let's style everything up in CSS.

Styling the Core App Elements

With the HTML in place, you can turn your attention to writing some CSS to present a workable interface. I always begin my work with Eric Meyer's Reset CSS.[1] There's no need to replicate that here, but you will see a minified version of it in the starter screen.css file for this app.

It's useful to begin by defining an app's basic typographic properties, usually on the html selector:

demos/basic-p2p/css/screen.css
```
html {
  font-family: "Lucida Grande", Arial, sans-serif;
  font-size: 18px;
  font-weight: bold;
  line-height: 22px;
}
```

That text setting might strike you as a bit large and bulky, especially because these are also meant to be mobile-first styles. But that's deliberate: think about your face's position relative to your screen when you're on a video call. Most of us move back from the screen so that the camera can capture at least our entire heads. And if your head is a prize-winning pumpkin like mine, you might have to move back. With users' eyes further from the screen, it's a more accessible choice to err on the side of an oversized, easily visible UI—especially for controls.

Let's also add some foundational layout styles that set box-sizing to the more intuitive border-box value, and add some padding around the interface and header elements:

demos/basic-p2p/css/screen.css
```
/* Layout */
* {
  box-sizing: border-box;
}
#interface {
  padding: 22px;
}
#header {
  margin-bottom: 11px;
}
#header > h1 {
  margin-bottom: 11px;
}
```

---

1. https://meyerweb.com/eric/tools/css/reset/

Because the "Streaming Videos" heading is meant to help low-vision users navigate the page's structures, let's use an accessible technique to hide the heading from sighted users while keeping it available in the accessibility tree. We will reuse this class on additional elements in later chapters:

demos/basic-p2p/css/screen.css

```
.preserve-access {
  position: absolute;
  left: -20000px;
}
```

Styling the Button Element

The <button> element, the only interactive UI on the page, is generally easier to style than other form elements. You can set up a basic look for it on the button element selector, opening with a bunch of font styles to inherit the look of all text on the page, as well as setting the cursor to display as a pointer:

demos/basic-p2p/css/screen.css

```
button {
  font-family: inherit;
  font-size: inherit;
  font-weight: inherit;
  line-height: inherit;
  cursor: pointer;
  /* Box Styles */
  display: block;
  border: 0;
  border-radius: 3px;
  padding: 11px;
}
```

For better control over the button's place in the layout, it's worth setting it to display as a block. You can also remove the default border that browsers draw, given the button rounded corners with a small border-radius. A little bit of margin and padding—derived from the page's 22px line-height value—provide some room around the text and some margins to offset the element. Nothing fancy. (And don't worry—if your familiarity with responsive design has you feeling a gnawing guilt for using pixel units, you're welcome to make those adjustments yourself. Or give yourself permission to work with pixel units while you're still learning WebRTC.)

The button's HTML currently has only the join class, but you can still set up some very basic colors on both the join and leave classes for the button:

demos/basic-p2p/css/screen.css

```
.join {
  background-color: green;
  color: white;
}
.leave {
  background-color: #CA0;
  color: black;
}
```

Finally, let's set a width on the #call-button selector:

demos/basic-p2p/css/screen.css

```
#call-button {
  width: 143px; /* 6.5 typographic grid lines */
  margin-right: 11px;
}
```

The 143px width value is tailored to comfortably fit the text for Join Call and Leave Call, while also being derived from the page's 22px line height. All the width does is ensure the button won't shift the layout around when the button's text changes from Join Call to Leave Call. That doesn't matter much when the button is on its own line, but as a small responsive touch, let's add a media query to display the contents of the <header id="header"> as flex items, all on the same line:

demos/basic-p2p/css/screen.css

```
@media screen and (min-width: 500px) {
  #header {
    display: flex;
    flex-direction: row-reverse;
    align-items: baseline;
    justify-content: flex-end;
  }
  #header > * {
    flex: 0 0 auto;
  }
  #header > h1 {
    margin-bottom: 0;
  }
}
```

If you're not familiar with flexbox and its properties, what's happening here is the page header is set to display as a flexbox with display: flex. Aligning the flex items—the first-level heading and the button—to the baseline keeps the text of each on the same invisible line.

Then, to move the join button so it sits to the left of the heading, flex-direction: row-reverse flips the order of the header's items, while justify-content: flex-end, on a row-reversed flexbox, will keep the flex items aligned to the *left* of the flexbox.

The child selector #header > * sets the behavior of the flex items (an <h1> and <button>, in this case). The shorthand flex sets the grow and shrink values to zero, meaning that neither element will grow or shrink from its auto width. For the first-level heading, that will be the width of its text. For the button, that will be the 143px value of the width property set on the #call-button selector.

The result is that on viewports 500 pixels and wider, the button and heading sit on the same line as in the figure on page 20. That will reduce how far down the viewport the header pushes the video elements. And speaking of the video elements, let's style them next.

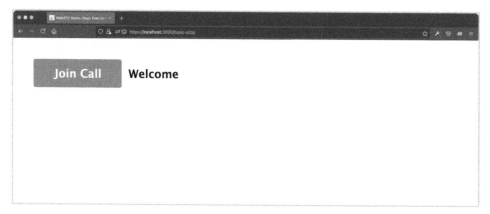

Styling the Video Elements

As embedded content, the <video> element displays inline by default, just like the <img/> tag does. Ethan Marcotte made famous the pairing of display: block and max-width: 100% for responsive images,[2] and we can do the same for videos. Setting the max-width property ensures the video element will be no wider than either its parent element's width or, in the case of this small app, the viewport:

demos/basic-p2p/css/screen.css

```
/* Video Elements */

video {
  background-color: #DDD;
  display: block;
  max-width: 100%;
}
```

_____

2.   https://alistapart.com/article/fluid-images/

You can set the background color on video elements to a very light shade of gray, which will show the exact boundaries of the video elements and work nicely with the transparent smiley face PNG set on the video element's poster attribute.

The peer video can display as is, but a few adjustments to the self video will make it obvious which video is which. That's helpful if you have just a single camera on your computer. The same streaming video image will appear in both video elements when you're testing out your app:

demos/basic-p2p/css/screen.css

```css
#self {
  width: 50%;
  max-width: 320px;
  margin-bottom: 11px;
}
```

That reduces the self video's width to 50 percent, and puts a half line-height of space between it and the peer video that sits below.

With all of that CSS in place, you can reload the page in your browser to see the button, heading, and video placeholders:

Adding Functionality to the Call Button in JavaScript

That's all the structure and styling your app needs. Now it's time to cozy up to JavaScript. We'll start by focusing on the call button's functionality.

The first thing we'll do in the main.js JavaScript file is invoke strict mode. That's as simple as writing strict mode as a string at the top of the file:

```
demos/basic-p2p/js/main.js
'use strict';
```

Invoking strict mode is good practice. Strict mode will often reveal errors and inconsistencies in your JavaScript that the browser would otherwise suppress or ignore. A strict browser turns out to be a real asset when you're trying to debug and track down errors in your JavaScript. If you're interested, you can read more about strict mode at MDN.[3]

Now onto the call button, which we'll handle as a one-off line of JavaScript in the "User Interface Setup" portion of the JavaScript file. You can use the querySelector() method on the document object to select the call button from the HTML. If you've not used querySelector() before, know that it accepts a string containing the same selector syntax that you'd write in CSS:[4]

```
document.querySelector('#call-button');
```

With the #call-button element selected, you can then call the addEventListener() method to respond to click events on the button. Start small and report in the console that the button has been clicked:

```
document.querySelector('#call-button')
  .addEventListener('click', function(event) {
    console.log('Call button clicked!');
  });
```

Reload your page in the browser and open the JavaScript console. You should see "Call button clicked!" appear in the console.

Writing Named Functions as Callbacks

While the querySelector method takes a single argument—the CSS selector #call-button—the addEventListener method takes two required arguments. The first argument is the name of the event, 'click', and the second argument is an *anonymous* callback function, also known as a *listener*. The function is

---

3. https://developer.mozilla.org/en-US/docs/Web/JavaScript/Reference/Strict_mode
4. https://developer.mozilla.org/en-US/docs/Web/API/Document/querySelector

anonymous because it doesn't have a name: the function keyword just defines the function in place. I like callback functions to have names and their own place to live in a JavaScript file. In this case, there is a "User-Interface Functions and Callbacks" area in the main.js file. So the first little improvement is to create a named function and pass its name in as the second argument to addEventListener():

```
/**
 *  User-Interface Setup
 */
document.querySelector('#call-button')
  .addEventListener('click', handleCallButton);

/**
 * User-Interface Functions and Callbacks
 */
function handleCallButton(event) {
  console.log('Call button clicked! Named callback function active!');
}
```

With the handleCallButton function passed in as a reference, the code looks a little cleaner: we can simply glance at the event, click, and the descriptive name of the function to be called in response to the event. Even better, the nitty-gritty details of handleCallButton are in their own spot a little further down in the JavaScript file. Maintaining those kinds of organizational habits will be even more important once the file includes more signaling and WebRTC code, which is almost entirely driven by events and their callbacks.

Reload your app in the browser and click the button once again. The console should show the longer message announcing that the named callback function is active.

If you saw the message in the console *before* you clicked, it's possible that you might have called the function by mistake, rather than passing it in by reference:

```
document.querySelector('#call-button')
  .addEventListener('click', handleCallButton()); // Oops!
```

If you included the opening and closing parentheses, (), on handleCallButton, what gets passed into addEventListener is not the reference to the callback function, but the *result* of the callback function after it runs prematurely. If that happened, make sure that you're passing in the name of the function only: handleCallButton, without parentheses. Then refresh the app in your browser and try again.

Working with Data Returned to Callback Functions

The addEventListener() method, like many methods that accept callback functions, passes along a chunk of data to the callback when its event fires. With addEventListener(), it's basically convention to pass that data into the callback as either event or simply e. Choose whichever you prefer, but note that the code you'll see throughout this book uses e for errors and spells out event for all events. The target property on event is a DOM object representing the element that was clicked. Because it's a DOM object, much like we'd get from using document.querySelector(), we can do DOM things with it, like determine its id:

```
function handleCallButton(event) {
  console.log('Button with ID', event.target.id, 'clicked!');
}
```

Refresh and click the button again, and watch for "Button with ID call-button clicked!" to appear in your console.

We can do even more with event.target to make the call button fully functional:

1. Change the button's class from join to leave, and vice versa
2. Change the button's text from "Join Call" to "Leave Call," and vice versa

Let's set that up. To make the code more readable, hang onto the event.target value in a local variable called call_button:

demos/basic-p2p/js/main.js
```
function handleCallButton(event) {
  const call_button = event.target;
  if (call_button.className === 'join') {
    console.log('Joining the call...');
    call_button.className = 'leave';
    call_button.innerText = 'Leave Call';
  } else {
    console.log('Leaving the call...');
    call_button.className = 'join';
    call_button.innerText = 'Join Call';
  }
}
```

Refresh your app once more. Now you can click the button again and again. Its text will change and, thanks to CSS that you wrote earlier, so will its appearance. The console will also log "Joining the call..." or "Leaving the call...," depending on what state the button is in.

Excellent. All of the foundational HTML, CSS, and JavaScript for the video-call app's interface is now in place. Up next, we need to start adding in logic for the signaling channel. But before we get to that, let's take a code break and look a little bit at WebRTC as implemented in the browser—and learn why a signaling channel is necessary for WebRTC.

Positioning WebRTC as a Front-End Technology

With an imposing name like *WebRTC: Real-Time Communication in Browsers*, the WebRTC specification sure sounds like a newfangled server-based technology.[5] As web developers, especially front-end developers, we've simply never seen browsers do much else than talk to a server, whether to make requests for static HTML pages, process data submitted from a form, or asynchronously request resources with the Fetch API. The traditional web has always been a 100 percent server-backed technology. Front-end developers are left to mush their faces against the windowpane to the server room, where all the cool new toys often are.

They're not wrong to feel that way: the web has always relied on the client-server architecture of HTTP, where the *client* part is usually synonymous with *browser*. (Web-standards documents refer to *user agents*—which are clients or browsers, too.) Client-server architecture means that even something as basic as a text-based chat application requires relaying each chat message from a browser, through a server, and over to the receiving browser. WebSockets have enabled persistent connections and push-like behavior, so chat messages appear to come across instantaneously from one user to another. But even with WebSockets, the basic architecture of the web remains unchanged, including the server as the central hub.

Not so with WebRTC. As a genuine peer-to-peer technology, the architecture of WebRTC as implemented in web browsers just about eliminates the need for an intermediary server. (True, there are server, OS, and even smart-device implementations of WebRTC, but they represent different use cases beyond the scope of this book.) Once a connection is established, WebRTC in the browser enables any two peers to directly exchange data, including streaming media, over an encrypted low-latency connection without their data ever touching a web server.

Previewing Peer-to-Peer Connection Negotiation

Of course, there's one little hitch: WebRTC is peer-to-peer *only* once a connection is established. RTC peer connections take a little bit of work to establish, as you'll see, and usually with the aid of a server that provides a signaling channel.

---

5.   https://www.w3.org/TR/webrtc/

As web developers, we're used to HTTP's request-response connection pattern: if you have a domain name or even just an IP address, you enter it in the address bar of the browser and boom—connection established and resource or error message delivered in response to the request. End of story. You've been doing that already with the little local web server for previewing your work on the video-call app's interface. Subsequent requests to the same website work the same way as the first request, but typically without a persistent connection between browser and server unless you're dealing with something fancy like WebSockets or a web server with keepalive functionality.

Establishing a connection over WebRTC is more involved than request-response. The two connecting peers have to negotiate the terms of the connection before it can be established. Instead of request-response, peer connections are negotiated by an offer-answer pattern over a signaling channel.

The offer-answer structure that establishes a peer connection is metaphorically no different from a conversation between two friends making plans to meet for coffee. Unless they share a remarkably strong psychic connection, the two friends won't show up the same day and time at the exact same coffee shop. They must first negotiate the details of the coffee date, using some kind of a signaling channel: email, phone, text, or something conventional like that. Even a remarkably strong psychic connection functions as a signaling channel, when it comes right down to it.

But let's stick with a more conventional example. One friend initiates the coffee date by opening a signaling channel: sending a text, making a phone call, or yelling up the street. The initiating friend provides proposed details on a plan to meet up, and the other friend responds. The friends go back and forth, offering and answering over their shared signaling channel, until they reach an agreement to meet at a specific time and place. Regardless of the signaling channel used (text, phone, email), their conversation goes something like this:

Friend A: *How about we meet for coffee next Tuesday at 10, at The Red Eye?*

Friend B: *I could do Tuesday, but not until 11.*

Friend A: *That works, but I have another meeting at 12:30 on the other side of town, so let's meet at Common Grounds instead.*

Friend B: *Okay! See you on Tuesday at 11 at Common Grounds.*

Friend A: *Sounds good!*

Again: all of that negotiation takes place over a signaling channel, which is independent of the destination coffee shop. The coffee shop itself cannot serve as a signaling channel, because even the question of *which* coffee shop may have to be negotiated—as was the case in the little exchange above.

Establishing a peer-to-peer connection between two browsers works much the same way. At least one browser will make an offer to connect, and the other browser will return some kind of response. The process continues like that over the signaling channel, like friends setting a coffee date over text, until the browsers agree on how to open the peer connection.

Using a Lightweight Signaling Channel

Browsers lack a signaling channel that enables a connection to be negotiated. The editors of the WebRTC specification have gone so far as to avoid requiring any specific signaling technology whatsoever: you have to bring your own. So to prepare the way to establish a WebRTC connection, we need first to select and set up a signaling channel.

A server-based signaling channel is the most convenient option. Even a very basic peer-to-peer application, like the one you're writing right now, requires both browsers to visit a URL pointing at some server on the web to download the HTML, CSS, and JavaScript necessary to establish and support the call. With a web server already in the mix, any server-side setup for passing a message from one browser to another would suffice.

Technically speaking, a server-based signaling channel isn't strictly necessary. Two peers connecting over WebRTC could, in theory, email or even handwrite and make no-contact delivery of their browsers' offers and answers to set up the peer connection—just like the two friends above could have set their coffee date using semaphore, tin cans on a string, a dead drop, or a whole bunch of other improbable signaling channels. But a server is going to provide the greatest flexibility and much lower latency. It would be possible, for example, to write your own signaling channel using WebSockets, in any server-side language you choose: PHP, Python, Ruby, and so on.

To prevent you from getting sidetracked by all of that work, I have written a very small server in ExpressJS[6] that includes a signaling channel based on Socket.IO.[7] It's included in the book's sample code you already downloaded. The signaling channel works out of the box. While you might find value in experimenting with it, you won't be writing much server-side code in this book. Our focus is in the browser, because that's where the real action is.

---

6. https://expressjs.com/
7. https://socket.io/

But before we get to work in the browser, you will better grasp the code you're about to write for using the signaling channel if we take a quick walking tour of the signaling channel itself. The channel is very little and very dumb: all it does is manage a few events and shuttle messages back and forth. It doesn't know about WebRTC or anything else that we might be doing. To the greatest extent possible, it's better to keep knowledge of WebRTC in and between browsers. The less your signaling channel does, the easier it will be to move your app to a different signaling channel in the future.

The server's signaling channel component is fewer than a dozen lines, all of which can be reproduced here. As you've seen, sometimes I walk through setting up a piece of code, line by line. Other times, I will do a dramatic reveal of the whole thing before talking through it with you. Like here:

```javascript
server.js
const namespaces = io.of(/^\/[0-9]{7}$/);

namespaces.on('connect', function(socket) {

  const namespace = socket.nsp;

  socket.broadcast.emit('connected peer');

  socket.on('signal', function(data) {
    socket.broadcast.emit('signal', data);
  });

  socket.on('disconnect', function() {
    namespace.emit('disconnected peer');
  });

});
```

Two features of the signaling channel set the stage for the code we'll write in the browser: a set of events and a precise seven-digit namespace. Let's look at the events first.

Exploring the Signaling Channel's Events

The signaling channel handles seven events: three that it listens for—connect, signal, and disconnect—and four that it emits—connected peer, signal, and disconnected peer, plus a connect event that Socket.IO emits automatically.

When a client connects, the signaling channel will broadcast the connected peer event to other connected clients. When a client sends a signal, the signaling channel will rebroadcast the signal event and its data, essentially acting as a repeater. And finally, when a client disconnects, the signaling channel will emit a disconnected peer event.

That captures everything a basic signaling channel needs to do: listen for connections, listen for and repeat signals, and listen for disconnections. That's it. The code we write in the browser to establish a peer connection will trigger or respond to each of those events.

Namespacing the Signaling Channel

The video-call app you're building is meant to scale: it will allow multiple different independent pairs of peers to connect to each other simultaneously. That is no different from how Zoom or Google Meet works. When you use Zoom, you and the person you want to talk to must share (over some *other* signaling channel!) a unique URL like https://fake-example.zoom.us/j/72072139453. You'll also be building unique URLs similar to that.

The opening lines of the signaling channel in server.js use a regular expression to verify the structure of a namespace, which is similar to a meeting code in Zoom. With a shared namespace, one pair of peers can negotiate their connection over the namespace /0000001, while another pair can connect simultaneously over /0000002. Their signals will never cross.

Those are very easy to guess patterns, of course, so we'll write a function in the browser to test or generate a random number that matches the namespace's expected seven-digit pattern on the server. We'll make the namespace easy for users to share by attaching it as a hash on the URL, something like https://localhost/basic-p2p/#1234567. (Later in the book, we'll use the server to generate namespaces using URL paths rather than hashes.)

At the very bottom of the main.js file, you will find a section for utility functions. Here I've written a function called prepareNamespace() that takes two arguments. The hash argument will work with an existing hash, likely as reported by the browser from window.location.hash. The second argument, set_location, is a Boolean value (true or false) for setting the prepared namespace on window.location.hash. Look through the whole thing, and then let's walk through it together.

demos/basic-p2p/js/main.js
```
/**
 *  Utility Functions
 */
function prepareNamespace(hash, set_location) {
  let ns = hash.replace(/^#/, ''); // remove # from the hash
  if (/^[0-9]{7}$/.test(ns)) {
    console.log('Checked existing namespace', ns);
    return ns;
  }
```

```
    ns = Math.random().toString().substring(2, 9);
    console.log('Created new namespace', ns);
    if (set_location) window.location.hash = ns;
    return ns;
}
```

The local variable ns uses the replace() string method with a regular expression and empty string to remove the # (octothorp) that window.location.hash always returns. With the octothorp removed, the function can check the namespace's value against another regular expression pattern: /^[0-9]{7}$/. That is almost identical to the signaling channel's pattern you already saw in server.js (its pattern must also check for the slash that Socket.IO prepends to namespaces).

Demystifying Regular Expressions

If you've never worked with regular expressions before, or if the phrase *regular expressions* makes your palms sweat and your chest tighten, please try to relax. Their basic purpose is pretty easy to summarize: regular expressions describe patterns.

Let's examine the regular-expression pattern /^[0-9]{7}$/ from the inside out. A pattern that matches a sequence of seven digits, 0 through 9, looks like this: [0-9]{7}. [0-9] represents all numbers in the range zero to nine. The seven in curly braces, {7}, means that we want the numbers in the range to appear seven times in a row. Easy enough, right? You'd think. The problem is that any string of text that includes seven digits in a row—no matter what other text the string includes—would still satisfy a regular expression pattern specifying seven sequential digits.

To make sure the namespace is only ever exactly seven digits and therefore prevent potentially malicious characters from ever reaching the signaling channel, the pattern opens with a caret: ^. The caret is a regular-expression symbol that marks the very beginning of a one-line string. Similarly, a dollar sign $ marks the very end of the string. Without the dollar sign, the namespace 0011222-EVIL-BUSINESS-HERE! would still match, because it opens with seven digits.

That kind of thing is probably why most people find themselves so confused and angered by regular expressions: they are incredibly, infuriatingly literal. *Hey, you said you wanted seven digits–I found you seven digits!* Ask regular expressions for a haircut, and they'll cut exactly one of your hairs. They are the dad jokes of computer programming.

Back to the pattern at hand: bookending the regular expression are slashes, /, which demarcate regular expressions in JavaScript, just like quotation marks or backticks demarcate strings. Put it all together, and this little creep should look a tad less imposing: /^[0-9]{7}$/. Seven digits in a row, and seven digits only. No more, no less—and nothing else. That's the pattern for our namespace.

Making Use of the Namespace

And now back to the prepareNamespace() function definition itself: With the regular expression in place, we call the test() method on it and pass along the namespace we have on hand, ns. If the test passes, we return the octothorp-free namespace, ns.

But if the test fails because either the hash doesn't match our pattern or there's no hash at all, the function generates a new random hash in a complex one-liner:

demos/basic-p2p/js/main.js
```
ns = Math.random().toString().substring(2, 9);
```

That generates a random number and converts it to a string. The substring() method gets called to remove the first two characters: numbers generated by Math.random() always begin with 0. The second argument to substring(), 9, ensures that we get a seven-digit number, thanks to the first two characters being discarded by the first argument, 2.

If set_location is true, the new namespace gets set on the URL by assigning it to window.location.hash.

Finally, the function returns the value of ns, which is the brand-new, randomly generated hash.

With the prepareNamespace() function definition in place, you can put it to work at the top of your file and assign its output–the returned namespace–to a namespace variable:

demos/basic-p2p/js/main.js
```
const namespace = prepareNamespace(window.location.hash, true);
```

Let's do something user-facing with the namespace variable. In the user-interface area of the JavaScript file, add another one-liner that sets the h1 text to welcome users to a correctly namespaced room:

demos/basic-p2p/js/main.js
```
/**
 *  User-Interface Setup
 */
document.querySelector('#header h1')
   .innerText = 'Welcome to Room #' + namespace;

document.querySelector('#call-button')
  .addEventListener('click', handleCallButton);
```

Reload the page at https://localhost:3000/basic-p2p/. You should see two things: a random, seven-digit hash appended to the URL, something like https://local-host:3000/basic-p2p/#4134610, and that same hash repeated in the text of the page's first-level heading, like this:

Those adjustments are basically cosmetic, changing only the appearance of the URL and page. Now let's use the namespace variable to connect to the signaling channel.

Connecting to the Signaling Channel

There are a few preliminary steps you'll need to take to connect to the signaling channel. The first is to return to the index.html file and add another <script> tag right above the one that loads the main.js file. Point it to the JavaScript file /socket.io/socket.io.js that Socket.IO automatically serves:

demos/basic-p2p/index.html
```
<script src="/socket.io/socket.io.js"></script>
<script src="js/main.js"></script>
</body>
</html>
```

The main.js file depends on the contents of the socket.io.js file, which is the Socket.IO client, so be sure to include the <script> tag that points at main.js second in the HTML.

Back in the main.js file itself, in the "Signaling-Channel Setup" area up top, let's connect to the signaling channel and attach some code to the connect event that will output a message to the browser console if the connection is successful. You can declare an sc variable to hold onto the namespaced signaling channel as returned by Socket.IO's io object's connect method:

```
/**
 *  Signaling-Channel Setup
 */

const namespace = prepareNamespace(window.location.hash, true);

const sc = io.connect('/' + namespace);

sc.on('connect', function() {
  console.log('Successfully connected to the signaling channel!');
});
```

If your browser's JavaScript console isn't already open, open it. Reload the page and you should see the success message logged in the console: "Successfully connected to the signaling channel!"

Right now, anyone using your app will automatically connect to the signaling channel by loading the page in the browser. That's not the behavior we want, though: the signaling channel's connect event will eventually start the process of establishing the WebRTC call. To give users better control, then, let's rewrite the code so users don't connect to the signaling channel until they click the Join Call button that we went to all the trouble of setting up.

Connecting to the Signaling Channel Manually

Remember how you set up a handleCallButton() function in Writing Named Functions as Callbacks, on page 22? Let's call two more functions from within it: joinCall() and leaveCall(). The definitions for those functions can go right below the handleCallButton function definition:

demos/basic-p2p/js/main.js
```
/**
 *  User-Interface Functions and Callbacks
 */

function handleCallButton(event) {
  const call_button = event.target;
  if (call_button.className === 'join') {
    console.log('Joining the call...');
    call_button.className = 'leave';
    call_button.innerText = 'Leave Call';
    joinCall();
  } else {
    console.log('Leaving the call...');
```

```
      call_button.className = 'join';
      call_button.innerText = 'Join Call';
      leaveCall();
    }
  }

  function joinCall() {
    sc.open();
  }

  function leaveCall() {
    sc.close();
  }
```

There will be more to add to both the joinCall and leaveCall functions. But to get started, they are responsible only for opening and closing the Socket.IO signaling channel, which provides its own open() and close() methods. We just need to call them on the sc object.

Now that your JavaScript is set to manually open and close the connection to the signaling server, you need to modify how the signaling channel is configured by passing in an options object that sets autoConnect to false:

demos/basic-p2p/js/main.js
```
const sc = io.connect('/' + namespace, { autoConnect: false });
```

Reload the page in your browser again. You shouldn't see the "Successfully connected to the signaling server!" in the JavaScript console until you click the Join Call button. If you click the button a few more times, joining and leaving the call, you'll see the success message each time you click Join Call. Nice!

Because the signaling channel is powered by Socket.IO, it has an active property that returns true when the signaling server is connected and false when it's not. If you like, hit the Join Call button and then type sc.active in your browser's JavaScript console and hit Return. It should report true. Hit the Leave Call button, type sc.active again, and it should report false. That's an easy way to verify that your button really is opening and closing the signaling channel.

Preparing Placeholders for the Remaining Signaling Callbacks

One more task, and then we'll have everything in place for writing the remaining signaling-channel code and WebRTC connection logic in the next chapter's coverage of Building Connection Logic to the "Perfect Negotiation" Pattern, on page 51. Find the "Signaling-Channel Functions and Callbacks" area of the JavaScript file. Let's write a wrapper function, registerScCallbacks() that will register callbacks for the four signaling-channel events that we saw in server.js (connect, connected peer, disconnected peer, and signal), and put placeholder function definitions for them on the lines below.

The anonymous callback on the connect event that logs "Successfully connected..." can also be rewritten as a named function, in case there's more to do with that event in the future. (Spoiler alert: there will be.) Putting it all together, your signaling callbacks will look like this:

```
/**
 *  Signaling-Channel Functions and Callbacks
 */

function registerScCallbacks() {
  sc.on('connect', handleScConnect);
  sc.on('connected peer', handleScConnectedPeer);
  sc.on('disconnected peer', handleScDisconnectedPeer);
  sc.on('signal', handleScSignal);
}

function handleScConnect() {
 console.log('Successfully connected to the signaling server!');
}

function handleScConnectedPeer() {
}

function handleScDisconnectedPeer() {
}

function handleScSignal() {
}
```

There are plenty of modifications to those function definitions on the way, of course, but for now they're enough to prevent the browser from complaining about missing references to them in the stack of sc.on events that registerScCallbacks() assigns.

And speaking of that wrapper function, the last thing to do is call it up at the top of the file. This completes your "Signaling-Channel Setup" area:

demos/basic-p2p/js/main.js
```
/**
 *  Signaling-Channel Setup
 */

const namespace = prepareNamespace(window.location.hash, true);

const sc = io.connect('/' + namespace, { autoConnect: false });

➤ registerScCallbacks();
```

Next Steps

You've now got several key foundational pieces in place for your peer-to-peer video-call app. You've constructed a user interface out of top-notch semantic HTML and modern CSS. You've written some important responsive-design features, which are essential to making your app accessible across the full range of web-enabled devices. You've also connected to your signaling channel and created a set of placeholder functions for triggering and responding to the signaling channel's events. In the next chapter, you'll complete the app by building out those functions to establish your first peer connection in WebRTC.

## CHAPTER 3

Establishing a Peer-to-Peer Connection

In the previous chapter, you constructed the basic interface for a video-call app. You also explored and wrote a number of placeholder callback functions to prepare the way for triggering and responding to the signaling channel's events.

In this chapter, you'll build on that work to enable two peers to set up a WebRTC connection and stream video directly to each other. At first, of course, the two peers will just be you and yourself with two different browser windows opened to the same namespace. To prevent skull-shattering feedback while you test things out, you'll start off with the audio disabled.

The goal is to to work systematically and get some foundational WebRTC code working as quickly as possible, which you'll further refine and make backward-compatible over the next few chapters. To get started, you'll learn how to request access to a user's camera and microphone. You'll then dive in to do meaningful work with the core pieces of a peer-to-peer app, including media streams and the WebRTC RTCPeerConnection interface. You'll also set up your peer-connection logic by writing a real-world implementation of the "perfect negotiation" pattern found in the WebRTC specification.

Requesting User-Media Permissions

Before we get into the heavy-duty WebRTC code, let's start off by handling an essential task that's also pretty awesome and fun: requesting permission for your app to access a user's camera and then displaying the camera's live video in the HTML's self video element.

Start by declaring a new variable called $self near the top of the main.js file. Note the variable name is prefixed with a dollar sign. While self would be a more convenient name, browsers have a built-in self property on the global window object.[1] So we will go with $self and assign it an object literal with a mediaConstraints property:

```
demos/basic-p2p/js/main.js
const $self = {
  mediaConstraints: { audio: false, video: true },
};
```

We'll talk about those constraints in a moment. For now, find the area of main.js labeled "User-Media Functions" and define a new function called requestUserMedia(). This time, though, you'll need to preface the function keyword with async. I'll explain that along with the rest of the function in a moment, but I promised fun first. So go ahead and build your function to look like this:

```
/**
 * User-Media Functions
 */

async function requestUserMedia(media_constraints) {
  $self.mediaStream = new MediaStream();
  $self.media = await navigator.mediaDevices
    .getUserMedia(media_constraints);
  $self.mediaStream.addTrack($self.media.getTracks()[0]);
  document.querySelector('#self')
    .srcObject = $self.mediaStream;
}
```

Now be sure to call that function, passing in the $self.mediaConstraints object, in the "User-Media Setup" area of your JavaScript file:

```
/**
 * User-Media Setup
 */

requestUserMedia($self.mediaConstraints);
```

When you reload the app, you should be greeted by your browser's dialog box for media permissions, such as the one for Firefox as shown in the first screenshot on page 39.

Be sure to click Allow on the permissions dialog. While you can opt to allow the browser to remember your decision, my own preference is to always be prompted for media permissions when I'm developing something for WebRTC. That serves as a frequent reminder of the flow of the interface for first-time users. Once you click allow, after a beat, you should see your very own face (as shown in the second screenshot on page 39), streaming in real time, staring right back at you from an otherwise static HTML page.

---

1.   https://developer.mozilla.org/en-US/docs/Web/API/Window/self

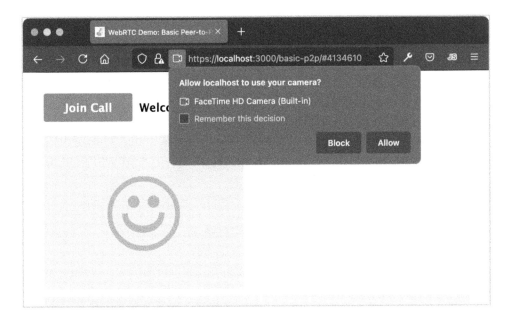

See? Fun stuff. But what's happening with that requestUserMedia() function you wrote?

Let's start by looking inside the body of the function. It sets two new properties on the $self object: stream and media. The stream property is assigned a new MediaStream object, which will hold onto any media tracks returned by the user's devices. The relationship between streams and tracks is a little compli-cated, but for now it's enough to think of a stream as a container for tracks. Tracks represent the actual audio and video data returned from a user's camera and microphone. Again, we're requesting only video for now.

Once a user grants permission, the media property holds onto a reference to the user's device returned by the navigator.mediaDevices.getUserMedia() method. More in the next section on what that await keyword is doing. The media con-straints passed to getUserMedia() are very basic. Recall how we set them up on the $self.mediaConstraints property:

```
demos/basic-p2p/js/main.js
const $self = {
  mediaConstraints: { audio: false, video: true },
};
```

Media constraints are always expressed as an object literal. At their most basic, constraints are about seeking a user's permission to access devices like the camera and microphone. In other words, constraints not necessarily about features: your app still needs to work with audio or video returned by a user's media devices—once they've granted permission. In Chapter 7, Managing User Media, on page 173, you'll test for and apply additional con-straints to the requested user media, but a simple set of constraints is all that's needed for now.

The constraints object you wrote specifies that your app is requesting permis-sion to access to the user's camera (video: true), but not the microphone (audio: false). Remember, for the time being, we're disabling audio in development by not even asking permission to access the mic. Doing that at the constraint level is to make darn sure that your computer doesn't go full Jimi Hendrix on the feedback. You'll build the necessary controls to safely develop audio-enabled WebRTC apps a little later in the book, in Adding Mic and Camera Toggles, on page 98.

Your requestUserMedia() function uses the getTracks() method on the $self.media object to access the data-containing tracks from the user's devices. Note that getTracks() returns an array of tracks; the [0] tacked onto the end means we're just interested in the very first, and in this case, the only track—the video coming off the user's camera. The function passes that track directly into the addTrack() method on the MediaStream object.

Once the track has been added to $self.mediaStream, the requestUserMedia() function uses document.querySelector to select the self video element from the DOM and set its srcObject property—that is, the video source for the element to play—to

$self.mediaStream. As you'll see, the technique for setting video on the remote peer's srcObject is almost identical. So much so that we can abstract that one-off document.querySelector line into a small, reusable user-media function:

demos/basic-p2p/js/main.js
```
function displayStream(stream, selector) {
  document.querySelector(selector).srcObject = stream;
}
```

Now we can call that function inside of requestUserMedia:

demos/basic-p2p/js/main.js
```
async function requestUserMedia(media_constraints) {
  $self.mediaStream = new MediaStream();
  $self.media = await navigator.mediaDevices
    .getUserMedia(media_constraints);
  $self.mediaStream.addTrack($self.media.getTracks()[0]);
  displayStream($self.mediaStream, '#self');
}
```

We'll make use of the displayStream() function later, when we're handling the incoming media stream from the remote peer in Receiving Media Tracks, on page 59.

Async, Await, Say What?

Stepping outside the function now: there's that curious async keyword hanging out in front of the more familiar function keyword. The async keyword is used to define the requestUserMedia function so it can make use of a related keyword, await.

Up to this point, we'd been using an old-school JavaScript pattern for handling asynchronous code: callback functions executed in response to events. The Join Call click event uses this pattern, as do all of the signaling-channel events we set up at the end of the previous chapter. In pseudocode:

```
waitForSomethingAsync('done', doSomething);
```

JavaScript syntax has evolved to make asynchronous code more readable. The old-school callback pattern looks pretty good in that simple case above, but it can lead to "pyramids of doom," with callbacks inside of callbacks inside of callbacks. JavaScript's evolution to address that problem came in the form of something called the Promise object. We don't need to go too deep on that here, but promises make async functions a little more readable with chainable methods like then():

```
waitForSomethingAsync()
  .then(doSomething)
```

The async and await keywords transform that pseudocode to look a little more familiar to developers used to functional programming in JavaScript. Functional programming is what we've been doing this whole chapter. Instead of chaining together a bunch of then() calls, we can use async and await:

```
async function waitForSomethingAsync() { return data; }
async function doSomething(data) { }

doSomething(await waitForSomethingAsync());
```

In that example, await appears right where the data argument gets passed into the doSomething() function. But await can also appear in the body of an outer asynchronous function:

```
async function someOuterAsyncFunction() {
  var data = await waitForSomethingAsync();
  doSomething(data);
}
```

In that case, the doSomething() function will not execute until data has been returned from waitForSomethingAsync(). In async-speak, it's not the data being returned, but rather a Promise resolving with the data the doSomething() function needs.

So why do we care about async and await in the context of media permissions? The power of asynchronous code is it doesn't bring your whole application to a halt. And the user-media API we used for the fun stuff, navigator.mediaDevices .getUserMedia(), is itself promise-based and asynchronous. Among other things, that means that even while the media permissions dialog is showing, users can continue to interact with the page: reload the app in your browser and try clicking the Join Call button while the permissions dialog box is open. The button keeps working, no problem.

The requestUserMedia() function, being async itself, will not move ahead until it has the permissions and stream from the user's media. Without await, the getTracks() method would be called on $self.media too soon, before its promise has resolved—resulting in no data. JavaScript would throw an error in that case, and you would be denied the chance to admire your own face in the browser window.

If you're intrigued by asynchronous JavaScript and want to learn more, check out Faraz Kelhini's *Modern Asynchronous JavaScript [Kel21]*.

Setting Up the Peer Connection

All right. Your video-call app is coming together. You've prepared the UI and set up the signaling channel for users to join whenever they are ready, and now you've got streaming video set up on the self side of the connection. It's time to put all of those pieces together and get a peer connection set up and established using WebRTC.

Let's kick things off by returning to the top of main.js. Once there, you can modify the $self object to include an rtcConfig property set to null. Eventually, $self.rtcConfig will include some important WebRTC configuration values (see Configuring a WebRTC App for Public Deployment, on page 198). But for testing WebRTC on a local network, initially setting the configuration to null will suffice. Immediately below $self, declare a new $peer variable and assign it an object literal—just like $self. All $peer should contain for now is a connection property to hold onto an instance of the RTCPeerConnection object:

```
demos/basic-p2p/js/main.js
const $self = {
  rtcConfig: null,
  mediaConstraints: { audio: false, video: true },
};

const $peer = {
  connection: new RTCPeerConnection($self.rtcConfig),
};
```

And that's it! App finished.

Okay, not really. Not by a long shot. I'm just being mean. There's so much more to come. Those few lines of code *are* accomplishing a lot, though. That's especially true for the $peer.connection property and its reference to a new RTCPeerConnection instance, which is the key piece of everything left to build.

But before we leave the enchanted land of variable assignment and make a triumphant return to the kingdom of callback function definitions, let's set a few more properties on $self, just below the rtcConfig property we added:

```
demos/basic-p2p/js/main.js
const $self = {
  rtcConfig: null,
  isPolite: false,
  isMakingOffer: false,
  isIgnoringOffer: false,
  isSettingRemoteAnswerPending: false,
  mediaConstraints: { audio: false, video: true },
};
```

We'll return to each of those new properties in time. Their purpose will be to track various states on $self as a WebRTC connection is established. But the one that is most interesting for the time being is the first one: $self.isPolite, which is initially set to false. That means we've admitted to the world that each of us, as $self, is surly and rude. But why?

Achieving Asymmetric Function from Symmetric Code

You're about to discover many mind-bending qualities of WebRTC. The primary source of its many mind-benders is loading the same codebase—HTML, CSS, and JavaScript—in the browsers on both ends of a WebRTC call. That means the code is symmetric: each browser loads the exact same code. There's no need to goof around writing server-side logic that sends different code to different peers.

As we established in Designing Peer-to-Peer UI Patterns, on page 12, everyone on the call is just a joiner. That choice frees us up to maintain just a single symmetric WebRTC codebase. Like the symmetric joiner interface it supports, our codebase will provide both peers (and eventually, in Chapter 6, Managing Multipeer Connections, on page 133, *all* peers) with the ability to initiate and answer offers to connect over WebRTC.

"But wait," you might say. "Why are we suddenly talking about initiating and answering 'offers to connect'? Didn't we explicitly set up a joiner pattern, rather than a caller pattern?" Yes, yes we did. The only real piece of UI in our interface—the Join Call button—means we aren't going to worry at all about who's calling whom. The peers just join the call. Your button doesn't lie.

But just because *we're* not going to worry about caller and answerer roles doesn't mean that WebRTC won't. I hate to talk about WebRTC behind its back like this, but you should know that it worries quite a lot—about caller and answerer roles and many other things that we'll get to soon enough. The RTCPeerConnection instance that we're hanging onto in $peer.connection is basically a giant worrywart. And like most worrywarts, it doesn't quite know how to cope on its own with all the things that might go wrong. We almost have to be like good therapists and give RTCPeerConnection some solid coping strategies to help manage its many worries.

That brings us back to the $self.isPolite value: it represents the core principle behind establishing a worry-free WebRTC connection. For each set of two peers connecting over your app, one peer will be polite ($self.isPolite === true), and one will be impolite ($self.isPolite === false). So even though the same code appears in both peers' browsers, each peer will behave a little differently, being either polite or impolite, depending on the circumstances of the call. And that's how we'll be able to pull off asymmetric behavior from symmetric code.

Establishing the Polite Peer

That all might sound reasonable. But if the code is still *exactly* the same in both browsers, including the opening lines of main.js that set $self.isPolite to false, what sorcery is required to establish that one of the peers is polite?

We can consider a few different approaches to establish politeness. We could write a function that plays a virtual game of rock-paper-scissors between the two peers over the signaling channel before they connect. Or we could make it weird and administer a short personality test to determine which of the two peers really *is* the rude one.

Or we could establish politeness based on the order peers join the call. The first person to click Join Call will be polite, being prompt and punctual (okay, actually, they'll be first to connect to the signaling channel), and the second person to join will be impolite. Probabilistically speaking, there is a very low chance that both peers might join the room at exactly the same fraction of a second. But it's so improbable that we don't have to worry about it.

Recall that the signaling channel broadcast emits a connected peer event. The broadcast emit is special, because it gets sent to everyone on the namespace *except* the person who triggered the event (otherwise, connecting peers would hear their own connected peer events). Every time a peer joins the namespaced signaling channel, the connected peer event fires. You've already written a callback function in the main.js file to handle the connected peer event. Let's open up its definition, and add a single line that sets $self.isPolite to true:

demos/basic-p2p/js/main.js
```
function handleScConnectedPeer() {
    $self.isPolite = true;
}
```

Here again, we appear to end up with another symmetric paradox: both peers join the call, meaning both peers will trigger the signaling server to broadcast the connected peer event to the other peer. That's true.

The trick is that when the first peer joins the call, the connected peer event winds up in Zen koan territory: *If a tree falls in the forest and no one is around to hear it, does it make a sound?* When the first peer triggers the connected peer broadcast-emit event, *the other peer isn't around to receive it.* The second peer hasn't connected yet, and likely will not connect in the nanosecond timeframe required to receive the event.

But—when the *second* peer connects, connected peer fires again—only this time, the first peer *is* around to receive it. And so the first peer becomes the polite one ($self.isPolite === true, as set in the handleScConnectedPeer() callback function), while the second peer stays impolite ($self.isPolite === false, as set near the top of the main.js file). Even though the second peer also has the handleScConnectedPeer function available, it will never execute, because the second peer will not hear a connected peer event.

Adding Peer-Connection Callbacks

Hold onto the fact that one peer on a call is polite, and the other is impolite, while you stack up a whole new collection of events tied to the RTCPeerConnection object. Find the "WebRTC Functions and Callbacks" area of the main.js file, and let's write these events inside their own wrapper function like we did with the signaling channel events on Preparing Placeholders for the Remaining Signaling Callbacks, on page 34. We'll execute this registerRtcCallbacks() function when a user connects to the signaling channel:

demos/basic-p2p/js/main.js
```
function registerRtcCallbacks(peer) {
  peer.connection.onnegotiationneeded = handleRtcConnectionNegotiation;
  peer.connection.onicecandidate = handleRtcIceCandidate;
  peer.connection.ontrack = handleRtcPeerTrack;
}
```

Those events use different syntax for registering callbacks from what we have seen so far. Because these three events—negotiationneeded, icecandidate, and track—are so commonly used, the RTCPeerConnection object gives us shorthand properties for each of them, prefixed with on. (You probably have seen this before with the DOM: you can use domObj.addEventListener('click', handleClick) or the shorthand domObj.onclick = handleClick. Both syntaxes achieve the same thing.)

Below the registerRtcCallbacks() definition, you can drop in the definition of handleRtcPeerTrack(). Because adding media tracks is necessary only for apps that include streaming media, we'll keep that function definition with the application-specific code:

```
function handleRtcPeerTrack() {
  // TODO: Handle peer media tracks
}
```

The onnegotiationneeded and onicecandidate events, however, are generic across any WebRTC apps you might build, so we'll isolate them in the "Reusable WebRTC Functions and Callbacks" area of the JavaScript file:

```
/**
 *  Reusable WebRTC Functions and Callbacks
 */
async function handleRtcConnectionNegotiation() {
  // TODO: Handle connection negotiation
}
function handleRtcIceCandidate() {
  // TODO: Handle ICE candidates
}
```

We'll build out those two reusable functions here, and return to the app-specific handleRtcPeerTrack() function later.

The handleRtcConnectionNegotiation() function will use await in its body, so we prefix it with async. It awaits a promise-based RTC peer connection method, setLocalDescription(), which prepares an offer according to the Session Description Protocol (SDP; see Making an Offer They Can't Refuse, on page 52). SDP offers include details on media capabilities on the self side of the call. While the body of the handleRtcConnectionNegotiation() function awaits the offer returned by setLocalDescription(), $self.isMakingOffer is set to true (recall we initially set the isMakingOffer property to false on $self). Once the offer—held in $peer.connection.localDescription—has been sent over the signaling channel, $self is no longer in the process of making an offer, so $self.isMakingOffer gets set back to its initial state, false:

demos/basic-p2p/js/main.js
```
async function handleRtcConnectionNegotiation() {
  $self.isMakingOffer = true;
  console.log('Attempting to make an offer...');
  await $peer.connection.setLocalDescription();
  sc.emit('signal', { description: $peer.connection.localDescription });
  $self.isMakingOffer = false;
}
```

Now don't be fooled by await, in that function or anywhere else: under most conditions, the wait is less than a blink of an eye. When we get to handling SDP offers (and answers) in Building Connection Logic to the "Perfect Negotiation" Pattern, on page 51, you'll see that blinks of an eye can still matter—especially to a worrywart WebRTC peer connection.

The handleRtcConnectionNegotiation() function generates and sends SDP offers, and the handleRtcIceCandidate() callback must do roughly the same for ICE candidates. I know, that name in all caps makes me think of awful things, too. But ICE in this case stands for Interactive Connectivity Establishment,[2] an IETF-defined protocol that enables browsers to describe how they can be reached

---

2. https://tools.ietf.org/html/rfc8445

Which Browsers Does This Code Support?

Elsewhere in the book, you've read that browser support for WebRTC is very good. But support isn't always uniform for all features—that's the case for any web API. Browsers must support two baselines for your code to work: RTCPeerConnection methods like setLocalDescription() must return a Promise (allowing them to work with await), and the standardized navigator.mediaDevices.getUserMedia() method must be available.

Those two features were implemented at different times in different browsers, but ultimately the code you're writing here works in at least Chrome 53, Edge 79, Firefox 66, and Safari 11. Those are all pretty ancient desktop browsers by almost any measure.

Safari lags all other browsers in regard to one feature: implicit rollback on setRemoteDescription, which didn't arrive until Safari 15.4 (elsewhere it showed up in Chrome 80, Edge 80, and Firefox 70). You can read about accommodating older Safaris in Appendix 1, Connection Negotiation in Legacy Browsers, on page 225. But apart from that, we'll write any other fallback code as needed throughout the book.

over the internet or a local network. While the offer in localDescription describes the media that will flow over the connection, ICE candidates describe possible peer-to-peer routes over the network. WebRTC needs both to establish a connection.

The handleRtcIceCandiate() callback is less complicated to write. Whenever a candidate becomes available, we just need to send it over the signaling channel, attached again to the signal event.

demos/basic-p2p/js/main.js
```
function handleRtcIceCandiate({ candidate }) {
  console.log('Attempting to handle an ICE candidate...');
  sc.emit('signal', { candidate: candidate });
}
```

Destructuring Assignment

Something might look odd to you in the handleRtcIceCandiate() callback function definition: the { candidate } in curly braces that gets passed into the function as an argument. Ordinarily, when we see curly braces surrounding a value, they look more like what gets sent over the signaling channel: { candidate: candidate }, with one value and another separated by a colon, :. Good, old-fashioned object literals, just like Grandmother used to make.

A newer feature available in JavaScript syntax is something called *destructuring assignment*. It's a shorthand way of pulling a value out of an object literal and assigning the value to its own variable. Here's a simple example:

```
const obj = { one: 1, two: 2 };
```

If we were interested in assigning the value of one to its own variable, we could write const one = obj.one; But destructuring assignment allows us to write this instead:

```
const {one} = obj;
console.log(one); //-> 1
```

In short, the value in the curly braces gets assigned as a standalone representation of whatever matching property exists in the object—assuming the property exists. If the property doesn't exist, the value is undefined:

```
const {three} = obj;
console.log(three); //-> undefined
```

So what function handleRtcIceCandidate({ candidate }) does is extract the value of candidate from the chunk of data returned by $peer.connection.onicecandidate and create a local candidate variable that we can use within the function itself.

Sending Media Tracks

We should test out those two RTC callbacks. The onnegotiationneeded event kicks off the establishment of a WebRTC call. But it's adding media to the peer connection that causes onnegotiationneeded to fire.

While you've already set your local stream to appear on the self <video> element, you need to also add the tracks from that stream to the peer connection so that the remote peer can ultimately receive them. We'll handle the receiving side in Receiving Media Tracks, on page 59. For now, let's write the track-sending logic as another little reusable function, below the other user-media functions:

```
demos/basic-p2p/js/main.js
function addStreamingMedia(stream, peer) {
  if (stream) {
    for (let track of stream.getTracks()) {
      peer.connection.addTrack(track, stream);
    }
  }
}
```

We'll pass the peer instance and the self media stream into that function. Assuming a media stream is set on self, a for loop runs through the tracks and adds them to the peer connection. Don't succumb to a false sense of *déjà vu* here: RTCPeerConnection has an addTracks() method, just like MediaStream does—as we saw in Requesting User-Media Permissions, on page 37. Here, though, we're adding media tracks to the call, not to a MediaStream.

While we could call addStreamingMedia() along with registerRtcCallbacks() directly inside of the handleScConnect() callback, let's take an opportunity to future-proof the code a bit. Streaming media is one possible feature of a WebRTC call. As you will see in Chapter 4, Handling Data Channels, on page 63, data channels represent other features. We can write a wrapper function called establishCallFeatures() which wraps registerRtcCallbacks() together with any app-specific call features, like adding streaming user-media. Add this function definition in the "Call Features & Reset Functions" area of the JavaScript file:

demos/basic-p2p/js/main.js
```
/**
 *  Call Features & Reset Functions
 */

function establishCallFeatures(peer) {
  registerRtcCallbacks(peer);
  addStreamingMedia($self.mediaStream, peer);
}
```

Note that it is essential to register the WebRTC callbacks before adding media or any other features to the connection. Adding the media to the RTCPeerConnection instance triggers the negotiationneeded event, which in turn sets the entire connection-negotiation process in motion. If media or other features are added before a callback is set to handle negotiationneeded, the event will fire without executing a callback, leaving users unable to initiate a WebRTC connection. So be sure to call registerRtcCallbacks() at the very top of the establishCallFeatures() function definition.

With the establishCallFeatures() function finished, call it from within the handleScConnect() callback, which is now complete, generic, and portable across any peer-to-peer WebRTC app you ever want to write:

demos/basic-p2p/js/main.js
```
function handleScConnect() {
  console.log('Successfully connected to the signaling server!');
  establishCallFeatures($peer);
}
```

Go ahead and refresh your browser and click the Join Call button. You'll now see some new messages logged to the console: one announcing "Attempting to make an offer...," followed by more than one announcing "Attempting to handle an ICE candidate...."

With the handleRtcConnectionNegotiation() and the handleRtcIceCandidate() callback functions defined and now tested out, you now have all of the sending logic in place for establishing a peer connection. The big piece remaining is the receiving logic, which will handle descriptions and ICE candidates coming in over the signaling channel.

Building Connection Logic to the "Perfect Negotiation" Pattern

We're going to build the connection's receiving logic according to the "perfect negotiation" pattern described in the WebRTC specification:

> This pattern has advantages over one side always being the offerer, as it lets applications operate on both peer connection objects simultaneously without risk of glare (an offer coming in outside of "stable" state). The rest of the application may use any and all modification methods and attributes without worrying about signaling state races.[3]

That's a dense quotation, but here's the essence: in symmetric WebRTC apps like the one you're building, both sides of the connection can pass an offer to the other. That's essential because it's impossible to know which peer is going to be able to run setLocalDescription() and pass an offer across the signaling channel first. It might not necessarily be the first peer to join the call. A slow browser, a poor network connection, and even a delay in granting media permissions can all factor into the timing of a peer's first offer.

The catch is once the RTCPeerConnection object on one side of a peer connection has prepared an offer to send over the signaling channel, it expects an answer in response. In fact, under typical conditions, the RTCPeerConnection object won't respond to anything *but* an answer. If both sides of a connection have prepared offers to send out, they basically end up in a stalemate—what the WebRTC spec calls "glare." It's a lot like a face-to-face conversation when two people start speaking at the same time, as Jan-Ivar Bruaroey points out.[4] Assuming the conversation doesn't escalate into a shouting match, one person in such a situation will usually say, "Oh, I'm sorry—I interrupted you." That's conceptually identical to the behavior of the polite peer in establishing the connection.

If you're wondering why we can't live in a harmonious world where we tell both peers to be polite, consider that we'd end up in the equivalent of a highly annoying, endless exchange like, "Sorry! Please go ahead!" "No, *you* go ahead!" "Oh, I couldn't!" "No, please!" "Really, whatever *you* have to say is much more important!" "No, my thing is stupid. I *insist* you talk first!" And on like that forever. The impolite peer is doing a heroic service by saving the connection from devolving into such tediousness.

---

3. https://www.w3.org/TR/webrtc/#perfect-negotiation-example
4. https://blog.mozilla.org/webrtc/perfect-negotiation-in-webrtc/

Making an Offer They Can't Refuse

Session Description Protocol (SDP) offers and answers are almost exclusively the business of the browsers producing them. There is no need to worry about the contents of SDP offers and answers when developing with the browser's WebRTC APIs. As WebRTC developers, we only need to make sure browsers correctly generate and pass them over the signaling channel.

For the dangerously curious, here is a tiny, reformatted portion of an SDP offer as generated by Firefox Developer Edition in a LAN environment:

```
RTCSessionDescription { type: "offer", sdp: "
    v=0
    o=mozilla...THIS_IS_SDPARTA-99.0 [...] 0 IN IP4 0.0.0.0
    s=-
    t=0 0
    a=sendrecv
    [...]
    m=video 64423 UDP/TLS/RTP/SAVPF 120 124 121 125 126 127 97 98
    c=IN IP4 0.0.0.0
    [...]
    a=rtpmap:120 VP8/90000
    a=rtpmap:124 rtx/90000
    a=rtpmap:121 VP9/90000
    a=rtpmap:125 rtx/90000
    a=rtpmap:126 H264/90000
    a=rtpmap:127 rtx/90000
    a=rtpmap:97 H264/90000
    a=rtpmap:98 rtx/90000
  " }
```

The opening lines describe the session. On the lines opening with m=video, we see a portion of the media description for video, including the CODECs the browser supports (VP8, VP9, and H264, in this case). Earlier in WebRTC's history, a modification technique called *SDP munging* was sometimes necessary to force the use of specific CODECs. SDP munging is generally no longer good practice—and was frankly pretty shady even at the time, especially for peer-to-peer connections.[a]

For the truly SDP obsessed, the IETF has an archived informational document called Annotated Example SDP for WebRTC.[b] It walks through the organization and semantics of a variety of SDP offers and answers, all with pointers to the galaxy of different specifications governing the correct form and content of each line. You can compare those against the contents of your own SDP offer by writing $peer.connection.localDescription and hitting return in your browser's JavaScript console after you click the Join Call button.

---

a. https://bloggeek.me/webrtc-sdp-munging-prohibited/
b. https://datatracker.ietf.org/doc/html/draft-ietf-rtcweb-sdp-14

Back to the code: all of the perfect-negotiation logic will appear inside the handleScSignal() callback, one of the callback functions you already defined for the signaling channel. Let's return to the function's definition, make it async, and pass into it the data received over the signaling channel. Inside the function, set up an if/else statement that will kick into action depending on whether it's an ICE candidate or description that's been received:

```
async function handleScSignal({ description, candidate }) {
  if (description) {
    // Work with an incoming description (offer/answer)
  } else if (candidate) {
    // Work with an incoming ICE candidate
  }
}
```

That sets the function up to handle either a description or a candidate, which we conveniently access using destructuring assignment again, this time with two values separated by a comma: {description, candidate}. If a description—an offer or an answer—comes across, candidate will be undefined and therefore false in the if statement. If it's a candidate, description will evaluate as false.

Determining Whether to Ignore Offers

If it turns out a peer is ignoring offers, all we need to do is exit the handleScSignal() function. So we'll write that logic first. To determine whether a peer is ignoring offers, we need to work through an unavoidably dense set of true/false conditions to either exit or, for the polite peer, continue on to an "Oh, I'm sorry—I interrupted you" state. Let's have another dramatic reveal, and then talk it through:

demos/basic-p2p/js/main.js
```
async function handleScSignal({ description, candidate }) {
  if (description) {

    const ready_for_offer =
        !$self.isMakingOffer &&
        ($peer.connection.signalingState === 'stable'
          || $self.isSettingRemoteAnswerPending);

    const offer_collision =
        description.type === 'offer' && !ready_for_offer;

    $self.isIgnoringOffer = !$self.isPolite && offer_collision;

    if ($self.isIgnoringOffer) {
      return;
    }
  } else if (candidate) {

  }
}
```

That's a dense chunk of code. What it's doing at every turn is looking for true and false conditions. It reads a little more sensibly by starting at the bottom, with the if ($self.isIgnoringOffer) block, and working back up to the top. What that if statement does is exit the function, thanks to that one-line return; statement, when $self is ignoring an incoming offer.

But to determine whether $self is ignoring offers, we need the line above, which assigns either a true or false value to $self.isIgnoringOffer:

```
$self.isIgnoringOffer = !$self.isPolite && offer_collision;
```

What that means is $self will ignore offers if it's impolite (!$self.isPolite === true) and (&&) if there's an offer collision (offer_collision === true). An impolite peer will evaluate as $self.isPolite === false, so adding an exclamation mark in front of $self.isPolite means *not.* In programming terms, recall that the exclamation mark returns the *opposite* value of $self.isPolite. So stick with it: with the exclamation point, the impolite peer will evaluate as true here, and the polite peer will evaluate as false. I find it helpful to say "not" aloud when I encounter an exclamation point in Boolean-happy code like this, and then remind myself that it's only ever the impolite peer who ignores offers.

The polite peer, by contrast, will never ignore offers: false on one side of an AND expression (&&) will always make the whole expression false. That's the polite peer saying, "Oh, I'm sorry—you go ahead" in the face of an offer collision.

Impolite peers do not simply ignore *all* offers. Determining whether there is an offer collision, then, is the other piece of information needed to set the $self.isIgnoringOffer state to either true or false. The value of offer_collision will be either true or false based on this line above $self.isIgnoringOffer:

```
const offer_collision =
    description.type === 'offer' && !ready_for_offer;
```

This will assign a value of true to offer_collision if two things are true: 1) the incoming description.type is offer (not answer) and 2) the $self side of the call is not ready to receive an offer: !ready_for_offer. The syntax looks a little wild, but just remember that a single = sign is for assignment—giving offer_collision a value— and a triple === is a strict-comparison operator: is description.type equal to and of the same type (string) as 'offer'? If that is true, and the peer is not ready to receive an offer, then there's an offer collision.

And that takes us to the top line of this mountainous climb, where there's one final tangle of Boolean values to straighten out:

```
const ready_for_offer =
    !$self.isMakingOffer &&
    ($peer.connection.signalingState === 'stable'
      || $self.isSettingRemoteAnswerPending);
```

Let's break this one down, too. The $self side of the connection will be ready for an offer (ready_for_offer === true) if it is not in the middle of making an offer of its own and if at least one of two other things is true: either 1) the peer-connection's signaling state is 'stable', or 2) the $self side of the connection is trying to set a remote answer. While the value of signalingState changes over the course of connection negotiation,[5] the only state we're interested in in this logic is stable. In that state, a peer connection can accept incoming offers.

The other two Boolean values—$self.isMakingOffer and $self.isSettingRemoteAnswerPending—are determined elsewhere in the connection logic. You have already seen the first one: you set $self.isMakingOffer in the handleRtcConnectionNegotiation() callback. To refresh your memory, here it is again:

```
demos/basic-p2p/js/main.js
async function handleRtcConnectionNegotiation() {
  $self.isMakingOffer = true;
  console.log('Attempting to make an offer...');
  await $peer.connection.setLocalDescription();
  sc.emit('signal', { description: $peer.connection.localDescription });
  $self.isMakingOffer = false;
}
```

The code in that example is the same as what you already wrote, but there's something new worth pointing out about it. As we saw in Establishing the Polite Peer, on page 45, the first peer triggers the connected peer event before the second peer joins the call. Similarly, the first peer will also immediately send off its initial offer over the signaling channel—again, almost certainly before the second peer is around to receive it. But on the outside chance the second peer *does* receive the first peer's offer, that would likely happen before the second peer generates its own offer—meaning there wouldn't be a collision.

And that's why it's smart to set the first-connecting peer as the polite one: by the time the second peer joins the call, the first is hopelessly awaiting an answer that will never come. And instead of sending the answer that the first peer expects, the impolite, second-connected peer fires off an offer of its own. That's glare: both sides have offers out, and both sides expect answers that ordinarily will never come. But because the first peer is polite, it will ditch its

---

5.   https://www.w3.org/TR/webrtc/#rtcsignalingstate-enum

own initial offer (a process called *rollback*) and immediately respond to the
second peer's offer with an answer. Let's write the code for that next.

Handling Offer and Answer Descriptions

If $self isn't ignoring offers, it has no choice but to respond. Add this code to
the bottom of the if (description){ } block inside of the handleScSignal() callback:

```
// inside the handleScSignal() function definition
if (description) {

  // snip, snip

  if ($self.isIgnoringOffer) {
    return;
  }
  $self.isSettingRemoteAnswerPending = description.type === 'answer';
  await $peer.connection.setRemoteDescription(description);
  $self.isSettingRemoteAnswerPending = false;
}
```

That's the code that sets $self.isSettingRemoteAnswerPending to true, for use in deter-
mining whether ready_for_offer is true or false. It's only set to true when the descrip-
tion.type is 'answer'. The description received, whether an offer or an answer, then
gets passed into the setRemoteDescription() method on the RTCPeerConnection object.
That's how incoming offers (and answers) are handled. The setRemoteDescription()
method is async, so it's necessary to await its completion. Once the remote
description has been set, $self.isSettingRemoteAnswerPending gets assigned back to
false, assuming it was set to true to begin with.

Below that, let's add one final block to the description-handling logic. When
an incoming description is an offer, not an answer, it's necessary to respond
with the answer the remote peer expects:

```
// inside the handleScSignal() function definition
if (description) {

  // snip

  if (description.type === 'offer') {
    await $peer.connection.setLocalDescription();
    sc.emit('signal', { description: $peer.connection.localDescription });
  }
}
```

This little block of code checks to see if the description is an offer. The received
description will have already been added to setRemoteDescription() on the lines
above, so this call to setLocalDescription() responds behind the scenes to whatever
was passed into setRemoteDescription(). After setLocalDescription() has done its work,

the resulting description—an answer—gets passed back over the signaling channel, care of the localDescription property on the peer connection object.

Putting it all together, the perfect-negotiation logic for handling incoming descriptions now looks like this:

```
demos/basic-p2p/js/main.js
async function handleScSignal({ description, candidate }) {
  if (description) {

    const ready_for_offer =
          !$self.isMakingOffer &&
          ($peer.connection.signalingState === 'stable'
            || $self.isSettingRemoteAnswerPending);

    const offer_collision =
          description.type === 'offer' && !ready_for_offer;

    $self.isIgnoringOffer = !$self.isPolite && offer_collision;

    if ($self.isIgnoringOffer) {
      return;
    }

    $self.isSettingRemoteAnswerPending = description.type === 'answer';
    await $peer.connection.setRemoteDescription(description);
    $self.isSettingRemoteAnswerPending = false;

    if (description.type === 'offer') {
      await $peer.connection.setLocalDescription();
      sc.emit('signal', { description: $peer.connection.localDescription });
    }
  } else if (candidate) {

  }
}
```

That's a lot of complex code you've written. The good news is that it's also completely portable: you can basically reuse this in any WebRTC app, independent of any other application logic you find yourself writing. You'll improve upon it and use it across all the other apps you build in this book. With incoming offers and answers now handled, let's finish the job and handle the incoming ICE candidates.

Handling Incoming ICE Candidates

Handling the ICE candidates received over the signaling channel is comparatively less complicated than handling descriptions, but ICE candidates still provide some interesting twists for our perfect-negotiation logic. Here's the complete else if (candidate) logic:

```
demos/basic-p2p/js/main.js
  } else if (candidate) {

    // Handle ICE candidates
    try {
      await $peer.connection.addIceCandidate(candidate);
    } catch(e) {
      // Log error unless $self is ignoring offers
      // and candidate is not an empty string
      if (!$self.isIgnoringOffer && candidate.candidate.length > 1) {
        console.error('Unable to add ICE candidate for peer:', e);
      }
    }

  }
}
```

This code uses a try/catch statement: whenever a candidate comes across it, we try passing it to the addIceCandidate method on the peer connection instance. That's an asynchronous operation, so it's necessary to call await on it. If the attempt at adding the ICE candidate throws an error, the error gets passed along as the e (error) argument to the catch block.

Inside the catch block, there's a little bit of protective logic for determining when to log errors returned from addIceCandidate. First, we see a return of the $self.isIgnoringOffer state property, this time with a negating ! in front of it. Saying "not" aloud again works here: *If we're not ignoring offers....* There's no value to logging ICE candidate errors if $self is ignoring offers, because in that state $self can harmlessly ignore errors on ICE candidates, too.

In addition to checking the state of $self.isIgnoringOffer, the if statement also tests the length property on the candidate string to make sure it's greater than one. Some browsers burp up empty ICE candidates as a single space when they have no more candidates left to offer. The empty candidate functions as an "end-of-candidates" indicator.[6] In browsers with modern WebRTC implementations, empty candidates are expected. But some older browsers will complain and throw an error from addIceCandidate() over an empty ICE candidate. Empty candidates don't prevent older browsers from establishing a connection, so there's no need for us to listen to their complaints about them.

Putting the error-logging logic all together in quick summary: if $self isn't ignoring offers and the candidate.candidate value isn't an empty string or a space, we log out the error to console.error().

---

6. https://developer.mozilla.org/en-US/docs/Web/API/RTCPeerConnection/addIceCandidate

And that, I'm delighted to tell you, is that. All of your WebRTC connection-negotiation logic is in place. Let's write one more short piece of code, and you'll be able to test your work out in full.

Receiving Media Tracks

Recall that we set up logic to attach media tracks to the call in Sending Media Tracks, on page 49. On the receiving side, we need logic that's going to listen for the remote peer's media coming in over the WebRTC connection and then set the peer <video>'s srcObject to the incoming stream. To do this, find the skeletal handleRtcPeerTrack() callback function you defined earlier and put some flesh on its bones:

```
demos/basic-p2p/js/main.js
function handleRtcPeerTrack({ track, streams: [stream] }) {
  console.log('Attempt to display media from peer...');
  displayStream(stream, '#peer');
}
```

Once more we see destructuring assignment at work: this time, it pulls out the returned track and stream from the event object returned by onaddtrack. To display the incoming stream, we reuse the displayStream() function we built earlier in Requesting User-Media Permissions, on page 37. Only this time, we pass in the peer's media stream coming in over the WebRTC connection and select the #peer video element to display it.

Avoid the Unmute Event

You'll often see WebRTC tutorials that add a callback to the unmute event when handling an incoming track.[a]

Code that waits for the unmute event to fire on a track will not display video until there are video frames streaming in from the peer. That can be frustrating in development, so I prefer to allow the empty frames from a video source to display immediately. Additionally, unmute was not properly supported in Safari until version 11—meaning that users running older versions of Safari would never see any video at all, as the unmute event would never fire.

---

a.   https://developer.mozilla.org/en-US/docs/Web/API/MediaStreamTrack/unmute_event

In a more sophisticated streaming-media setup, we might manage individual media tracks and add them to a custom peer MediaStream object, like we did for self in the requestUserMedia() code on page 41. (In fact, that's exactly the sophisticated streaming-media setup we'll build later in the book, in Adding

Mic and Camera Toggles, on page 98.) But working with the stream is perfectly acceptable for now. There's only the one video track to this stream anyway.

Testing Out Your First Peer-to-Peer App

Now it's time to test it all out. Reduce the size of the browser window you've been working in so there's room to open a second just like it. Be sure to copy and paste the URL from the first window into the second, so you're communicating over the same namespace on the signaling channel. Refresh both windows, grant permissions for the camera, and then hit Join Call in one window, then the other. Then get ready to see a whole lot of your own face on the screen.

If things aren't working, don't lose heart. Check your console for any errors and messages, including the ones from the calls to console.log that you sprinkled in along your journey through this chapter. You might also want to check your work against the completed example in the demos/basic-p2p/ directory.

Leaving and Rejoining a Call

One more task and this basic app will be feature-complete. We need to make it so the Leave Call button works as advertised for peers who want to leave. The peer remaining on the call must also know what to do when the other peer leaves—especially in the event that the leaving peer rejoins the call.

To manage the steps for tearing down the call, let's create a function called resetPeer() right below establishCallFeatures(). The resetPeer() function should set the incoming peer's video stream to null (without that, the last frame received would continue to display someone's face frozen in an unflattering grimace for the rest of time) as well as close the existing peer connection:

demos/basic-p2p/js/main.js

```
/**
 *  Call Features & Reset Functions
 */

function establishCallFeatures(peer) {
  registerRtcCallbacks(peer);
  addStreamingMedia($self.mediaStream, peer);
}
function resetPeer(peer) {
  displayStream(null, '#peer');
  peer.connection.close();
  peer.connection = new RTCPeerConnection($self.rtcConfig);
}
```

Calling the close() method on the peer connection instance, peer.connection, tells the browser that that instance is no longer in use. (Closing the peer connection happens in addition to closing the signaling channel at the top of the leaveCall() function, which you wrote earlier—we will return to it in a moment.) And then in a move of pure optimism, the last line of resetPeer() initializes a new RTCPeerConnection object in case the leaving peer decides to rejoin the call. That's why we named the function resetPeer(), rather than something ominous and destructive like obliteratePeer().

We need to call resetPeer() in two different places. Start with the leaving peer, who clicks the Leave Call button. Open up the leaveCall() function, and add the following line:

demos/basic-p2p/js/main.js
```
function leaveCall() {
  sc.close();
  resetPeer($peer);
}
```

When the remote peer leaves, the remaining peer needs to know about it, and be told what to do, too. You could write some heavy-duty logic for the remaining peer to detect a closing RTCPeerConnection, but you already have an empty handleScDisconnectedPeer() callback function in place to handle the signaling channel's disconnected peer event. The logic is already there and triggered by the Leave Call button. A dropped network connection on either side of the call will also trigger the disconnected peer event, which makes tying the reset logic to the signaling channel a robust choice. So let's build out the handleScDisconnectedPeer() callback:

```
demos/basic-p2p/js/main.js
function handleScDisconnectedPeer() {
➤   resetPeer($peer);
➤   establishCallFeatures($peer);
}
```

As we did inside of leaveCall(), we call the resetPeer() function from within the handleScDisconnectedPeer() callback, where we also call the establishCallFeatures() function. Note that we didn't have to reestablish the call features for the leaving peer: rejoining the call by clicking the Join Call button will register the callbacks and add the media, care of establishCallFeatures() on the signaling channel's connect event, like when the peer joined the call initially. But for a peer remaining on the call, we quietly call establishCallFeatures() so that there is no need for the remaining peer to click Leave Call and then Join Call again.

One more time, refresh both of your browser windows. Try leaving and rejoining the call from either window. You can even leave the call from both windows, and then rejoin. Everything should be working as expected on both ends of the call when one or both peers decide to leave—and come back.

Next Steps

With all of this working, congratulate yourself. This is a huge feat, and you've now mastered all of the fundamental techniques for establishing, tearing down, and resetting peer-to-peer connections with WebRTC. You're streaming live video like a pro. As cool as that is, you can stream more than audio and video over a peer-to-peer connection. In the next chapter, you will open up and manage pipelines for streaming application data over the RTCDataChannel interface.

## CHAPTER 4

Handling Data Channels

Over the last two chapters, you built the essential core of all WebRTC applications: you connected to a signaling server and established a peer connection according to the perfect-negotiation pattern. You also successfully implemented WebRTC's most famous feature, which is the ability to stream user media from one peer to another in real time.

But streaming media is only one facet of WebRTC's capabilities. WebRTC connections can also stream any application data you like, directly from one peer to another, over the RTCDataChannel interface. This chapter picks up right where you left off and will have you adding a couple of features to your video-call app for streaming application data, too.

The first feature you'll build will enable your users to set filters on their videos. For example, users will be able to set it so that their video streams display in black and white, instead of the normal color coming off of their cameras. We'll use a data channel to tell the remote peer to set the same filter as the local peer selects. The video-filter feature will help you familiarize yourself with an asymmetric method for adding data channels to a call, and the events that data channels fire as they are added, opened, and closed.

We'll follow that up with a second, more involved feature backed by data channels: a chat box that will give users the ability to send text messages to each other. In setting up the chat feature, we'll employ a symmetric method for adding data channels to a call and look more closely at how data is sent and received over WebRTC data channels.

In this chapter, we'll be sending data in the form of simple strings, which is enough to build these two features. You'll extend your skills to stream more sophisticated forms of data in Chapter 5, Streaming Complex Data, on page 93.

Adding Basic Visual Effects to User Videos

Let's get down to work, and do something fun and lightweight with data channels to trick out the streaming videos: we'll enable users to apply one of a small set of visual-effects filters to their video streams, and have that same filter applied to their stream on the remote peer's side of the call.

We're going to squeeze as much as we can out of very little data. Sometimes all that's needed to complete a task is to share only the tiniest bit of information. People like me who grew up in the age just before cell phones relied on all sorts of clever hacks to avoid paying for phone calls, including from pay phones. One of the most famous of those hacks was to use a pay phone to make a collect call home for Mom or Dad to come and pick you up from somewhere. When the automated operator would prompt you for your name, you instead said your message as fast as you could: "Mall! Pick me up!" And then when your parents got the call, they declined the charges but still got the recorded message. It was a simpler time. I have a friend who worked in college as a DJ on local radio, and he loves to talk about how prisoners at the nearby jail would use that same trick, breathlessly saying, "Play the new Soundgarden" in collect calls to the station.

Nostalgia aside, the first thing we'll do with data channels is modeled on the collect call hack. We're going to write a little bit of CSS that uses the filter property to build a set of visual effects to apply to the HTML elements displaying the video streams. We won't be adding any new interface components for this, like a button for choosing filters. Instead, we'll build an unadvertised feature: curious or even just bored users who click their own video elements will discover that they can cycle through the set of filters we provide them. We'll use a data channel to let the remote peer know to apply the same filter to the incoming user's stream. And then, like a parent-chauffeur or a radio DJ receiving a collect call, the remote peer will just hang up. Technically, we won't be streaming any data for this feature—we'll let the label for the data channel do all of the work.

Duplicating the Peer-to-Peer Example

You're welcome to keep working in last chapter's basic-p2p/ directory, but I'm going to duplicate that code into a new directory, dc-filters/, to keep my work organized. I do the same for other examples. If you keep working in basic-p2p/, make sure you use that path in your development browser's URLs, and not https://localhost:3000/dc-filters/ like I will.

Building Video Filters in CSS

The CSS filter property[1] will help keep this nice and simple. We will set up styles that describe four filters: grayscale, sepia, noir, and psychedelic. You can add these to your CSS file:

```
demos/dc-filters/css/screen.css
/*  Video Effects */

.filter-grayscale {
  filter: grayscale(100%);
}
.filter-sepia {
  filter: sepia(100%);
}
.filter-noir {
  filter: grayscale(100%) contrast(300%) brightness(60%);
}
.filter-psychedelic {
  filter: hue-rotate(180deg) saturate(400%) contrast(200%);
}
```

If you want to test the filters before you write any JavaScript, add one of the classes by hand to your HTML, on the #self video element, like <video id="self" class="filter-sepia">, and refresh your browser. As always, make sure that you have disabled caching in your browser's developer console so you get the latest copy of your CSS file. And don't forget to remove the class you manually added to the HTML once you've tested it out.

Cycling Through and Applying the Filters Locally

We need to build an array of filters in JavaScript that matches the CSS class selectors, and cycle through them. One way to cycle through an array in JavaScript while also avoiding global variables is to create a class. Classes are easier than ever to write in JavaScript with the class keyword, which is supported in all browsers that support WebRTC. If you decide to go even wilder with video effects later, you'll have their foundations all neatly encapsulated in this class.

One thing to note about JavaScript class declarations is they aren't hoisted the way function declarations are. That means any class declarations must be written near the top of your JavaScript file, before you reference them. You might find it useful to declare classes using the variable-assignment syntax (const VideoFX = class {}, rather than class VideoFX {}) to remind yourself of that:

---

1. https://developer.mozilla.org/en-US/docs/Web/CSS/filter

```
demos/dc-filters/js/main.js
/**
 * Classes
 */

const VideoFX = class {
  constructor() {
    this.filters = ['grayscale', 'sepia', 'noir', 'psychedelic', 'none'];
  }
  cycleFilter() {
    const filter = this.filters.shift();
    this.filters.push(filter);
    return filter;
  }
};
```

In the constructor(), we set an instance property—this.filters—to hold an array of the filters to match the ones described in the CSS. A none filter will return the video to a filterless state, because there's no equivalent class selector with that name in the CSS. For brevity's sake, the array members don't include the filter- prefix used in the CSS. We'll add that elsewhere.

The VideoFX class includes just a single method, cycleFilter(), which uses the array shift() method to grab the filter from the front of the array and the push() method to then stick that filter onto the end of the array. That's how users will cycle through all the filters in a never-ending loop. The cycleFilter() method also returns the shifted array element, which we'll use in a moment to set a class in the HTML and apply the video effect.

With the class written, we can assign an instance of it to a filters property on the $self object:

```
demos/dc-filters/js/main.js
/**
 *  User-Media Setup
 */

requestUserMedia($self.mediaConstraints);

$self.filters = new VideoFX();
```

Great. Now let's write a little more JavaScript to use $self.filters when the self video element is clicked. An anonymous function is fine for now—we'll turn it into a named callback shortly:

```
document.querySelector('#self')
  .addEventListener('click', function(event) {
    const filter = `filter-${$self.filters.cycleFilter()}`;
    e.target.className = filter;
  });
```

All that does is listen for click events on the self video, and then apply the filter-prefixed class name to the video. But the effect is pretty satisfying. Here is the noir filter applied:

Preparing to Apply the Video Filters Remotely

With that code in place, both peers can set filters on their own videos. The next step is to instruct the remote peer to apply the same filter to the incoming stream. The actual video stream is unaffected; we're applying CSS filters to the video elements on both sides of the call. We'll make use of the RTCDataChannel API to accomplish that and see again how WebRTC knits together the states and behavior of remote interfaces: data channels can be more than a conduit for data.

Opening a data channel on a peer connection can be more time- and state-sensitive than adding streaming media. Recall how in Sending Media Tracks, on page 49, we attached the streaming-media tracks to the connection by calling the establishCallFeatures() function in the handleScConnect() callback:

demos/dc-filters/js/main.js
```
function handleScConnect() {
  console.log('Successfully connected to the signaling server!');
  establishCallFeatures($peer);
}
```

Once the peer connection is negotiated and established, the video and audio begin streaming almost immediately. Users know to wait until they can see or hear the remote peer before they begin speaking. As developers, we don't have to worry about the content of audio or video streams that simply aren't received by the remote peer before the connection is established.

That's not always the case with data channels. It's sometimes better to ensure the peer connection is established before activating any user-interface elements that allow users to interact with each other over data channels. For the video-filter feature, that means not enabling users to set filters until the other peer is connected.

Determining Peer-Connection States

The RTCPeerConnection interface provides two features that simplify working with peer-connection states: an onconnectionstatechange property for attaching a callback function, and a connectionState property for determining what state the connection is in. (Note the WebRTC connectionState differs from the signalingState that appeared as part of the the perfect-negotiation code in the last chapter on page 55).

You can define a handleRtcConnectionStateChange() callback function, right alongside the other peer-connection callbacks you've already written. To start, write a call to console.log to get a sense of how the connection state changes as a call is established. A local connection_state variable will make it easier to reference the connection state multiple times over the life of the function:

demos/dc-filters/js/main.js
```
function handleRtcConnectionStateChange() {
  const connection_state = $peer.connection.connectionState;
  console.log(`The connection state is now ${connection_state}`);
}
```

Be sure to register the callback inside of your registerRtcCallbacks function, too:

demos/dc-filters/js/main.js
```
function registerRtcCallbacks(peer) {
  peer.connection.onconnectionstatechange = handleRtcConnectionStateChange;
  peer.connection.onnegotiationneeded = handleRtcConnectionNegotiation;
  peer.connection.onicecandidate = handleRtcIceCandidate;
  peer.connection.ontrack = handleRtcPeerTrack;
}
```

On each connection-state change, the handleRtcConnectionStateChange() function will log to the console one of six possible states defined in the low-level RTCPeerConnectionState enumerable: new, connecting, connected, disconnected, failed, and closed.[2] We can use descendent selectors in CSS to apply styles based on the connection state, so let's also set a utility class on the <body> element that will always reflect the current connection state:

demos/dc-filters/js/main.js
```
function handleRtcConnectionStateChange() {
  const connection_state = $peer.connection.connectionState;
  console.log(`The connection state is now ${connection_state}`);
  document.querySelector('body').className = connection_state;
}
```

With only that code in place, reload your app in both browser windows. Make sure you've got the console visible. Then join the call, and see what the console reports.

Template Literals

You might have noticed a different style of demarcating strings in this chapter's examples. Instead of using the familiar single or double quotes, template literals are wrapped in backticks, `like this`.

One of the powerhouse features that comes with template literals (sometimes also called template strings) is expression interpolation. Within a template literal, you can write any JavaScript expression you like, and the evaluated expression's string representation will become part of the string. The result is syntax that is more readable than the string concatenation that's long been used in JavaScript:

```
// concatenation:
console.log('The area of the square is ' + 5 * 5 + ' meters');
// interpolation:
console.log(`The area of the square is ${5 * 5} meters`);
```

Any JavaScript expression, including variables, is permissible inside the ${} placeholder. All browsers with modern WebRTC implementations also support template literals.[a]

---

a. https://developer.mozilla.org/en-US/docs/Web/JavaScript/Reference/Template_literals

Loading adapter.js

If you're running an up-to-date version of Chrome or Firefox, you'll see messages in the console that the connection state is connecting and then connected. If you're using or testing an older version of Firefox, you will see that the connection is undefined. That will put an undefined state class on <body>, too. As

---

2. https://www.w3.org/TR/webrtc/#rtcpeerconnectionstate-enum

good as Firefox's implementation of WebRTC is, the connectionState property was missing prior to version 113.[3]

So here comes a small compatibility enhancement for browsers that need it. It's a simple one: we're going to load up a separate JavaScript file called adapter.js[4] that patches and polyfills certain parts of the RTCPeerConnection interface, including a missing connectionState property that can help us determine when it's safe to begin attaching and working with asymmetric data channels. Even if you've been hacking on the latest browsers, be sure to add this for the sake of older ones. Open up your HTML file, and add this <script> tag just before the one that loads your main.js file:

demos/dc-filters/index.html
```
<script src="/socket.io/socket.io.js"></script>
➤ <script
➤   src="https://webrtchacks.github.io/adapter/adapter-latest.js"></script>
<script src="js/main.js"></script>
```

Note well the URL for the script. An outdated version of adapter.js hosted under an old GitHub account is often referenced on even current examples on the web. You want to make sure you're loading the one hosted by the webrtcHacks GitHub account, as in the example above. You can find instructions for serving your own copy of adapter.js, but you'll prefer the simplicity of loading up a hosted copy of adapter-latest.js. Let someone else worry about keeping it up to date.

With adapter.js in place, reload your app. Just like Chrome, older versions of Firefox should now report the connection state, not undefined. If you want to see the initial connection state, new, make a similar call to console.log on the line below where you assigned new RTCPeerConnection() to the connection property on $peer. The browser will announce right away that the connection state is new.

Using the Connection-State Class

With the connection state correctly reporting in the console, you can now return to the state class on the <body> element and put it to work in your CSS. Recall that the video-effects feature is unadvertised. Let's give users with pointer devices a little clue about it by changing the cursor to a button/link-style pointer when hovering over the #self video:

demos/dc-filters/css/screen.css
```
.connected #self {
  cursor: pointer;
}
```

---

3. https://developer.mozilla.org/en-US/docs/Web/API/RTCPeerConnection/connectionState
4. https://github.com/webrtcHacks/adapter

That little .connected #self descendent selector ensures that the pointer-style cursor only appears when the peer connection is in a connected state. Refresh both of your browser windows and test it out. Make sure, too, that you've activated the window you're checking, because your operating system might only display the default arrow cursor otherwise.

Applying Filters Remotely with Data Channels

Having made that detour to improve the WebRTC code with adapter.js, let's get back to work on the goal of applying video filters remotely. Take the anonymous click-event handler you wrote earlier and rewrite it as a handleSelfVideo() callback. Start by immediately exiting the callback function when the peer connection state is anything other than connected:

demos/dc-filters/js/main.js
```
document.querySelector('#self')
  .addEventListener('click', handleSelfVideo);

function handleSelfVideo(event) {
  if ($peer.connection.connectionState !== 'connected') return;
  const filter = `filter-${$self.filters.cycleFilter()}`;
  event.target.className = filter;
}
```

Now the click event won't apply any filters to the self video until after the connection is established and reporting a connected state.

You're now set up to build data-channel logic into the handleSelfVideo() callback. You'll do that by calling the createDataChannel() method on the peer connection, passing in the value of the filter variable as the channel's label.[5] A label is nothing more than a string to identify the channel by name, as you'll read about in Uniquely Identifying Data Channels, on page 73. As a diagnostic, you can also listen for the onclose event on the data channel and log a message to the console when the peer closes it:

demos/dc-filters/js/main.js
```
function handleSelfVideo(event) {
  if ($peer.connection.connectionState !== 'connected') return;
  const filter = `filter-${$self.filters.cycleFilter()}`;
  const fdc = $peer.connection.createDataChannel(filter);
  fdc.onclose = function() {
    console.log(`Remote peer has closed the ${filter} data channel`);
  };
  event.target.className = filter;
}
```

---

5. https://developer.mozilla.org/en-US/docs/Web/API/RTCPeerConnection/createDataChannel

The label for the data channel that opens—something like filter-noir—determines the filter that'll be set for the incoming video stream on the remote peer's side of the call. We're not even really sending any data here. It's just metadata—data channel's label—that the remote peer will use to set a class on the incoming peer's video element. All that's missing is logic to listen for incoming data-channel events.

Listening for the Filter Data Channel on the Remote Peer

First, let's review what we've done so far: we've built an event listener that registers click events on the self video. Each time the video is clicked, if the peer connection is in a connected state, the active filter changes and gets applied to the local peer's self video. The local peer also opens a data channel with the name of the filter. The final step, then, is to listen for data channel events and respond to them.

You'll do that by creating another RTC connection callback function and attaching it to the peer connection's ondatachannel property. The datachannel event will fire any time a data channel is added to the connection. Because an app can open multiple data channels for handling different tasks, it's often necessary to do some checks on the data channel's label value, and trigger the appropriate action based on the label. Here, the startsWith string method works nicely to check for filter-related data channels:[6]

demos/dc-filters/js/main.js
```
function registerRtcCallbacks(peer) {
  peer.connection.onconnectionstatechange = handleRtcConnectionStateChange;
  peer.connection.ondatachannel = handleRtcDataChannel;
  peer.connection.onnegotiationneeded = handleRtcConnectionNegotiation;
  peer.connection.onicecandidate = handleRtcIceCandidate;
  peer.connection.ontrack = handleRtcPeerTrack;
}

function handleRtcDataChannel({ channel }) {
  const label = channel.label;
  console.log(`Data channel added for ${label}`);
  if (label.startsWith('filter-')) {
    document.querySelector('#peer').className = label;
  }
}
```

Note how destructuring assignment is lifting the channel object off of the returned event object, giving us a local channel variable within the function. Any time a data channel opens with a label that starts with filter-, we set the label as

---

6.   https://developer.mozilla.org/en-US/docs/Web/JavaScript/Reference/Global_Objects/String/startsWith

the class name on the peer video element. Once that happens, the local peer's self video and the remote peer's incoming video will have the same filter applied.

That code will work as expected, but as curious users cycle through the various filters, a whole bunch of data channels will be left attached to the call with nothing to do. They'll almost certainly get into some kind of mischief. So let's do a little cleanup and, like parents receiving a collect call from their stranded kids, wait for the incoming data channel's onopen event to fire, at which point we'll hang up by closing it:

```
demos/dc-filters/js/main.js
function handleRtcDataChannel({ channel }) {
  const label = channel.label;
  console.log(`Data channel added for ${label}`);
  if (label.startsWith('filter-')) {
    document.querySelector('#peer').className = label;
    channel.onopen = function() {
      channel.close();
    };
  }
}
```

With that all wired up, refresh your browser windows and give it a try. As you cycle through the filters on the self video on one side of the connection, you should see the same filter applied to the incoming video on the other side. In the JavaScript console, you'll see messages like "Remote peer has closed the filter-grayscale data channel" logged each time you cycle through to a new filter, confirming each short-lived filter channel has been closed.

Uniquely Identifying Data Channels

Data channels can be opened asymmetrically or symmetrically. For setting video filters remotely, data channels are opened asymmetrically: the peer wishing to set a new video filter adds the channel to the call, and the receiving peer listens for the ondatachannel event. We labeled the data channel by passing in the name of a filter, like filter-grayscale, to the peer connection's createDataChannel() method.

Useful as they are, labels do not uniquely identify data channels. It's the stuff of debugging nightmares that multiple data channels can end up with the same label. You can experiment with this by writing a little diagnostic code and joining a call in two browser windows. First, open up an else statement in the handleRtcDataChannel callback:

```
} else {
  console.log(`Opened ${channel.label} channel with an ID of ${channel.id}`);
}
```

Refresh the pages in both of your browser windows and join the call. Run $peer.connection.createDataChannel('experiment').id in each window's console. The labels will be the same, but you'll see different numbers returned in each window. For example, just now I got an id of 3 in one console, and an id of 2 in another. Even though the label, experiment, was exactly the same, the id values differ. And the id value is what actually uniquely identifies a data channel.

For that reason, an asymmetric channel must only ever be opened by one peer—even if both peers are allowed to send data over it. (That's not a great idea for asymmetric channels, because you then need to write logic to ensure both peers can't open the channel simultaneously.) The other peer will listen for the channel to be opened, and then preserve a reference to the channel in a variable—just as you've done for the data channels that handle filters. Asymmetric channels are excellent choices for data channels that are either short-lived or that only handle data sent by a peer on one side of the call, which again is the case for the video-filter channels.

Opening Symmetric Data Channels

Asymmetric data channels aren't the only game in WebRTC town, though. Data channels can also be opened symmetrically, which is a better option for channels that permit both peers to send and receive data. The RTCDataChannel interface refers to symmetric data channels as *negotiated*. To create a negotiated data channel, we have to pass in a label as well as an options object to createDataChannel(). At a minimum, the options object includes two values. First, it must set a negotiated property to true. And second, it must specify a unique id for the data channel. Try running this code to create a negotiated data channel (ndc) in the consoles of two connected browsers:

```
const ndc = $peer.connection
  .createDataChannel('negotiated', { negotiated: true, id: 100 });
console.log(`Label: ${ ndc.label }, ID: ${ ndc.id }`);
```

Both browsers will report a data channel with a negotiated label and an ID of 100. But importantly, you will not see a logged message of Opened negotiated channel with an ID of 100. That's because negotiated or symmetric data channels do not fire the ondatachannel event. The negotiated: true option means that both sides of a call are expected to add the same data channel independently. This is exactly what we will do to set up the data channel for supporting a text chat in the call: because both users can send data over it, and because we don't want to have to write a ton of logic to manage an edge case where both users might open the channel simultaneously, a negotiated, symmetric data channel is the better choice.

ID Values for Data Channels

The WebRTC specification notes that the value of a data channel ID is an "unsigned short."[a] If you're struggling to remember that day in kindergarten class when you learned about maximum values of unsigned short integers, it's usually around 65,535 or 2^{15}-1. However, after testing this extensively across Firefox and Chrome, I can report that you'll want to set your IDs well under 1000. 500, to be safe. And there's nothing at all wrong with assigning IDs in the single digits. My preference is to assign negotiated data-channel IDs starting at 100. That helps me with debugging when there are lots of data channels in play: if I have an ID that is 100 or above, I know that I am dealing with a negotiated data channel.

Asymmetrically added data channels will be opened with the lowest ID value the browser has available. In the case of peers opening more than one channel simultaneously, the first peer to add a data channel will increment ID values by odd numbers, starting with 1 (1, 3, 5, 7...), and the peer that is second will increment by even numbers, starting with zero (0, 2, 4, 6...). That prevents ID-value collisions from ever happening on asymmetric data channels. Note that browsers release and can reuse ID values as soon as the data channels using them have been closed and garbage-collected, so a given ID value is in no way guaranteed to be unique over the life of a call.

---

a.   https://www.w3.org/TR/webrtc/#dom-rtcdatachannel-id

Adding a Text-Chat Feature

Let's add a more useful feature to the app: a text chat. Anyone who's ever shared a URL in a text chat on a video call already knows how useful text chats can be, independent of full audio and video capabilities. A text chat also makes a call more accessible to users who cannot speak or hear, or be heard, for any reason.

By building a text chat, we're going to learn how to work with negotiated data channels. As you read in the last section, the method for adding negotiated channels to a call differs somewhat from the asymmetric data channels we used for the video filters. We'll also learn how to send data over data channels, which works the same way on symmetric and asymmetric data channels. And to make for a more robust interface, we'll add a message-queueing system that enables users to compose messages whenever they like—even before a call—and the app will send any queued messages as soon as the data channel opens.

We'll start things off by quickly building the chat's interface components as another example of the tight bond between UI and WebRTC. I'm going to copy the dc-filters/ directory to one called dc-chat-basic/. You can do the same, if you'd like, or keep working in whatever directory makes you happiest.

Building the Text-Chat Interface

Pull open your HTML file to start. Just below the article element containing the streaming videos, but still inside of <main>, open up an <aside id="chat"> element for holding the chat-related components: an accessibility-minded heading, plus an empty ordered list for logging the chat messages and a small form for composing them. Remember that we've got reset CSS in place that strips numbers off of ordered lists and bullets off of unordered lists, so we don't have to worry about numbers appearing. Semantically, an ordered list makes good sense, because chat messages will be appended to the list in the order that they are composed and received:

demos/dc-chat-basic/index.html
```
<aside id="chat">
  <h2 class="preserve-access">Text Chat</h2>
  <ol id="chat-log"></ol>
</aside>
```

Below the empty ordered list, you can create a basic form with three elements: a <label> associated via the for attribute with an <input> where users can type a message, and a send <button> for users who prefer to click something instead of hitting Return to send the message. It's important to disable autocomplete or users might be shown an annoying drop-down with all their previous messages. If you like, you can explicitly set type="submit" on the button element, even though it's associated with a <form> and takes that type implicitly:

demos/dc-chat-basic/index.html
```
<aside id="chat">
  <h2 class="preserve-access">Text Chat</h2>
  <ol id="chat-log"></ol>
➤ <form id="chat-form" action="#null">
➤   <label for="chat-msg" class="preserve-access">Compose Message</label>
➤   <input type="text" id="chat-msg" name="chat-msg" autocomplete="off" />
➤   <button type="submit" id="chat-btn">Send</button>
➤ </form>
</aside>
```

We'll be handling the form's behavior in JavaScript, of course, and you might find it useful to include action="#null" on JavaScript-dependent forms as a reminder of that.

Improving the Chat App's CSS

Over in the CSS, let's refine some existing styles and add some new ones. The goal here is to try and manage the elements on the page—the header and its button, the videos, and the new chat box—to keep them responsive but also visible at all times without users needing to scroll away from the video streams. To achieve that, we'll use viewport units as well as CSS grid and flexbox.

Setting an exact height, such as 100vh, gives us some vertically responsive superpowers with CSS grid, which you can set up for both narrow screens and a larger 680px viewport:

demos/dc-chat-basic/css/screen.css

```
/* Layout */

* {
  box-sizing: border-box;
}
#interface {
➤  height: 100vh;
   padding: 22px;
➤  display: grid;
➤  grid-gap: 11px;
➤  grid-template-rows: auto auto 1fr; /* heading videos chatbox */
}
➤ #header { /* Can discard this selector; superseded by grid-gap. */ }

   /* Media Queries */

➤ @media screen and (min-width: 680px) {
➤    #interface {
➤      grid-template-columns: 1fr 1fr;
➤      grid-template-rows: auto 1fr;
➤    }
➤    #header {
➤      grid-column: 1 / 3;
➤    }
➤ }
```

At the mobile scale, we set three rows: auto for the first two means that the header and the article element containing the videos should be sized according to the size of their content. The third row, however, is set to 1fr. That's the row the chat box will sit on. The magic of 1fr coupled with a 100vh on the grid results in a chat box that will always be perfectly sized to occupy whatever vertical space remains—regardless of how many messages it contains. You can completely remove the old #header style declaration, because its 11px bottom-margin is now handled by the 11px value on the grid-gap property.

At the 680px breakpoint, there's room to introduce a second column, which is where the chat box will appear. The header occupies its own row, above the two equally-sized columns containing the videos and chat box, which will automatically appear in the correct rows and columns without us having to write any CSS explicitly placing them there.

Because the interface now has to accommodate a chat box, let's reduce the overall footprint of the videos. We'll further shrink the size of the self video and use CSS positioning so that it overlays the peer video's top lefthand corner:

demos/dc-chat-basic/css/screen.css

```css
#videos {
  position: relative;
}
#self {
  width: 30%;
  position: absolute;
  top: 11px;
  left: 11px;
  z-index: 1000; /* Prevent remote filters from hiding #self */
  border: 1px solid #CCC;
}
```

The reason for setting a z-index on self is to stave off a rendering bug on any incoming video filters: in Firefox, for example, once a filter has been applied to an incoming video, the self video seems to disappear. A high z-index value on the self video prevents that from happening.

Finally, let's anticipate callers joining from phones or other devices that might have portrait-oriented video streams. With the videos now more neatly contained, we'll change the max-width property to width. This will keep the size of the video consistent, even if network conditions change. We'll also set the CSS aspect-ratio property to 4:3,[7] which will always display video boxes in that aspect ratio. To make sure that video streams always fill the entirety of their designated boxes, we can set the object-fit property to cover,[8] and the object-position property to center:[9]

demos/dc-chat-basic/css/screen.css

```css
video {
  background-color: #DDD;
  display: block;
  width: 100%;
  aspect-ratio: 4 / 3;
  object-fit: cover;
  object-position: center;
}
```

---

7. https://developer.mozilla.org/en-US/docs/Web/CSS/aspect-ratio
8. https://developer.mozilla.org/en-US/docs/Web/CSS/object-fit
9. https://developer.mozilla.org/en-US/docs/Web/CSS/object-position

Styling the Chat Box

Let's add some styles to make an attractive chat box. The form element should be anchored to the very bottom of the box, and the log of messages should appear above it. The log of messages should also scroll once there are more messages than fit in the box. We'll use CSS flexbox in tandem with the overflow property to achieve that effect:

demos/dc-chat-basic/css/screen.css

```css
#chat {
  height: 100%;
  min-height: 220px; /* Accommodate small, squarish screens */
  border: 1px solid #999;
  padding: 5.5px;

  display: flex; /* Use columnar flexbox to constrain log */
  flex-direction: column;

  font-weight: normal;
}
#chat-log {
  flex-grow: 1;
  overflow: auto;
  padding-bottom: 11px;
  margin-bottom: 5.5px;
  min-height: 0; /* Firefox fix */
}
#chat-form {
  flex-grow: 0;
  display: flex;
}
```

What we're doing in that CSS is setting up a vertical flexbox (flex-direction: column), which gains some vertically responsive superpowers in a parent element with a set height, which your app has, thanks to the CSS grid you set up on the main element, along with its 100vh height. The vertical flexbox will simply fill the remaining space of the containing grid line. It does that by placing the chat form at whatever size its input and button render at before allotting the remaining space to #chat-log, thanks to flex-grow: 1. As you can see in the CSS comments, we set min-height: 0 to stave off yet another rendering bug in certain versions of Firefox.[10]

By setting overflow: auto, any content that doesn't fit within the chat-log box will simply scroll out of view. On larger viewports, the empty box will look something like the screenshot on page 80.

---

10. https://medium.com/@stephenbunch/how-to-make-a-scrollable-container-with-dynamic-height-using-flexbox-5914a26ae336

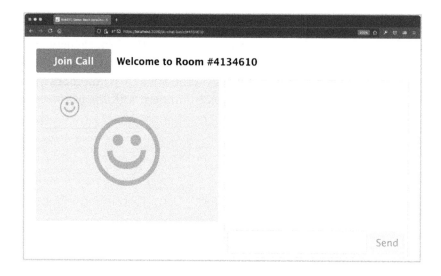

To finish up, let's provide styles for the individual chat messages and the chat form. Here is a chunk of styles to handle how messages are displayed:

demos/dc-chat-basic/css/screen.css
```
#chat-log li {
  border-radius: 5.5px;
  padding: 5.5px;
  margin-bottom: 5.5px;
  max-width: 60%;
  clear: both;
}
#chat-log .peer {
  background: #EEE;
  float: left;
}
#chat-log .self {
  background: #009;
  color: #EEE;
  float: right;
}
```

That will give the messages the look of a texting app: the peer's own messages will hold to the right of the chat log and have a blue background. The incoming, remote peer's messages will be gray and hold to the left. Old-school floats are enough to accomplish that.

And finally, because you set #chat-form to display: flex, it's its own flex container. That will make it very easy to allow the chat-message input to grow as needed to the left of the send button, which will always be the same size—neither growing nor shrinking:

```
demos/dc-chat-basic/css/screen.css
#chat-form button {
  cursor: pointer;
  flex: 0 0 auto;
  background: #009;
  color: #EEE;
}
#chat-form input {
  flex: 1 1 100%;
  padding: 9px;
  margin-right: 5.5px;
  border: 2px solid #999;
  outline: 0;
}
```

That's it for our work with CSS. With the HTML structures and a responsive design in place, let's carry this over the finish line and wire up the data-channel logic for sending and receiving messages.

Adding Logic to Handle Chat Events

With the user interface in pretty awesome, responsive shape, let's shift focus to JavaScript and handle a few important tasks to prepare the chat's behavior for use with a data channel. We'll need to listen for submit events on the form element and append chat messages to the chat log. And of course we will need to decide how and when to attach a data channel to the call, and provide logic for both peers to send and receive messages over it.

Appending Messages to the Chat Log

Messages need to be appended to the chat log when users either send or receive messages. Let's define a function that handles both cases. The function will take a few arguments: the message sender (self or peer), the element for the chat log, and the message itself. Because we're appending user input to the DOM, let's keep things ultra-safe for now and create text nodes with innerText to present the messages, rather than worry about sanitizing rogue HTML that users might try to inject:

```
demos/dc-chat-basic/js/main.js
function appendMessage(sender, log_element, message) {
  const log = document.querySelector(log_element);
  const li = document.createElement('li');
  li.className = sender;
  li.innerText = message;
  log.appendChild(li);
}
```

Now we need to listen for submit events on the chat form, and use those to trigger the appendMessage() function. The handleMessageForm() callback function must prevent the browser's default form-submission behavior and also check that the chat-message box has some content in it. It will then call the appendMessage() function and set the chat-message box's input value to an empty string—readying it for the next message a user composes:

demos/dc-chat-basic/js/main.js
```
document.querySelector('#chat-form')
  .addEventListener('submit', handleMessageForm);

function handleMessageForm(event) {
  event.preventDefault();
  const input = document.querySelector('#chat-msg');
  const message = input.value;
  if (message === '') return;

  appendMessage('self', '#chat-log', message);

  input.value = '';
}
```

Take a moment to test this out on one side of a call. Try typing some messages into the chat box. You should see them appended to the chat log above the form, as in this figure:

But if you type enough messages, you'll stop seeing them appear in the chat log, and you'll have to manually scroll down to find them. What a pain. Let's use the scrollTo property to automatically scroll to the bottom of the chat log on each appended message. For browsers that don't support scrollTo,[11] we'll add a fallback that uses old-school scrollTop instead:

demos/dc-chat-basic/js/main.js
```js
function appendMessage(sender, log_element, message) {
  const log = document.querySelector(log_element);
  const li = document.createElement('li');
  li.className = sender;
  li.innerText = message;
  log.appendChild(li);
  if (log.scrollTo) {
    log.scrollTo({
      top: log.scrollHeight,
      behavior: 'smooth',
    });
  } else {
    log.scrollTop = log.scrollHeight;
  }
}
```

Reload the app and try entering more messages. On browsers that support the options object on scrollTo, you'll see the effect of messages appearing to slide into view at the bottom of the chat log. On all other browsers, the message will appear—but it won't require users to do any scrolling. Not bad for a few lines of CSS and JavaScript.

Setting Up the Text-Chat Data Channel

With all of that in place, we can get down to work on the data-channel logic. Let's use a symmetric data channel, meaning that both peers will open the data channel as part of joining the call:

demos/dc-chat-basic/js/main.js
```js
/**
 *  User-Media and Data-Channel Functions
 */

function addChatChannel(peer) {
  peer.chatChannel =
    peer.connection.createDataChannel('text chat',
      { negotiated: true, id: 100 });
```

---

11. https://developer.mozilla.org/en-US/docs/Web/API/Element/scrollTo

```
peer.chatChannel.onmessage = function(event) {
  appendMessage('peer', '#chat-log', event.data);
};

peer.chatChannel.onclose = function() {
  console.log('Chat channel closed.');
};
}
```

Everything here should look at least a little familiar from the video-filters example: we're creating a data channel with the createDataChannel() method on the peer connection and giving it a label, text chat. But we're also passing in configuration options declaring that the channel is negotiated and that it will take an id of 100. We're also handling onmessage and onclose events, with the onmessage event calling the appendMessage() function just like the form handler does. Three cheers for function reuse!

Your last task is to call the addChatChannel() function inside of your establishCallFeatures() function:

demos/dc-chat-basic/js/main.js
```
/**
 *  Call Features & Reset Functions
 */

function establishCallFeatures(peer) {
  registerRtcCallbacks(peer);
  addChatChannel(peer);
  addStreamingMedia($self.mediaStream, peer);
}
```

Both peers will now set up the chat channel automatically, like they both add streaming media to the connection. Sweet! Thanks, establishCallFeatures(), for living up to your name.

Sending Messages over the Text-Chat Data Channel

Prepare to be a tad underwhelmed: to send messages over the chat data-channel, all we need is one line of JavaScript tucked into the handleMessageForm() callback. The line uses the data channel's send() method to transmit the message to the remote peer:

```
function handleMessageForm(event) {
  event.preventDefault();
  const input = document.querySelector('#chat-msg');
  const message = input.value;
  if (message === '') return;
  appendMessage('self', '#chat-log', message);
```

```
➤      $peer.chatChannel.send(message);
       input.value = '';
     }
```

That's literally it for the sending logic. The onmessage event you already set up in addChatChannel() handles the receiving logic, and it too runs the appendMessage() function, but with the messaging coming in over the data channel, rather than text in an input element. CSS applies color and position styles to the self and peer classes, visually distinguishing sent and received messages.

Testing the Text Chat with a Second Device

Let's test this out. But as a twist, consider using a second device on your local network for one end of the connection. If you've got a spare laptop or an Android phone running Chrome or Firefox, or an iPhone or iPad running at least Safari 15.4, give it a try. (If you keep older devices around, have a look at the fallbacks you'll need to write in Appendix 1, Connection Negotiation in Legacy Browsers, on page 225.)

You can't connect a second device over https://localhost:3000/ or https://127.0.0.1:3000/ on the second device, though. Recall that there are multiple IP addresses listed when you start the signaling server:

```
signaling-server:    ** Serving from the www/ directory. **
signaling-server:
signaling-server:    App available in your browser at:
signaling-server:
signaling-server:      -> https://127.0.0.1:3000/
signaling-server:      -> https://192.168.1.6:3000/
signaling-server:
signaling-server:    Hold CTRL + C to stop the server.
signaling-server:
signaling-server:    +0ms
```

Use that second IP address to reach your app from your other device, using a URL like https://192.168.1.6:3000/dc-chat-basic/, as with the example IP address above. And, of course, make sure the namespaces are identical on both your development machine and other device, too. You can manually set a seven-digit namespace like #0001111 in the address bar of each browser to make life easier on yourself. Once you machete your way through the security warnings you first dealt with in your development browser in Getting Past Browser Security Warnings, on page 8, you should be able to join the call and send and receive messages as shown in the screenshot on page 86.

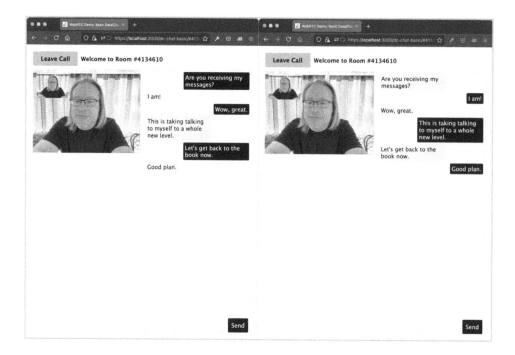

Building a Message Queue

Joining a call and sending messages works great. But there's a problem that you might have already discovered: the way you've written the chat feature, it's possible for users to compose and attempt to send messages outside of a connected state. Go ahead and reload one of your browser windows and, before joining the call, compose and send a message. You'll see the message appended in the chat box as though everything's hunky-dory, but the input box will not be cleared and your console will report an error like Uncaught TypeError: can't access property "send", $peer.chatChannel is undefined.

We need to decide what to do when users compose and send messages outside of a connected call state. While we could do something similar to what we did with the video filters and test the connectionState property before allowing users to enter a message in the chat form, let's attempt a more robust solution and build a message-queueing system instead.

What the queueing system will do is let users compose and attempt to send messages independent of the call's connection state or the data channel's own readyState. If the call is connected and the data channel is open, we will send along the message. But if the call or the data channel is out of service, maybe because the remote peer dropped out or either peer is experiencing connectivity problems, we'll hold onto their messages and queue them up for sending as soon as the data channel next becomes available.

First, let's add a messageQueue property to $self and assign it an empty array. You can do this right in the user-media setup part of your JavaScript file:

demos/dc-chat-basic/js/main.js
```
/**
 *  User-Media Setup
 */

requestUserMedia($self.mediaConstraints);

$self.filters = new VideoFX();

$self.messageQueue = [];
```

Then you can write the beginnings of a small queueMessage() function that initially takes a message argument, and pushes the message onto the end of the queue. That will result in a queue where the oldest queued message will be at the beginning of the queue—with the newest message at the end:

```
function queueMessage(message) {
  $self.messageQueue.push(message);
}
```

Next, let's write another function that will begin to neatly encapsulate the logic for queue-backed calls to send() on the data channel. It will take a peer and message as arguments:

```
function sendOrQueueMessage(peer, message) {
  const chat_channel = peer.chatChannel;
  if (!chat_channel || chat_channel.readyState !== 'open') {
    queueMessage(message, push);
    return;
  }
  try {
    chat_channel.send(message);
  } catch(e) {
    console.error('Error sending message:', e);
    queueMessage(message, push);
  }
}
```

That function starts by checking both the existence and readiness of the chatChannel data channel, which won't be set up until the call is joined. The if statement examines the channel's readyState—a property available on the RTCDataChannel interface.[12]

---

12. https://developer.mozilla.org/en-US/docs/Web/API/RTCDataChannel/readyState

If the channel does not yet exist, or if the readyState is anything other than open, the message gets queued and the function exits, care of the return statement. But if the readyState is open, the message gets sent using the data channel send() method, which appears in a try/catch statement. Should the message fail to send for any reason, it will be queued for sending later.

Let's put the sendOrQueueMessage() function to work in the context of the handleMesssageForm() callback:

```
demos/dc-chat-basic/js/main.js
function handleMessageForm(event) {
  event.preventDefault();
  const input = document.querySelector('#chat-msg');
  const message = input.value;
  if (message === '') return;

  appendMessage('self', '#chat-log', message);

➤  sendOrQueueMessage($peer, message);
  input.value = '';
}
```

If you want, you can test out your new queue-backed logic for sending messages. At the moment, it will queue any messages composed outside of a connected state. But because we have yet to write a means to send any queued messages, they'll never reach their intended recipient. Let's fix that.

Sending Queued Messages

Adding messages is only half of a queueing task, of course. We also need to be able to send any queued messages as soon as a data channel becomes available. We'll do that by assigning a callback to the chat channel's onopen event. It will be responsible for looping through the queue and sending any queued messages, beginning with the very first message that was queued: FIFO, or first in, first out.

That's a slightly trickier proposition than it sounds, in part because you will need to empty the queue of any messages that are successfully sent.

The good news is you've already written a nice sendOrQueueMessage() function, which can also be used for sending queued messages. However, you'll need to add an argument that determines what happens to a message that's already in the queue, but that still cannot be sent, for whatever reason.

Recall your original queueMessage() function:

```
function queueMessage(message) {
  $self.messageQueue.push(message);
}
```

That works well for queueing at the time of composing: more recent messages are added to the end of the queue. But as we work through a queue of previously composed messages, any message that still cannot be sent should be replaced where it came from, at the front of the queue. Otherwise, the messages appearing on the receiving side will appear all out of order, once they're ultimately sent.

To put that line of thinking into code: instead of calling the .push() method on the array, which would queue the message to the end of the array, we'll need to call the .unshift() method instead—which will add it to the beginning.[13]

Rewrite queueMessage() to take an optional push argument, which defaults to true. When push is false, the queued message should be placed at the start of the queue, courtesy of unshift():

demos/dc-chat-basic/js/main.js
```
function queueMessage(message, push = true) {
  if (push) $self.messageQueue.push(message); // queue at the end
  else $self.messageQueue.unshift(message); // queue at the start
}
```

You'll also need to add the push argument onto your sendOrQueueMessage() function, too, and pass in push to both queueMessage() calls:

demos/dc-chat-basic/js/main.js
```
function sendOrQueueMessage(peer, message, push = true) {
  const chat_channel = peer.chatChannel;
  if (!chat_channel || chat_channel.readyState !== 'open') {
    queueMessage(message, push);
    return;
  }
  try {
    chat_channel.send(message);
  } catch(e) {
    console.error('Error sending message:', e);
    queueMessage(message, push);
  }
}
```

To finish things up, you can assign an anonymous callback to peer.chatChannel.onopen inside the addChatChannel() function:

demos/dc-chat-basic/js/main.js
```
function addChatChannel(peer) {
  peer.chatChannel =
    peer.connection.createDataChannel('text chat',
      { negotiated: true, id: 100 });
```

---

13. https://developer.mozilla.org/en-US/docs/Web/JavaScript/Reference/Global_Objects/Array/unshift

```
      peer.chatChannel.onmessage = function(event) {
        appendMessage('peer', '#chat-log', event.data);
      };

      peer.chatChannel.onclose = function() {
        console.log('Chat channel closed.');
      };

➤     peer.chatChannel.onopen = function() {
➤       console.log('Chat channel opened.');
➤       while ($self.messageQueue.length > 0 &&
➤           peer.chatChannel.readyState === 'open') {
➤         console.log('Attempting to send a message from the queue...');
➤         // get the message at the front of the queue:
➤         let message = $self.messageQueue.shift();
➤         sendOrQueueMessage(peer, message, false);
➤       }
➤     };
      }
```

The heart of that callback is the while loop that works through any messages
in the queue. To avoid setting ourselves up for an infinite loop, the while loop
also checks that the chat channel's readyState is open. No good and a lot of hurt
will come from trying to loop through a message queue if we're outside a data
channel's open state: messages will bounce off the queue and back for eternity.

Inside the while loop, we pull the oldest-queued message off of the queue
using the .shift() method.[14] The message then gets passed right back into
sendOrQueueMessage(), but this time with push set to false: if it's not possible to
send the message, it needs to go right back to the front of the queue where
it came from. The next time through the loop, or the next time the open event
fires on the chat channel, we pick up and try to send that same message all
over again.

Reload your browser windows once more. This time, try sending some messages from one or both sides before joining the call. In the JavaScript console,
type $self.messageQueue.length and check that the returned number matches the
number of messages you see queued in your chat window.

Then, join the call: you should see your queued messages appear on the
other side, in exactly the order you originally wrote them. Awesome. Typing
$self.messageQueue.length in the JavaScript console should return 0, an empty
queue. You can even leave the call, compose more messages, and rejoin. Same
deal: the queued messages will always be sent as soon as possible.

---

14. https://developer.mozilla.org/en-US/docs/Web/JavaScript/Reference/Global_Objects/Array/shift

Next Steps

You've accomplished and learned a lot in this chapter: you've added short- and long-lived data channels to an RTC peer connection, and learned about the lifecycles and management of both asymmetric and symmetric data channels. You've also seen how to send basic strings over data channels. On top of all of that, you've learned how to build a robust queueing function to make it possible to send messages outside of an active peer connection.

In the next chapter, you'll do even more with data channels, including sending structured JSON data and binary data for streaming image files, which you'll be adding to your chat feature. You will also see how data channels and streaming media can work together: you'll be enabling streaming audio for the first time, with data-channel-backed controls to toggle mics on and off. Cameras too!

## CHAPTER 5

Streaming Complex Data

Sending simple messages is pretty great: it's a small but satisfying taste of what WebRTC data channels enable us to build. Bask in your success for a moment, and think about all that is happening in your browser at this point: you've built an app that streams video and allows two connected peers to set and share filters on their videos. You've enhanced the app further by providing the interface and logic for those peers to exchange text messages with each other, including outside of a connected call, thanks to the message queue you wrote.

In short, you're now able to do some pretty fancy things with WebRTC. And they're only going to get fancier: in this chapter alone, you will be pushing the capabilities of data channels even further to exchange more complex data, including JSON strings and binary data. You're also going to learn how to add audio to the video you've been streaming. To keep your users happy, you'll also be adding buttons to toggle their mics and cameras on and off. You'll use your knowledge of JSON and data channels to share mic and camera state with the other peer on a call.

To prepare the way for all of those tasks, let's begin by taking a look at sending and receiving JSON as a way to enrich the chat messages you learned to send last chapter.

Structuring Chat Messages in JSON

Instead of sending messages as unadorned strings, as we did in the last chapter, let's use JSON to structure some metadata with each message sent over the chat. To start with, the remote peer will use the metadata's content to acknowledge each message received. We can even add a little CSS so that, on the sender's side, there is a visual difference between messages that have been received by the remote peer and those that have not.

Preparing and Sending JSON

Sending JSON isn't much different from sending strings: JSON, or JavaScript Object Notation, is a fancy kind of string. Let's rework handleMessageForm() so that it builds a small object literal on message in place of the message strings we relied on in the previous chapter. We'll set up two properties on the message object: the text of the message, and a timestamp, which uses the Date.now() class method to generate a Unix timestamp in milliseconds.[1] The timestamp will uniquely identify each sent message:

demos/dc-chat-json/js/main.js
```
function handleMessageForm(event) {
  event.preventDefault();
  const input = document.querySelector('#chat-msg');
➤ const message = {};
➤ message.text = input.value;
➤ message.timestamp = Date.now();
➤ if (message.text === '') return;

  appendMessage('self', '#chat-log', message);

  sendOrQueueMessage($peer, message);

  input.value = '';
}
```

If you're like me, you much prefer working with JavaScript objects directly. Let's set up the sendOrQueueMessage() function to make a JSON string out of the message object at the last possible moment. We'll do that by calling JSON.stringify() inside the call to the data channel's send() method:

demos/dc-chat-json/js/main.js
```
function sendOrQueueMessage(peer, message, push = true) {
  const chat_channel = peer.chatChannel;
  if (!chat_channel || chat_channel.readyState !== 'open') {
    queueMessage(message, push);
    return;
  }
  try {
➤   chat_channel.send(JSON.stringify(message));
  } catch(e) {
    console.error('Error sending message:', e);
    queueMessage(message, push);
  }
}
```

Messages that wind up in the queue will remain as JavaScript objects. That's the benefit of stringifying objects within the send() method, even if it makes

---

1. https://developer.mozilla.org/en-US/docs/Web/JavaScript/Reference/Global_Objects/Date/now

the method call look a bit crowded: an object is only JSON when it's sent. At the same time, you can glance at a call like chat_channel.send(JSON.stringify(message)) and know that there's JSON involved. Best of all, JSON.stringify() relieves you of the error-prone business of constructing a JSON string yourself by hand.

With handleMessageForm() now handling messages and objects, and sendOrQueueMessage() properly sending messages as JSON, we need to update how messages are appended to the chat log. Two changes are all we need: referencing message.text from the new message object that we're passing in and preserving a reference to the Unix timestamp in a data-timestamp attribute.

```
demos/dc-chat-json/js/main.js
function appendMessage(sender, log_element, message) {
  const log = document.querySelector(log_element);
  const li = document.createElement('li');
  li.className = sender;
➤ li.innerText = message.text;
➤ li.dataset.timestamp = message.timestamp;
  log.appendChild(li);
  if (log.scrollTo) {
    log.scrollTo({
      top: log.scrollHeight,
      behavior: 'smooth',
    });
  } else {
    log.scrollTop = log.scrollHeight;
  }
}
```

If you've not used data- attributes before,[2] they are a super useful feature for storing out-of-band data in HTML. The HTMLElement.dataset property that you referenced as li.dataset.timestamp makes it pretty straightforward to read and write data- attributes using JavaScript too.[3]

Acknowledging Received Messages

Let's set up the logic to send a response that acknowledges each message a peer receives. This will take two steps: first, the receiving peer must parse the JSON message and check the resulting object for an id attribute. Only responses will have id attributes—messages have only text and timestamp attributes. When a message comes in, we create a response object whose id will take the timestamp value of the incoming message. The response object will also include its own timestamp, which captures the moment the message

---

2. https://developer.mozilla.org/en-US/docs/Web/HTML/Global_attributes/data-*
3. https://developer.mozilla.org/en-US/docs/Web/API/HTMLElement/dataset

was received. Let's also reference a handleResponse() function that we'll build next for—you guessed it!—handling incoming responses:

```
demos/dc-chat-json/js/main.js
function addChatChannel(peer) {
  peer.chatChannel =
    peer.connection.createDataChannel('text chat',
      { negotiated: true, id: 100 });

  peer.chatChannel.onmessage = function(event) {
    const message = JSON.parse(event.data);
    if (!message.id) {
      // Prepare a response and append an incoming message
      const response = {
        id: message.timestamp,
        timestamp: Date.now(),
      };
      sendOrQueueMessage(peer, response);
      appendMessage('peer', '#chat-log', message);
    } else {
      // Handle an incoming response
      handleResponse(message);
    }
  };

  peer.chatChannel.onclose = function() {
    console.log('Chat channel closed.');
  };

  peer.chatChannel.onopen = function() {
    console.log('Chat channel opened.');
    while ($self.messageQueue.length > 0 &&
        peer.chatChannel.readyState === 'open') {
      console.log('Attempting to send a message from the queue...');
      // get the message at the front of the queue:
      let message = $self.messageQueue.shift();
      sendOrQueueMessage(peer, message, false);
    }
  };
}
```

Should the call or data channel fail in the time it takes to respond, the sendOrQueueMessage() function steps in and queues the response. Responses will of course be sent from the queue like any other message, as soon as the data channel opens again. Pretty snazzy, right?

Now you can turn your attention to building out the handleResponse() function. What it will do is use document.querySelector(), backed by CSS attribute selectors,[4] to hunt down in the DOM the exact list item for the appended message that

---

4. https://developer.mozilla.org/en-US/docs/Web/CSS/Attribute_selectors

the remote peer is acknowledging. That message will take a received class. If more than a second elapses between the message being composed and the acknowledgment, the list item also takes a delayed class:

```
demos/dc-chat-json/js/main.js
function handleResponse(response) {
  const sent_item = document
    .querySelector(`#chat-log *[data-timestamp="${response.id}"]`);
  const classes = ['received'];
  if (response.timestamp - response.id > 1000) {
    classes.push('delayed');
  }
  sent_item.classList.add(...classes);
}
```

If you've been quietly irritated by my use of the old-school className property across all the earlier code, I hope you can now breathe easier with the call to the modern classList API.[5] Note also the use of the fancy spread syntax,[6] ...classes, to ease passing in the array's values as a series of comma-separated arguments like .add() expects. The delayed class is only pushed onto the classes array if there is more than 1000 milliseconds difference between the timestamps for when a message was composed and when it was acknowledged.

Let's reference and style both the received and delayed classes in CSS:

```
demos/dc-chat-json/css/screen.css
#chat-log .self {
  background: #009;
  color: #EEE;
  opacity: 0.3;
  float: right;
}
#chat-log .self.received {
  opacity: 1;
}
#chat-log .self.received.delayed {
  transition: opacity 0.4s;
}
```

A user's sent messages might now appear faded out when appended to the chat log, thanks to a semi-transparent opacity value. The received class restores full opacity (opacity: 1.0). For the delayed class, however, let's add a nice little touch to the interface: delayed messages will appear to fade up from semitransparency to full opacity over a little less than half a second, thanks to

---

5. https://developer.mozilla.org/en-US/docs/Web/API/Element/classList
6. https://developer.mozilla.org/en-US/docs/Web/JavaScript/Reference/Operators/Spread_syntax

the CSS transition property.[7] Messages with less than a one-second delay will appear appended at full opacity. That prevents users from being annoyed by messages always fading up during a low-latency call—which would make the message interface feel like molasses. Here you can see acknowledged and queued messages sent after leaving the call:

Excellent. You're now sending and receiving JSON over data channels. You've also implemented a simple method for acknowledging messages as a peer receives them. And thanks to some carefully crafted DOM attributes and CSS, you've seen once more how tight the connection is between WebRTC and interface design.

Let's apply that same tightly connected approach to a fundamental feature of WebRTC applications: giving users the ability to toggle their cameras and microphones on and off.

Adding Mic and Camera Toggles

So far in your work with WebRTC, you've streamed only silent video from one peer to the other. (Raise your hand if you've grown sick and tired of looking at yourself.) Video has been great for setting up and testing out peer connections, but no app streaming user media is complete if it can't stream audio, too.

As you have read in earlier chapters, there are some genuine safety concerns to consider when you are developing with streaming audio coming off a

---

7.   https://developer.mozilla.org/en-US/docs/Web/CSS/transition

microphone. The possible feedback is not just unpleasant: in the worst cases, it could damage your hearing and your audio equipment.

With your knowledge of data channels, you're now prepared to build logic and controls to toggle audio on and off. That logic is essential not only for your safety as a developer, but also for giving your users fuller control over what media they stream and when.

As you'll see, data channels can play a central role in the construction of device toggles and other features that stitch together interfaces over peer-to-peer connections. But before we get into building toggles, we'll need to refine how your app requests permission for user media—and in turn, how it manages separate tracks for audio and video as returned by users' mics and cameras.

To safely introduce streaming audio into your app, we'll proceed together in three stages:

1. We'll refine and build out some media-related properties on $self and $peer. As a companion task to that, you'll rework the requestUserMedia() function that you built way back in Requesting User-Media Permissions, on page 37 and other track- and stream-related functions.

2. We will add some safety-minded logic for working with audio in development. We'll tie that logic to a set of buttons that users can click to turn their mics and cameras on and off.

3. We'll build some new data-channel functionality for sharing call features with the remote peer. Specifically, you'll alert the remote peer whenever the local peer toggles the camera or mic on or off.

That list represents some intricate work and your first real taste of rewriting some WebRTC code you've written in earlier chapters, but I think you'll enjoy yourself. Let's find out.

Refining the Initial Properties on Self and Peer

Let's refresh our memories about the requestUserMedia() function you built back in Requesting User-Media Permissions, on page 37. Recall that it looked like this:

```
async function requestUserMedia(media_constraints) {
  $self.mediaStream = new MediaStream();
  $self.media = await navigator.mediaDevices
    .getUserMedia(media_constraints);
  $self.mediaStream.addTrack($self.media.getTracks()[0]);
  displayStream($self.mediaStream, '#self');
}
```

That function has the effect of requesting user permission to access the devices you include in $self.mediaConstraints. So far, that's been a single video device. Once a user grants permission for your app to access the camera, the function goes on to use some very brittle code ($self.media.getTracks()[0]) to grab the lone video track and attach it to a new MediaStream object on $self.mediaStream. That stream is then passed along to displayStream() so that users can see themselves.

In a bit, we're going to alter that function significantly by building more logic around $self.mediaStream. To prepare the way for those alterations, let's move $self.mediaStream out of requestUserMedia() and up to where the $self object is initially declared, at the top of the main.js file.

While we're looking at the $self object, let's make a couple more adjustments to it. First, set audio to true in the mediaConstraints object. That will ensure that your app asks users for permission to access their microphones in addition to their cameras. Users granting full access to their devices will return an audio track as well as a video track from navigator.mediaDevices.getUserMedia().

Next, let's establish two brand-new properties on $self: mediaTracks and features. Assign an empty object to mediaTracks. Eventually, you'll use that property to manage the media tracks that are available for sending to the remote peer. The features property can take an object of its own with one property, audio, set to false. That property will serve two purposes: we'll use it to mute user mics when a call starts, so that there is no opportunity for instant, unexpected feedback. And we'll also use it to track a user's mic state so that it can be shared with the remote peer.

With these adjustments in place, your $self object should look like this:

```
demos/dc-media/js/main.js
/**
 *  Global Variables: $self and $peer
 */

const $self = {
  rtcConfig: null,
  isPolite: false,
  isMakingOffer: false,
  isIgnoringOffer: false,
  isSettingRemoteAnswerPending: false,
  mediaConstraints: { audio: true, video: true },
  mediaStream: new MediaStream(),
  mediaTracks: {},
  features: {
    audio: false,
  },
};
```

Great. And so long as we're up at the top of the file, let's modify $peer to also take mediaStream, mediaTracks, and an empty features object—all of which will serve the same purpose that they do on $self:

```
demos/dc-media/js/main.js
const $peer = {
  connection: new RTCPeerConnection($self.rtcConfig),
➤ mediaStream: new MediaStream(),
➤ mediaTracks: {},
➤ features: {},
};
```

Let's also improve the resetPeer() function to re-establish the properties we just added to the $peer object:

```
function resetPeer(peer) {
  displayStream(null, '#peer');
  peer.connection.close();
  peer.connection = new RTCPeerConnection($self.rtcConfig);
➤ peer.mediaStream = new MediaStream();
➤ peer.mediaTracks = {};
➤ peer.features = {};
}
```

You might be wondering why the features property is always set to an empty object on $peer, rather than with audio: false as on $self. Eventually, you will write media-toggling logic that will use a special data channel to send audio and any other features one peer might want to communicate to the other. We can't know in advance what features the remote peer will have set, but the placeholder object is there to receive them.

With all of those initial properties set on $self and $peer, and with resetPeer() properly resetting the new $peer properties, we can turn to reworking the requestUserMedia() function for better control over streaming media.

Managing Audio and Video Tracks in requestUserMedia()

So here's a little fact about the call to navigator.mediaDevices.getUserMedia(): what it returns is a promise that resolves to a media stream. So in that sense, the creation of a MediaStream of your own on $self.mediaStream might seem redundant. And in the simpler case of a stream with a lone video track, it kind of was. But now that you're assuming responsibility for multiple tracks that a peer will be able to toggle on and off at will, it's essential to maintain a MediaStream of your own.

Let's look at the complete revised requestUserMedia() function, and talk about what its changes are doing:

```
demos/dc-media/js/main.js
async function requestUserMedia(media_constraints) {

  $self.media = await navigator.mediaDevices
    .getUserMedia(media_constraints);

  // Hold onto audio- and video-track references
  $self.mediaTracks.audio = $self.media.getAudioTracks()[0];
  $self.mediaTracks.video = $self.media.getVideoTracks()[0];

  // Mute the audio if `$self.features.audio` evaluates to `false`
  $self.mediaTracks.audio.enabled = !!$self.features.audio;

  // Add audio and video tracks to mediaStream
  $self.mediaStream.addTrack($self.mediaTracks.audio);
  $self.mediaStream.addTrack($self.mediaTracks.video);

  displayStream($self.mediaStream, '#self');
}
```

The first group of changes uses the getAudioTracks()[8] and getVideoTracks() methods.[9] Those pull the first ([0]) and, in this case, only audio and video tracks off of the $self.media stream. Those are each in turn stored as references in the new $self.mediaTracks object that you created in the previous section.

Then comes the line inside requestUserMedia() that's all about safety:

```
// Mute the audio if `$self.features.audio` evaluates to `false`
$self.mediaTracks.audio.enabled = !!$self.features.audio;
```

That sets the enabled property on the audio track to the value you set on the audio property in $self.features. The double-bang operator means that enabled will be set to false even if you forget to set the property at all (in which case, $self.features.audio will be undefined, which evaluates to false). Note, though, that an erroneous string value will evaluate to true here, so be sure you're setting the Boolean false on the audio value in $self.features.

From a user's perspective, setting enabled to false mutes a track.[10] What happens behind the scenes, though, is that the track continues to send frames of silence for audio, and frames of black pixels for video. We'll be addressing the video frames in just a bit.

Finally, the revised requestUserMedia() function adds the tracks referenced in $self.mediaTracks.audio and $self.mediaTracks.video to $self.mediaStream, which continues to get passed along to the displayStream() function.

---

8. https://developer.mozilla.org/en-US/docs/Web/API/MediaStream/getAudioTracks
9. https://developer.mozilla.org/en-US/docs/Web/API/MediaStream/getVideoTracks
10. https://developer.mozilla.org/en-US/docs/Web/API/MediaStreamTrack/enabled

> ## Looping Through Media Tracks
>
> The getAudioTracks() and getVideoTracks() methods make for code that is still a tad on the brittle side, which is the price of their readability. Another approach would be to continue using getTracks() and loop through the tracks it returns:
>
> ```
> for (let track of $self.media.getTracks()) {
>   $self.mediaTracks[track.kind] = track;
> }
> ```
>
> That loop makes use of the read-only kind property on MediaStreamTrack,[a] which will be "audio" for audio tracks and "video" for video tracks.
>
> While that loop is potentially more elegant than longhand assignments using media-specific methods like getAudioTracks(), note that there is never any guarantee of the order of multiple tracks on any given media stream. That means that, whether you grab the first track from getAudioTracks() or, effectively, the last track from a loop, in the presence of multiple video tracks or audio tracks, you cannot know for certain which audio or video track you're grabbing.
>
> If that makes your head hurt, don't worry: we'll return to this topic and unique identifiers for media tracks in Chapter 7, Managing User Media, on page 173.
>
> ---
>
> a.   https://developer.mozilla.org/en-US/docs/Web/API/MediaStreamTrack/kind

Revising the addStreamingMedia() function

The displayStream() function is not the only destination for user media, which also gets passed to the remote peer in the addStreamingMedia() function. Let's update that as well. Previously, it expected stream and peer parameters. But in the new track-centered logic, we can remove the stream parameter and loop directly over tracks on the $self.mediaTracks object:

```
demos/dc-media/js/main.js
function addStreamingMedia(peer) {
  const tracks_list = Object.keys($self.mediaTracks);
  for (let track of tracks_list) {
    peer.connection.addTrack($self.mediaTracks[track]);
  }
}
```

Be sure also to update the establishCallFeatures() function call to addStreamingMedia() by removing the old reference to the self stream. JavaScript being JavaScript, that extra argument will be ignored, but it's always good to keep code references up to date:

```
function establishCallFeatures(peer) {
  registerRtcCallbacks(peer);
  addChatChannel(peer);
  addStreamingMedia(peer);
}
```

Now we can look at the media-receiving logic, and update it to handle multiple incoming media tracks.

Updating the handleRtcPeerTrack() callback

Let's take one more walk down memory lane and recall how the handleRtcPeer-Track() has looked up to this point:

```
function handleRtcPeerTrack({ track, streams: [stream] }) {
  console.log('Attempt to display media from peer...');
  displayStream(stream, '#peer');
}
```

Even though that callback destructured the track values from the event object, we only ever used the stream value. That was basically a shortcut: now that we are getting into multiple tracks, we can rewrite the handleRTCPeerTrack() callback to destructure track values from the track event payload. We'll then attach each track to the stream we already prepared on $peer.mediaStream:

demos/dc-media/js/main.js
```
function handleRtcPeerTrack({ track }) {
  console.log(`Handle incoming ${track.kind} track...`);
  $peer.mediaTracks[track.kind] = track;
  $peer.mediaStream.addTrack(track);
  displayStream($peer.mediaStream, '#peer');
}
```

The handleRtcPeerTrack() callback is track-agnostic: it uses the kind property on MediaStreamTrack objects to figure out what type of track has come in.[11] Keep in mind, too, that the track event fires per track, not per stream, so it will now fire at least twice: once for the audio track, and once for the video track. That's why the stream provided with addTrack() is no longer of any use: it will never include both audio and video, which is why it's up to you to now manually manage the stream on $peer.mediaStream.

The end result? The new track and stream properties you added to $peer, like those you added to $self, have set the stage to provide finer-grained control over user media. Let's turn now to see what that control looks like in terms of providing users the ability to toggle mics and cameras on and off.

---

11. https://developer.mozilla.org/en-US/docs/Web/API/MediaStreamTrack/kind

Building A/V Toggles

So far, you've updated your app's core logic for managing audio and video tracks. You've also implemented a developer-safety feature by muting the audio track as soon as your app loads. Your next task is to build the controls and logic for toggling mics and cameras on and off. Initially, those controls will trigger the intended effects—they'll indeed toggle the user's mic and camera—but once we've finished them, we'll use data channels to communicate media changes to the remote peer.

Adding A/V Controls to the HTML

Let's begin in the HTML and add a "Remote peer is muted" message below the peer video. Begin by hiding the message from assistive technologies by setting its aria-hidden attribute to true:[12]

demos/dc-media/index.html
```
<video id="peer"
  autoplay
  playsinline
  poster="img/placeholder.png">
</video>
➤ <p id="mic-status" aria-hidden="true">Remote peer is muted.</p>
```

In a bit, we'll write CSS to hide the message from sighted users, too. Later, we'll use JavaScript to set the aria-hidden value to false when a remote peer is actually muted.

First, let's introduce a couple buttons for controlling user media. We'll tuck them inside of a new <footer> element, too, right before the app's closing </main> tag:

demos/dc-media/index.html
```
<footer id="footer">
  <button
    aria-label="Toggle microphone"
    role="switch"
    aria-checked="true"
    type="button"
    id="toggle-mic">Mic</button>
  <button
    aria-label="Toggle camera"
    role="switch"
    aria-checked="true"
    type="button"
    id="toggle-cam">Cam</button>
</footer>
```

---

12. https://developer.mozilla.org/en-US/docs/Web/Accessibility/ARIA/Attributes/aria-hidden

Accessible Rich Internet Applications (ARIA) Attributes

ARIA attributes are a part of the Web Accessibility Initiative's ARIA suite of web standards.[a] They are meant to build additional information into HTML elements to provide a more accessible experience on the web for everyone, especially users of screen readers and other assistive technologies.

While some ARIA roles and attributes are implicit in certain HTML elements,[b] others— such as aria-hidden—provide a powerful mechanism for expressing interface states that HTML alone can't always convey.

---

a.   https://www.w3.org/WAI/standards-guidelines/aria/
b.   https://www.w3.org/TR/html-aria/

You might notice some unusual attributes on both of those buttons (see Accessible Rich Internet Applications (ARIA) Attributes, on page 106): aria-label provides a more accessible description for what each button does.[13] And another pair of ARIA attributes—role="switch"[14] and aria-checked="true"[15]—work in tandem to help assistive technologies present the buttons as toggles, each with an on and off state.

Enhancing the A/V Controls in CSS

With the HTML set up, let's now add a few enhancements in the CSS. We can begin by adding a utility style that will always visually hide any element with the aria-hidden attribute set to true:

demos/dc-media/css/screen.css
```
*[aria-hidden="true"] {
  visibility: hidden;
}
```

Unlike display: none, which treats an element as though it no longer exists, visibility: hidden preserves the space the element would otherwise appear in, were it not hidden. The advantage to that is revealing a hidden element will not cause any layout shifts or other unintended weirdness.

Let's look at another example of writing CSS to ARIA attributes. Recall the aria-checked attribute on <button>: when that attribute's value is "false", let's turn the button to white-on-red, and even strike out the text of the button—just to hammer home the idea that self's mic or camera is off:

---

13. https://developer.mozilla.org/en-US/docs/Web/Accessibility/ARIA/Attributes/aria-label
14. https://developer.mozilla.org/en-US/docs/Web/Accessibility/ARIA/Roles/switch_role
15. https://developer.mozilla.org/en-US/docs/Web/Accessibility/ARIA/Attributes/aria-checked

```
demos/dc-media/css/screen.css
button[aria-checked="false"] {
  text-decoration: line-through;
  color: white;
  background: red;
}
```

Let's also put 11 pixels of padding around the new #mic-status element that will reveal the remote peer's mic status:

```
demos/dc-media/css/screen.css
/* Video Elements */

#videos {
  position: relative;
}
video {
  background-color: #DDD;
  display: block;
  width: 100%;
  aspect-ratio: 4 / 3;
  object-fit: cover;
  object-position: center;
}
➤ #mic-status {
➤   padding: 11px;
➤ }
```

Finally, make a small modification to the CSS grid you built in Improving the Chat App's CSS, on page 76. You can add an auto-size row onto the grid, which will hold the new <footer> element:

```
demos/dc-media/css/screen.css
#interface {
  height: 100vh;
  padding: 22px;
  display: grid;
  grid-gap: 11px;
➤  grid-template-rows: auto auto 1fr auto;
}
```

We can style the footer element itself to display as a flexbox, with an 11px column gap to separate the individual buttons:

```
demos/dc-media/css/screen.css
#footer {
  display: flex;
  column-gap: 11px;
}
```

We'll also add a row to the grid inside the 680px media query and explicitly declare where in the grid the chat box and footer will sit:

demos/dc-media/css/screen.css
```
@media screen and (min-width: 680px) {
  #interface {
    grid-template-columns: 1fr 1fr;
    grid-template-rows: auto 1fr auto;
  }
  #header {
    grid-column: 1 / 3;
  }
  #chat {
    grid-column: 2 / 3;
    grid-row: 2 / 4;
  }
  #footer {
    grid-column: 1 / 2;
  }
}
```

Refresh your app in the browser now. It should look something like this, with the mic-status message hidden but the mic and camera toggles visible:

Wiring up the A/V Toggle Logic in JavaScript

Now that you've built the HTML structures and CSS styles that will power your media toggles, you can wire everything together in JavaScript.

First, as soon as the page loads, make sure that the mic-toggle state accurately reflects the false Boolean value you set on $self.features.audio:

demos/dc-media/js/main.js
```
/**
 *  User-Interface Setup
 */
➤ document.querySelector('#toggle-mic')
➤   .setAttribute('aria-checked', $self.features.audio);
```

Further down in the User-Interface Setup portion of the JavaScript file, you can write some flexible logic to listen for clicks on the toggle buttons. We'll do a little JavaScript jujitsu here and set the listener up on the containing footer element—rather than on the individual buttons. Because click events bubble in JavaScript, it's possible to listen for clicks on elements higher up in the DOM:

demos/dc-media/js/main.js
```
document.querySelector('#footer')
  .addEventListener('click', handleMediaButtons);
```

The trade-off for having a single listener is that the handleMediaButtons callback must inspect what's been clicked. When it's a button, we'll use a little Java-Script switch statement to route each actual button-click to the correct toggle function:

demos/dc-media/js/main.js
```
function handleMediaButtons(event) {
  const target = event.target;
  if (target.tagName !== 'BUTTON') return;
  switch (target.id) {
  case 'toggle-mic':
    toggleMic(target);
    break;
  case 'toggle-cam':
    toggleCam(target);
    break;
  }
}
```

That's pretty cool, isn't it? If you need additional toggle buttons, you can add them without attaching any new event listeners.

You still have to write the toggle functions themselves, of course. In the name of clarity, these will be a tad repetitious to start. Their purpose is to determine the enabled state of the corresponding media track (audio or video), toggle it, and then update the button's aria-checked state in the HTML. Let's start with the toggleMic() function:

```
function toggleMic(button) {
  const audio = $self.mediaTracks.audio;
  const enabled_state = audio.enabled = !audio.enabled;

  $self.features.audio = enabled_state;

  button.setAttribute('aria-checked', enabled_state);
}
```

That function holds onto a reference to $self.tracks.audio. It then captures the track's new enabled state by negating its current state: if audio.enabled is true (the mic is on), enabled_state will evaluate to false (the user is turning off the mic). The function then preserves the new enabled_state on $self.features.audio and also sets it on the <button> element's aria-checked attribute. That's why it's necessary to pass the button element in as the target value from the handleMediaButtons() callback.

The toggleVideo() function is almost identical to toggleMic(), but with one key difference: by disabling a video track (video.enabled = false), the video will appear to be frozen when in reality the peer will stop sending new frames of video. But a frozen video frame will make a live stream appear broken. So we'll need an additional piece of logic to add or remove the video track on $self.mediaStream:

```
function toggleCam(button) {
  const video = $self.mediaTracks.video;
  const enabled_state = video.enabled = !video.enabled;

  $self.features.video = enabled_state;

  button.setAttribute('aria-checked', enabled_state);

➤  if (enabled_state) {
➤    $self.mediaStream.addTrack($self.mediaTracks.video);
➤  }
➤  else {
➤    $self.mediaStream.removeTrack($self.mediaTracks.video);
➤  }
}
```

If the new enabled_state is true, the if/else statement will add the video track referenced by $self.mediaTracks.video back onto $self.mediaStream. Conversely, if the camera is switched off, the track is removed.

Great. Give this all a test. Turn your speakers or system volume way down, and then you can even join the call from a second browser window as shown in the screenshot on page 111. Give it a try from a second device, too, especially if you didn't try that back in Testing the Text Chat with a Second Device, on page 85.

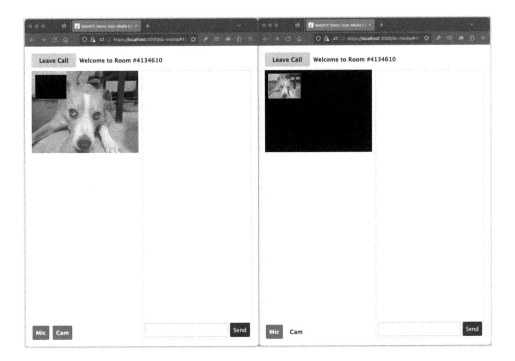

Pretty great. On the self side of the call, things are functioning pretty well. The black boxes rendered in place of disabled videos look a little jarring, though. The good news is you already have a function in place to correct those, at least for the self side of the call: displayStream(). Go ahead and call it inside the else statement:

```
demos/dc-media/js/main.js
function toggleCam(button) {
  const video = $self.mediaTracks.video;
  const enabled_state = video.enabled = !video.enabled;

  $self.features.video = enabled_state;

  button.setAttribute('aria-checked', enabled_state);

  if (enabled_state) {
    $self.mediaStream.addTrack($self.mediaTracks.video);
  } else {
    $self.mediaStream.removeTrack($self.mediaTracks.video);
    displayStream($self.mediaStream, '#self');
  }
}
```

It's only necessary to call displayStream() when there is no video track. Without a video track, the poster image will display—not the empty black video frame.

However, when a video track is added to the peer stream, it will automatically replace the poster image and play as expected.

There are now two things left to do to complete your A/V toggles, which we'll use data channels to implement: giving the self side of the call an indication that the remote peer is muted (we'll finally reveal that status message), and displaying the smiley-face poster image instead of the black video box when the remote peer's camera is off, too.

Sharing Features over Data Channels

Just like we did to power the chat, let's write another symmetric data channel whose only purpose will be to exchange feature information between two peers.

Start off by creating an addFeaturesChannel() function that resembles the add-ChatChannel() function you created in Setting Up the Text-Chat Data Channel, on page 83. The features channel will be negotiated and established with an id of 110. Inside the function, add an onopen event whose callback immediately sends along a JSON version of $self.features to the remote peer:

```
demos/dc-media/js/main.js
function addFeaturesChannel(peer) {
  peer.featuresChannel =
    peer.connection.createDataChannel('features',
      { negotiated: true, id: 110 });

  peer.featuresChannel.onopen = function() {
    console.log('Features channel opened.');
    // send features information just as soon as the channel opens
    peer.featuresChannel.send(JSON.stringify($self.features));
  };
}
```

We'll of course need to be able to send and update additional features as needed, but this will help share known features—like a muted mic—as soon as possible.

Let's think a moment about the receiving side as represented by the onmessage event. At a minimum, we should update the $peer.features object with each feature that comes in. But updating that object is only part of the story: it'll often be necessary to take action based on the incoming feature and its value.

For example, when a remote peer shares the $self.features.audio feature, the local peer needs to show or hide the "Remote peer is muted" status. But rather than create a bunch of free-floating functions, let's set things up programmatically and build a featureFunctions object literal that we'll populate with functions to be executed for specific features.

For starters, let's write an audio-feature function that updates the aria-hidden property to show or hide the remote peer's mic-status message:

```
const featureFunctions = {
  audio: function() {
    const status = document.querySelector('#videos #status');
    // reveal "Remote peer is muted" message if muted (aria-hidden=false)
    // otherwise hide it (aria-hidden=true)
    status.setAttribute('aria-hidden', $peer.features.audio);
  }
}
```

To programmatically call that and any other functions housed in the feature-Functions object, let's prepare the onmessage callback inside the addFeaturesChannel() function:

```
demos/dc-media/js/main.js
function addFeaturesChannel(peer) {
  peer.featuresChannel =
    peer.connection.createDataChannel('features',
      { negotiated: true, id: 110 });

  peer.featuresChannel.onopen = function() {
    console.log('Features channel opened.');
    // send features information just as soon as the channel opens
    peer.featuresChannel.send(JSON.stringify($self.features));
  };

➤  peer.featuresChannel.onmessage = function(event) {
➤    const features = JSON.parse(event.data);
➤    const features_list = Object.keys(features);
➤    for (let f of features_list) {
➤      // update the corresponding features field on $peer
➤      peer.features[f] = features[f];
➤      // if there's a corresponding function, run it
➤      if (typeof featureFunctions[f] === 'function') {
➤        featureFunctions[f]();
➤      }
➤    }
➤  };
  }
```

What that function does is, first, parse the incoming JSON data as a Java-Script object called features. A for loop then iterates over each of that object's properties. Inside the loop, there is logic to update the value on the locally stored $peer.features object and then use typeof to test for a function on feature-Functions that matches the incoming feature name.

We have just about enough of the code set up to test this out. But we first need to call addFeaturesChannel() from inside the establishCallFeatures() function. To improve the chances that any existing features are sent as soon as possible, call it before the addChatChannel() function, which might have queued messages to send:

```
demos/dc-media/js/main.js
function establishCallFeatures(peer) {
  registerRtcCallbacks(peer);
  addFeaturesChannel(peer);
  addChatChannel(peer);
  addStreamingMedia(peer);
}
```

Go ahead and give it a try. If everything is working, you should almost immediately see the "Remote peer is muted" status below the remote peer's video.

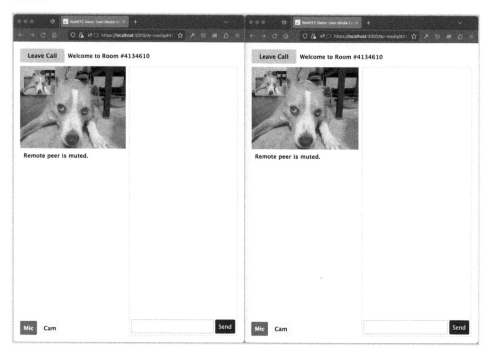

All right. That's great for features, like a muted mic, that are set at the start of a call. But to make the features channel complete, we also need to be able to share new features or changes to existing ones.

Sharing Features as Needed

While we could make things kind of simple and share the entire $self.features object, let's take a finer-grained approach and share only those features we specifically need to. Since you now have logic in place to fire callbacks for specific features, you'll want to be really smart and economical about sharing features. Let's look at the entire shareFeatures() function, and then consider what it's doing:

demos/dc-media/js/main.js

```
function shareFeatures(...features) {
  const featuresToShare = {};

  // don't try to share features before joining the call or
  // before the features channel is available
  if (!$peer.featuresChannel) return;

  for (let f of features) {
    featuresToShare[f] = $self.features[f];
  }

  try {
    $peer.featuresChannel.send(JSON.stringify(featuresToShare));
  } catch(e) {
    console.error('Error sending features:', e);
    // No need to queue; contents of `$self.features` will send
    // as soon as the features channel opens
  }
}
```

The function takes a rest parameter, ...features, so that it's possible to share more than one feature at a time.[16] A rest parameter looks similar to the spread syntax you used with classList above in Acknowledging Received Messages, on page 95, but while the spread syntax makes it possible to pass an array to a function as individual values, a rest parameter makes individual values available as an array within the function. Rest-parameter syntax is supported in all browsers that ship with WebRTC.

Inside the function, a featuresToShare object will be responsible for managing the features to be shared and of course their values. Their values are taken directly from the object referenced from $self.features.

In case a user does something like toggle the camera on or off before joining the call, the shareFeatures() function will quietly exit, care of a return statement. It's worth noting that there is no need to queue the features the way we do with chat messages, because the onopen callback inside of addFeaturesChannel() will always transmit the complete $self.features object as soon as the channel opens.

With that all set, let's call shareFeatures() from inside the toggleMic() function:

---

16. https://developer.mozilla.org/en-US/docs/Web/JavaScript/Reference/Functions/rest_parameters

demos/dc-media/js/main.js
```
function toggleMic(button) {
  const audio = $self.mediaTracks.audio;
  const enabled_state = audio.enabled = !audio.enabled;

  $self.features.audio = enabled_state;

  button.setAttribute('aria-checked', enabled_state);

➤ shareFeatures('audio');
}

function toggleCam(button) {
  const video = $self.mediaTracks.video;
  const enabled_state = video.enabled = !video.enabled;

  $self.features.video = enabled_state;

  button.setAttribute('aria-checked', enabled_state);

➤ shareFeatures('video');

  if (enabled_state) {
    $self.mediaStream.addTrack($self.mediaTracks.video);
  } else {
    $self.mediaStream.removeTrack($self.mediaTracks.video);
    displayStream($self.mediaStream, '#self');
  }
}
```

Reload your app in two browser windows, and then toggle the mic from one side of the call. On the remote side, you should see the "Remote peer is muted" message appear and disappear as you click it. Nice!

Now let's get things working for a toggleable video, too. You're already calling shareFeatures() from within the toggleCam() function. To bring it on home, add a video member to the featureFunctions object, whose complete form to this point will look like this—complete with a call to displayStream() when the remote peer's camera toggles off:

demos/dc-media/js/main.js
```
const featureFunctions = {
  audio: function() {
    const status = document.querySelector('#mic-status');
    // reveal "Remote peer is muted" message if muted (aria-hidden=false)
    // otherwise hide it (aria-hidden=true)
    status.setAttribute('aria-hidden', peer.features.audio);
  },
➤ video: function() {
➤   // This is all just to display the poster image,
➤   // rather than a black frame
➤   if (peer.mediaTracks.video) {
➤     if (peer.features.video) {
➤       peer.mediaStream.addTrack(peer.mediaTracks.video);
```

```
        } else {
          peer.mediaStream.removeTrack(peer.mediaTracks.video);
          displayStream(peer.mediaStream, '#peer');
        }
      }
    },
  };
```

One more time, give things a test across two browser windows or devices. Your mic and camera toggles should be working as expected. And you should be feeling pretty great about yourself: you now have audio as well as video streaming in your app.

Sending Images over the Chat

Let's return to the chat feature now one last iteration: enabling users to send and receive images.

Text messages will continue to be sent over the symmetric, negotiated chat channel. But in a return to the short-lived data channels you wrote for the video-filter feature in Applying Filters Remotely with Data Channels, on page 71, each image a user sends will be delivered over its own asymmetric, short-lived data channel.

Your use of multiple data channels will be invisible to users: images will be appended to the chat log just like text messages are already. But by using one data channel per image, we will avoid congestion on the primary text-chat data channel. It would become a lot less performant for sending text messages if it were also used to stream binary data. As a bonus, using a dedicated data channel for each image sent will actually simplify the logic for receiving images.

Setting Up the User Interface for Images

To build an interface for sending any kind of file, we need to make use of HTML file inputs. The native HTML file input element is regrettably uggo, as the kids say. Let's look at a method for avoiding including one in your interface by instead adding a button with an accessible <label> element:

```
demos/dc-chat-images/index.html
<form id="chat-form" action="#null">
  <label for="chat-msg" class="preserve-access">Compose Message</label>
  <input type="text" id="chat-msg" name="chat-msg" autocomplete="off" />
  <label for="chat-img-btn" class="preserve-access">Send Image</label>
  <button type="button" id="chat-img-btn">Image</button>
  <button type="submit" id="chat-btn">Send</button>
</form>
```

We're about to write JavaScript to enable clicks on that button to create and trigger an artificial click on a file input behind the scenes. But first, adjust your CSS to style the new button:

demos/dc-chat-images/css/screen.css

```css
#chat-form button {
  cursor: pointer;
  flex: 0 0 auto;
  background: #009;
  color: #EEE;
}
#chat-img-btn {
  background: #EEE;
  color: #000;
  margin-right: 5.5px;
}
```

To finish up the UI, let's write a little bit of JavaScript that creates and effectively passes clicks on the image button along to a hidden file input. Note that Firefox's security policy prohibits passing an artificial click() on a file input that has been written in the actual HTML. That's not a problem, because we'll set this one up entirely in JavaScript, inside the handleImageButton() callback. In another twist, Safari ignores artificial click events on JavaScript-created file inputs unless they're appended to the DOM. So we have to do that, too:

demos/dc-chat-images/js/main.js

```javascript
document.querySelector('#chat-img-btn')
  .addEventListener('click', handleImageButton);

/**
 *   User-Interface Functions and Callbacks
 */

function handleImageButton() {
  let input = document.querySelector('input.temp');
  input = input ? input : document.createElement('input');
  input.className = 'temp';
  input.type = 'file';
  input.accept = '.gif, .jpg, .jpeg, .png';
  input.setAttribute('aria-hidden', true);
  // Safari/iOS requires appending the file input to the DOM
  document.querySelector('#chat-form').appendChild(input);
  input.addEventListener('change', handleImageInput);
  input.click();
}
```

That function looks for an existing file input with a class of temp. If none exists, it creates a new one. A file input might already exist if a user clicks the Image button but clicks Cancel in the OS file-selector box before choosing a file.

Regrettably, there is no standard event we can hook into to detect when someone has canceled selecting a file. So the file input will stay in the DOM in that case. In a bit, we'll remove the temporary file input from the DOM in the handleImageInput() callback. But that callback will only ever run when someone selects a file.

File inputs take an optional accept attribute, which is useful for describing allowable files by their extension or MIME type. Extensions are a little more human-readable, not to mention memorable for weary developers, so we can write extensions as a comma-separated list of the most web-friendly image types: GIFs, JPEGs, and PNGs. Many operating systems prevent users from selecting non-matching files. But note that that is an interface nicety, not anything like a security policy.

The handleImageButton() function sets the aria-hidden ARIA attribute, which will again hide the temporary file input from assistive technologies. But unlike the "Remote user is muted" message you hid with visibility: hidden in Adding A/V Controls to the HTML, on page 105, we want to completely remove the temporary file input from the document flow. That's a job for display: none, coupled with a very fancy two-attribute CSS selector:

```
demos/dc-chat-images/css/screen.css
.preserve-access {
  position: absolute;
  left: -20000px;
}

*[aria-hidden="true"] {
  visibility: hidden;
}
➤ input[type="file"][aria-hidden="true"] {
➤   display: none;
➤ }
```

So that you can test out the logic for choosing a file, add a placeholder function definition for the handleImageInput() callback on the file input's change event. It will fire when users select an image from the operating-system file picker:

```
function handleImageInput(event) {
  // TODO: Handle image input
}
```

Open your work in the browser, and try clicking on the image button. You should be greeted by your operating system's file picker. On most operating systems, GIF, JPEG, and PNG files will be highlighted in some way. On MacOS, files that aren't of those types appear grayed out and cannot be selected as shown in the screenshot on page 120.

If you select a file, nothing happens yet: we still have to write the logic that takes a chosen file and appends it to the chat log. So let's do that.

Appending Images to the Chat Log

We're going to build a slightly dangerous interface pattern for sending images, to keep our focus on how to send binary data over the chat: as soon as users select a file, we'll append it to the user's chat log and send it over a data channel. (I invite you to polish this bit of interface on your own later, by previewing the image and pairing it with its own Send and Cancel buttons.)

To create the dangerous form of this UI, let's build out the handleImageInput() callback:

```
demos/dc-chat-images/js/main.js
function handleImageInput(event) {
  event.preventDefault();
  const image = event.target.files[0];
  const metadata = {
    kind: 'image',
    name: image.name,
    size: image.size,
    timestamp: Date.now(),
    type: image.type,
  };
  appendMessage('self', '#chat-log', metadata, image);
  // Remove appended file input element
  event.target.remove();
}
```

That function grabs only the first file users might have selected (event.target .files[0]) and builds a nice chunk of metadata describing the file, including its name, size, and type. While we can read those properties off of the file itself on the sending side, we want to send them ahead of the file itself to the receiving side. Along with the properties pulled off the file, a hard-coded kind: 'image' will help prefix each data channel for sending along an image. And just like you did for the chat's text messages, you can generate another Unix timestamp and send it along with the image metadata.

You can also reuse your appendMessage() function by updating it to take a fourth argument—image—that will handle the actual image file. At the very bottom of the handleImageInput() function, event.target.remove() swoops in and removes the temporary file input we appended to the DOM in the handleImageButton() callback.

Having called appendMessage() with a fourth argument, we need to update its function definition. Remember that JavaScript, for good or ill, does not complain about mismatched numbers of arguments. You can add the image argument onto the end of the function definition without angering JavaScript or any of the previous three-argument calls to it for appending chat messages:

demos/dc-chat-images/js/main.js

```
function appendMessage(sender, log_element, message, image) {
  const log = document.querySelector(log_element);
  const li = document.createElement('li');
  li.className = sender;
  li.innerText = message.text;
  li.dataset.timestamp = message.timestamp;
  if (image) {
    const img = document.createElement('img');
    img.src = URL.createObjectURL(image);
    img.onload = function() {
      URL.revokeObjectURL(this.src);
      scrollToEnd(log);
    };
    li.innerText = ''; // undefined on images
    li.classList.add('img');
    li.appendChild(img);
  }
  log.appendChild(li);
  scrollToEnd(log);
}
```

Inside the appendMessage() function, we check for the presence of an image value. If one exists, it creates a new <img /> element. We can then employ the URL API and its createObjectURL() method[17] to take the image file's raw data and write it to an object. We'll then set that object on the <img /> element's src attribute to display the image. The image's onload event then revokes the object URL's

---

17. https://developer.mozilla.org/en-US/docs/Web/API/URL/createObjectURL

reference in JavaScript, which frees up the considerable space the image data would otherwise occupy in memory. Don't worry: the image will continue to display on screen even after its URL object has been revoked.

Wrapping up the revisions for handling images, we set the innerText value to an empty string and add a class of img onto the message's containing list item before appending the newly created image element.

Notice that appendMessage() calls a new scrollToEnd() function that keeps the chat box scrolled to its bottom every time a new message arrives. That creates the illusion of messages being appended to the bottom of the chat, which is the behavior of most other messaging apps.

The scrollToEnd() function also gets called on the img.onload callback. That is necessary for the scrollHeight value to accurately reflect the dimensions of the image, which are only known once the image has actually loaded. Without an accurate scrollHeight value, the image would appear to be cut off at the bottom of the chat box. Expressed as a reusable function, scrollToEnd() looks like this:

demos/dc-chat-images/js/main.js
```
function scrollToEnd(el) {
  if (el.scrollTo) {
    el.scrollTo({
      top: el.scrollHeight,
      behavior: 'smooth',
    });
  } else {
    el.scrollTop = el.scrollHeight;
  }
}
```

Let's hop back into the CSS file and make a couple of adjustments to the way list items and images are styled in the chat log:

demos/dc-chat-images/css/screen.css
```
/* Chat Elements */

➤ img {
➤   display: block;
➤   max-width: 100%;
➤ }
  #chat-log li {
    border-radius: 5.5px;
    padding: 5.5px;
    margin-bottom: 5.5px;
    max-width: 60%;
    clear: both;
➤   overflow: hidden;
  }
```

```
#chat-log .img {
  padding: 0;
}
```

Those adjustments prepare images to display responsively and fit within their containing chat <li> element, which gets its own enhancements. First, we set the overflow property to hidden, which is a little trick to preserve the list item's rounded corners when displaying the child <img /> element. To complete the effect and avoid presenting a colored frame around the image, we set the padding to 0 for the .img class, which you added in the appendMessage() callback with li.classList.add('img'). The image will now take up the entire message bubble *and* have rounded corners.

Let's give this a try. Reload your browser, hit the Image button, and choose a file: you'll see it appended to the chat log, with reduced opacity just like the text messages—nice, right?!

With the interface all wired up to handle images, it's time to invite data channels to the party and wire them up to send and receive binary data.

Exchanging Feature-Detection Information

In your WebRTC journey so far, Google Chrome has been something of a hero: a modern WebRTC implementation, with no need for adapter.js on properties like connectionState, as we saw in Loading adapter.js, on page 69. But like any hero, Chrome has its tragic flaws. The big one we need to address right away is how Chrome handles binary data over WebRTC data channels—something currently not covered by adapter.js.

The WebRTC specification provides for sending one of two binary types over data channels:[18] arraybuffer, which is part of the ECMAScript specification behind JavaScript, and binary large object, better known as blob, which browsers implement according to the W3C File API specification.[19] All browsers support the arraybuffer type over data channels. Modern browsers—including Safari but surprisingly excluding Chrome—support the blob type. Chrome supports the Blob API—which we'll be using in a bit—but Chrome does not currently support sending blobs over WebRTC data channels.

In order to send binary data as a blob over an RTCDataChannel, both peers must support doing so. The trick is that we need to know whether both peers support the blob binary type *before* sending even the first byte of binary data. Thanks to the feature-channel logic you wrote for handling mic and camera toggles, you can piggyback on the addFeaturesChannel() logic and check the default binaryType on the features channel itself:

```
demos/dc-chat-images/js/main.js
function addFeaturesChannel(peer) {

  // snip, snip, snip

  peer.featuresChannel.onopen = function() {
    console.log('Features channel opened.');
    $self.features.binaryType = peer.featuresChannel.binaryType;
    // send features information just as soon as the channel opens
    peer.featuresChannel.send(JSON.stringify($self.features));
  };

  // snip, snip, snip

}
```

All that's doing is setting up another features property—$self.features.binaryType—and assigning it the browser-default value of the binaryType on the features data channel.

In Chrome and Chrome-based browsers like Edge, the binaryType will be array-buffer; in all other modern browsers, the default will be blob. That new feature then gets passed along with the rest of the features object over the features channel. The logic you already built in Sharing Features over Data Channels, on page 112, is all set to receive the same feature information from the remote peer, which will be stored in the features object on $peer.

Beautiful. What a graceful way to detect and share feature availability between peers. Now let's use that shared-feature information to send binary data.

---

18. https://www.w3.org/TR/webrtc/#dom-datachannel-binarytype
19. https://www.w3.org/TR/FileAPI/

Sending and Receiving Binary Data

You have now written all of the foundational logic to send and receive binary data along with a custom JSON payload of metadata for each file sent over a data channel. Let's set up a sendFile() function that opens a data channel for each file a user wants to send.

To start with, create a function that takes two arguments, peer and payload, and a handful of variables:

```
function sendFile(peer, payload) {
  const { metadata, file } = payload;
  const file_channel =
    peer.connection.createDataChannel(`${metadata.kind}-${metadata.name}`);
  const chunk = 16 * 1024; // 16KiB chunks
}
```

The body of the function opens by destructuring metadata and file from payload. As you'll see, that will simplify the sending of images that wind up in the queue. The function then sets up an asymmetric data channel whose label will comprise of the value in metadata.kind followed by a hyphen and the file's name.

Next comes that curious chunk constant. It represents the maximum size for the pieces of data that we'll be sending. There won't be any need to share it with your RTCPeerConnection or any other WebRTC API, though: it's a value that will be used only in your logic for sending binary data.

Maximum Message Sizes in WebRTC

WebRTC data channels cannot send messages larger than a certain size. You can inspect this value for a given browser by running $peer.connection.sctp.maxMessageSize in your browser console when you're connected to a call. Two connected browsers will often report different sizes. And sometimes, especially on Firefox, the maxMessageSize will be a very large number.

Generally speaking, though, we want to go with a very conservative, small number. Although they also fire more calls to the send event, smaller chunks are generally more interoperable with older browsers. On data channels that enable both users to send binary data, large message sizes can cause congestion if both peers are attempting to send very large messages. The sendFile() function uses a very modest 16KiB chunk, which should be interoperable with all browsers.[a]

If you'd like, you can add chunk as a third argument on your function to make it easier to experiment with different chunk sizes.

---

a. https://developer.mozilla.org/en-US/docs/Web/API/WebRTC_API/Using_data_channels#understanding_message_size_limits

With that all set, let's actually dig into the logic for chunking up and sending binary data.

Sending Binary Data

Start by setting up an anonymous asynchronous function on the data channel's onopen handler. We want to get down to business as soon as the per-file data channel has opened.

demos/dc-chat-images/js/main.js

```
function sendFile(peer, payload) {
  const { metadata, file } = payload;
  const file_channel =
    peer.connection.createDataChannel(`${metadata.kind}-${metadata.name}`);
  const chunk = 16 * 1024; // 16KiB chunks
  file_channel.onopen = async function() {
    if (!peer.features ||
        ($self.features.binaryType !== peer.features.binaryType)) {
      file_channel.binaryType = 'arraybuffer';
    }
    // Prepare data according to the binaryType in use
    const data = file_channel.binaryType ===
      'blob' ? file : await file.arrayBuffer();
    // Send the metadata
    file_channel.send(JSON.stringify(metadata));
    // Send the prepared data in chunks
    for (let i = 0; i < metadata.size; i += chunk) {
      file_channel.send(data.slice(i, i + chunk));
    }
  };
}
```

The onopen callback opens with a small bit of Boolean logic that checks whether the features property is missing for $peer. That could happen if someone tried to send a file before the remote peer has shared feature information. If that's the case, we fall back to the arraybuffer binary type, which all browsers support, by setting it explicitly on the data channel instance, file_channel.binaryType.

The line comparing self and peer binary types is slicker than it looks. If there is a difference between them, we manually set the the data channel's binary type to arraybuffer. Any difference between browsers means that we need to fall back to arraybuffer. When there's no difference, we don't need to set anything at all—regardless of what the browsers support. If *both* browsers are Chrome, for example, they'll default to arraybuffer without needing to explicitly set it on file_channel.binaryType. All other browsers will default to blob automatically. See? Pretty slick.

Still inside the anonymous callback to file_channel.onopen, we hit these interesting lines:

```
const data = file_channel.binaryType ===
  'blob' ? file : await file.arrayBuffer();
```

Browsers that support the blob binary type can handle the file object as is (surprise! the file gets passed into the browser from the OS as a blob). But when an arraybuffer is needed, we create one from the blob object. That happens asynchronously, which is why this anonymous callback must be defined as async.

Then it's onto the sending logic: we stringify the metadata into some wholesome JSON goodness and send it across, like we've done with the chat's JSON-enhanced text messages. But sending the file's binary data requires a little old-school for loop:

```
// Send the prepared data in chunks
for (let i = 0; i < metadata.size; i += chunk) {
  file_channel.send(data.slice(i, i + chunk));
}
```

Extremely happily for us, blobs and array buffers alike have an identically constructed slice() method. That saves us from worry about whether we're dealing with a blob or an array buffer in the body of the loop. The slice() method takes start and end values to carve off a generous portion of binary data, still warm from the oven. The for loop increases the i value by the chunk size on each iteration, so the loop can send along the next 16KiB chunk of data over the data channel until there's no data left.

To finish off the sendFile() function, let's also include a callback for the onmessage event, which will reuse the handleResponse() function before closing out the file's data channel after the response has come in. (We'll craft and send the response from the receiveFile() function, which we'll build next.)

demos/dc-chat-images/js/main.js
```
function sendFile(peer, payload) {
  const { metadata, file } = payload;
  const file_channel =
    peer.connection.createDataChannel(`${metadata.kind}-${metadata.name}`);
  const chunk = 16 * 1024; // 16KiB chunks
  file_channel.onopen = async function() {
    if (!peer.features ||
      ($self.features.binaryType !== peer.features.binaryType)) {
      file_channel.binaryType = 'arraybuffer';
    }
```

```
    // Prepare data according to the binaryType in use
    const data = file_channel.binaryType ===
      'blob' ? file : await file.arrayBuffer();
    // Send the metadata
    file_channel.send(JSON.stringify(metadata));
    // Send the prepared data in chunks
    for (let i = 0; i < metadata.size; i += chunk) {
      file_channel.send(data.slice(i, i + chunk));
    }
  };
  file_channel.onmessage = function({ data }) {
    // Sending side will only ever receive a response
    handleResponse(JSON.parse(data));
    file_channel.close();
  };
}
```

With the sendFile() function complete, let's call it in the context of sendOrQueue-
Message(). That will require checking for a file member on message, and calling
sendFile() if the file member exists:

demos/dc-chat-images/js/main.js
```
function sendOrQueueMessage(peer, message, push = true) {
  const chat_channel = peer.chatChannel;
  if (!chat_channel || chat_channel.readyState !== 'open') {
    queueMessage(message, push);
    return;
  }
  if (message.file) {
    sendFile(peer, message);
  } else {
    try {
      chat_channel.send(JSON.stringify(message));
    } catch(e) {
      console.error('Error sending message:', e);
      queueMessage(message, push);
    }
  }
}
```

Note that the message-queueing logic still applies, even to image files. If the
main data channel is out of service or hasn't been created yet, the image file
and its metadata will be queued, too. Nice!

Pulling it all together, we can now call sendOrQueueMessage() from inside the
handleImageInput() callback. You can build a little payload object with metadata and
file properties:

demos/dc-chat-images/js/main.js

```
function handleImageInput(event) {
  event.preventDefault();
  const image = event.target.files[0];
  const metadata = {
    kind: 'image',
    name: image.name,
    size: image.size,
    timestamp: Date.now(),
    type: image.type,
  };
➤ const payload = { metadata: metadata, file: image };
  appendMessage('self', '#chat-log', metadata, image);
  // Remove appended file input element
  event.target.remove();
  // Send or queue the file
➤ sendOrQueueMessage($peer, payload);
}
```

Boom. The sending-side logic is all complete. Let's switch gears and write the logic for the receiving side.

Receiving Binary Data

With all of the file-sending logic fresh in our heads, let's get right to work building a complementary receiveFile() function:

demos/dc-chat-images/js/main.js

```
function receiveFile(file_channel) {
  const chunks = [];
  let metadata;
  let bytes_received = 0;
  file_channel.onmessage = function({ data }) {
    // Receive the metadata
    if (typeof data === 'string' && data.startsWith('{')) {
      metadata = JSON.parse(data);
    } else {
      // Receive and squirrel away chunks...
      bytes_received += data.size ? data.size : data.byteLength;
      chunks.push(data);
      // ...until the bytes received equal the file size
      if (bytes_received === metadata.size) {
        const image = new Blob(chunks, { type: metadata.type });
        const response = {
          id: metadata.timestamp,
          timestamp: Date.now(),
        };
        appendMessage('peer', '#chat-log', metadata, image);
```

```
      // Send an acknowledgement
      try {
        file_channel.send(JSON.stringify(response));
      } catch(e) {
        queueMessage(response);
      }
    }
  }
};
}
```

That looks like a lot of code, but you've seen almost all of it before! We're setting up variables for a receiving-side chunk array, the processed metadata, and the number of bytes received. We then inspect the data coming in. If it opens with a curly brace, {, we know it's the JSON metadata coming in. So we parse it. No sweat.

But then comes the exciting part, where we reassemble the chunks of binary data coming in over the data channel. Blobs and array buffers both have a .slice() method, as we saw for sending the file, but their implementations in RTCDataChannels use different properties for reporting the amount of data a chunk contains. To abstract away that difference, we again use a ternary operator—this time to keep track of how many bytes have been received:

```
bytes_received += data.size ? data.size : data.byteLength;
```

As each binary chunk comes in, we add its total bytes (data.size for blobs, data.byteLength for array buffers) to the total on bytes_received.

The data itself gets pushed onto the end of the chunk array until finally the bytes_received matches the value on the metadata payload. At that point, we reassemble the array chunks into a blob for passing into appendMessage(). Again, despite Chrome's lack of support for sending blobs over data channels, it implements the new Blob() constructor just fine. We also construct a response object, just like for acknowledging text messages. When the file transfer is complete, we try to send the response, or at least queue it for sending later.

To wire up the receiving logic, we need to register the receiveFile() callback on the handleRtcDataChannel() event handler we set up way back in Listening for the Filter Data Channel on the Remote Peer, on page 72:

demos/dc-chat-images/js/main.js
```
function handleRtcDataChannel({ channel }) {
  const label = channel.label;
  console.log(`Data channel added for ${label}`);
  if (label.startsWith('filter-')) {
    document.querySelector('#peer').className = label;
```

```
    channel.onopen = function() {
      channel.close();
    };
  }
➤ if (label.startsWith('image-')) {
➤   receiveFile(channel);
➤ }
}
```

Testing Out Your Image-Capable Chat

Now for the moment of truth. Go ahead and open your app in two browser windows, and join the call. Click the Image button, choose an image of one of the allowed types (GIF, JPEG, or PNG) on your file system, and watch for it to append to both the local and remote peer's chat logs. Try sending one from the other side, too. You should see something like this, but of course with a photo of your own ride-or-die house pet. (His name's Hank, and he's a rescue—yes, he's that cute, and no, he never leaves my side. He's also the official spokesdog for *Programming WebRTC*.)

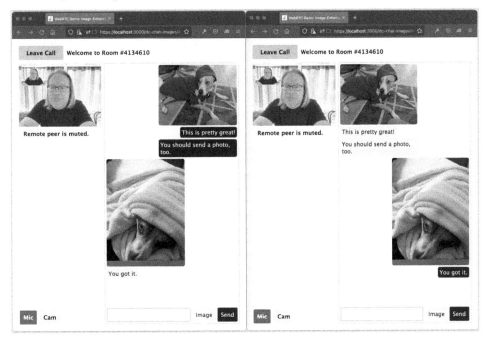

Awesome. Just awesome. I wish I could high-five you right now. This is a another huge achievement, and your WebRTC journey through the fundamentals of all aspects of data channels is now complete.

Next Steps

When I said your journey with WebRTC fundamentals is nearing its end, that wasn't hyperbole. You've now mastered all of the major pieces: signaling, establishing a peer connection, sending and receiving user media, and now sending and queueing all possible forms of data over a WebRTC data channel. You even know how to abstract away the differences between blob and arraybuffer binary types, so that there's no need to think deeply about them again.

You could stop reading this book now and have a fairly complete WebRTC education. But I hope you'll keep going. In the coming chapters, you'll be digging deeper into WebRTC-powered interfaces, especially for accessibility, and how to optimize streaming media. Plus you'll learn how to deploy your WebRTC apps so you can test them out with friends, family, and colleagues well beyond the cozy comfort of your local network.

But before we get to all that, it's time to tackle a serious limitation to our work with WebRTC: so far, we have been limited to connecting exactly two peers over a WebRTC call. In the next chapter, you'll have the chance to seriously level up your skills by establishing WebRTC calls between three or more peers. Much of the work to come will feel very familiar, but don't be surprised if more than a few lightbulbs flicker on above your head about WebRTC generally when you learn to manage calls with multiple peers. Your journey continues.

## CHAPTER 6

Managing Multipeer Connections

If you're like me and have a habit of opening way too many browser windows and tabs while you're working, you might have encountered mysterious problems and errors at some point during your peer-to-peer WebRTC work. Perhaps you thought your app had stopped working, only to discover two browser windows connected on your app's namespace already—before you accidentally connected a third.

But even if you've been more careful than that, let's prove the connection limits on a peer-to-peer app. Fire up the starter app for this chapter—which contains peer-to-peer logic and the audio features you built in the last chapter—by running npm run start and pointing to the same namespace off of https://localhost:3000/multipeer/ in three browser windows. Join the call in the first two windows, and ensure that the peer-to-peer connection is successful:

Then let that evil, interloping third peer join.

What you'd *hope* would happen, of course, is that suddenly the call will show all three peers, in all three windows. Magic.

But what really happens is probably even worse than you could've imagined: not only can't the third peer join the call (that truly *would* be magical, given the logic we've written so far), but the first two peers have their connection severed, and the consoles of all three browser windows fill up with new and exotic errors. What a mess. From two connected peers to no connected peers, thanks to an unwelcome, evil third peer's attempt to connect:

However multipeer connections are created and maintained, hoping for code to suddenly turn magical ain't it.

Learning from a Failed Peer-to-Peer Call

Still, there are some things to learn about signaling and WebRTC connections in general from this failed three-way call. Step back and consider what's happening when a peer-to-peer call is established between exactly two peers: as soon as the JavaScript loads, each side of the call creates a single instance of RTCPeerConnection on the $peer object for the remote peer. That one instance enables two peers to negotiate a connection with each other over the signaling channel.

When a third peer's browser joins the same peer-to-peer namespace as the first two, there's a serious problem: each peer has exactly one instance of RTCPeerConnection to work with, representing exactly one remote peer. When the signaling channel kicks in, care of the interloping third peer, the two connected peers' browsers get hopelessly confused: their connection with each other is all set, stable, and established. Then suddenly and without warning, the signaling channel goes berserk for both connected peers, who receive a flurry of incoming SDP descriptions and ICE candidates.

The logic you've written so far happily relays new incoming descriptions and ICE candidates, because it assumes that any signals will originate from exactly one remote peer. That's why you'll now see errors in the console when the third peer joins—things like DOMException: Unknown ufrag (76d5a562) on attempts to add an ICE candidate, or DOMException: Cannot set remote answer in state stable when ill-fated offers and answers arrive.

In short, the WebRTC logic you've built so far operates on something of a social cliché: three's a crowd. That logic, stemming from the single instance of RTCPeerConnection on either side of a call, limits each peer only to ever connect successfully with exactly one remote peer. Add a third peer to the call, and suddenly signals will be exchanged wildly. No one knows who to signal to, or whether incoming signals are even meant for the peer receiving them.

It's like walking down a busy street and noticing someone waving in your direction from across the way: as a sociable and generally friendly human, you instinctively wave back even as you wonder, "Who the heck is that person?" I usually discover too late that the wave was meant for someone else, naturally, and now I look like an even bigger weirdo than usual for continuing to wave back at a disinterested stranger. Except someone else, a fellow weirdo on the stranger's side of the street, sees *me* waving—and now they're waving back at me. I might try to comfort myself that at least the weirdo torch has been passed, but my social anxiety will race at full tilt until I can disappear back into the crowd and get far, far away.

Okay. Enough about my social awkwardness. To build a multipeer WebRTC application, it'll be necessary to restructure the fundamental peer-to-peer application logic we've written so far. Just for starters, each connected peer will need to know how to create and maintain a separate instance of RTCPeerConnection for each remote peer that connects. No more random waving strangers on a call. We'll also need to ensure that connection negotiation only ever involves two peers, each working with a specific instance of RTCPeerConnection—no matter how many peers end up on the call.

Although the finished app will appear to have multiple peers streaming media to each other all in real time, each peer must first directly negotiate a connection with every other remote peer in what's known as mesh-network topography as shown in the image to the right.

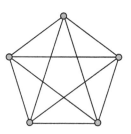

In a mesh network, sometimes also called a star network, each node is connected to every other node. Applied to WebRTC, each of the connections between two nodes must be negotiated—just as you've been doing for one-to-one calls. To create a mesh network for people connecting over your app, you'll need to extend your peer-to-peer foundations in WebRTC to manage the additional complexity that multipeer calls represent. You'll do that not by starting from scratch, but by rewriting the starter peer-to-peer app in www/multipeer/. So let's get to it.

Working with a Multipeer-Ready Signaling Channel

The first thing that's needed to prepare the way for multipeer calls is a reworked signaling channel. We need one that is capable of coordinating the signals between any set of two peers. The signaling channel we've used so far isn't capable of that, really. But don't worry: if you examine the server.js file, you'll see a different namespace—mp_namespace—that is set up for multipeer connections. Let's look through this code line by line, just like we did in Using a Lightweight Signaling Channel, on page 27, and use what we learn to improve upon the logic we've already written for one-to-one signaling:

```
server.js
const mp_namespaces = io.of(/^\/[a-z]{4}-[a-z]{4}-[a-z]{4}$/);

mp_namespaces.on('connect', function(socket) {

  const namespace = socket.nsp;

  const peers = [];

  for (let peer of namespace.sockets.keys()) {
    peers.push(peer);
  }

  // Send the array of connected-peer IDs to the connecting peer
  socket.emit('connected peers', peers);

  // Send the connecting peer ID to all connected peers
  socket.broadcast.emit('connected peer', socket.id);

  socket.on('signal', function({ recipient, sender, signal }) {
    socket.to(recipient).emit('signal', { recipient, sender, signal });
  });
```

```
  socket.on('disconnect', function() {
    namespace.emit('disconnected peer', socket.id);
  });

});
```

First off, the multipeer signaling channel uses a namespace pattern that's a lot harder for an interloper to guess or loop their way through: three groups of four lowercase letters, a through z, which produce a pattern that looks something like abcd-efgh-ijkl. Make a mental note that that change in the namespace pattern will require a revision to the client-side prepareNamespace() function.

As with the original peer-to-peer signaling channel, this one holds onto the socket.nsp value in a namespace variable. Then things get more interesting. Whenever a peer connects on the multipeer namespace, the callback creates an empty peers array. Socket.IO exposes a JavaScript Map object that tracks all the clients connected to the namespace.[1] We're interested only in the map's keys, which represent the unique IDs for all connected peers on any one namespace. To build a list of IDs, the signaling channel loops through the map's keys and pushes them onto the peers array.

Each peer ID is assigned by Socket.IO on a per-connection basis: Socket.IO assigns a brand-new ID to each connected peer, each time they connect. So even returning peers—those disconnecting from and reconnecting to the same namespace—will always be treated as brand new. Leaving peers are simply forgotten to history, by decree of the town elders, and their unique IDs never spoken of again on pain of death.

Continuing onward through the signaling logic, you'll see that the multipeer signaling channel emits a new connected peers event—which differs from its singular counterpart, connected peer. The connected peers event is emitted only when someone first joins the namespace. The event also transmits some data: the array of peer IDs for everyone already connected on the namespace.

Anyone already connected to the namespace will be notified of each new connecting peer, thanks socket.broadcast.emit and a repurposed connected peer event. The multipeer namespace's connected peer event now also sends along a small payload of data containing the ID of the new connecting peer. Skipping over the signal event for a moment, we can see that the disconnected peer event includes a similar payload, representing the ID of the disconnecting peer.

---

1. https://developer.mozilla.org/en-US/docs/Web/JavaScript/Reference/Global_Objects/Map

Fixing the Peer-to-Peer Signaling Channel

The failed multipeer-call attempt at the beginning of the chapter revealed a huge weakness in the basic signaling channel you've been using so far. A third peer cannot successfully join a peer-to-peer WebRTC call. But that connection attempt will still ruin the party for the two peers already on the call. That weakness makes for good WebRTC book-learnin', but it's unacceptable for anything you might deploy to production.

If you're looking to build a true peer-to-peer application, rather than a multipeer one, you need to add a small fix to this Socket.IO-backed code. In the 'server.js' file, add this line right below where the signaling channel declares the namespace variable:

```
// server.js
namespaces.on('connect', function(socket) {
  const namespace = socket.nsp;
➤ if (namespace.sockets.size > 2) return;

  // snip...
}
```

That line uses the size property on the JavaScript Map object held by namespace.sockets.[a] A size value greater than two means there are already two peers using the namespace. The return statement exits the callback function and quietly prevents any interlopers from using that particular namespace. That ensures that the two connected peers can carry on their call without even realizing anyone tried to crash their private, peer-to-peer party.

---

a. https://developer.mozilla.org/en-US/docs/Web/JavaScript/Reference/Global_Objects/Map/size

Destructuring the Signal Event's Data

So far, so good. Your signaling code in the browser has always listened for connections and disconnections. But notice the big difference from the peer-to-peer namespace that can be found on the multipeer signal event. You might recall that the peer-to-peer signal event looked like this:

```
// server.js, peer-to-peer namespace
socket.on('signal', function(data) {
  socket.broadcast.emit('signal', data);
});
```

That worked fine on the peer-to-peer namespace, because socket.broadcast.emit sends the signal to what it assumes is a single other connected peer.

In a multipeer WebRTC application, though, the signaling channel needs to route each signal to a specific peer. That's how the mesh-network topography of multipeer WebRTC calls gets established: each peer on the call has to negotiate a connection with every other peer. While the multipeer signaling channel could continue along the lines of the socket.broadcast.emit route, that would leave us having to write a lot of thankless client-side logic to instruct each local peer to ignore signals intended for someone else. The result would be a lot of noise over the signaling channel—and almost certainly slower performance for establishing multipeer connections.

Instead of being noisy like that, the multipeer signaling channel uses the Socket.IO .to() method for routing each signal—an ICE candidate or an SDP description—only to its intended recipient:

```
// server.js, multipeer namespace
socket.on('signal', function({ recipient, sender, signal }) {
  socket.to(recipient).emit('signal', { recipient, sender, signal });
});
```

The routing logic on the signal event requires making the multipeer signaling channel a tad less dumb than its peer-to-peer counterpart. But not by much. The peer-to-peer signaling channel did nothing more than pass along a chunk of data containing a signal. The multipeer signaling channel goes a step further and destructures the data received from the peer sending the signal. The destructured data will ultimately have recipient and sender components, in addition to the signal data (again, a description or a candidate).

Note that the signaling channel itself does nothing with the sender value but send it along. As we'll see, when it comes time to revise the handleScSignal() callback in Working with Peer IDs in the handleScSignal() Callback, on page 156, the peer receiving the signal is only interested in the sender value. Although it can be useful for debugging purposes in the browser, the recipient value is only needed for the signaling channel to route each signal to the correct peer—and no one else.

That's it for the multipeer signaling channel. With a better understanding of how it works, you can turn now to revising the logic in the browser that triggers and responds to the signaling channel's events.

Revising the Signaling Logic on the Client

We're going to follow almost the same process for working up the multipeer app as we did for the original one-to-one, peer-to-peer app in Chapter 3, Establishing a Peer-to-Peer Connection, on page 37. You can work from the starter peer-to-peer app for you to work from in www/multipeer/, which will help you see more clearly how a peer-to-peer app becomes a multipeer one.

Stripping Back Self and Peer

To ease into things, let's revisit the $self and $peer objects and prepare them for a multipeer app. By doing this work first, you'll be able to improve the signaling-channel logic without filling your JavaScript console with a bunch of wacky errors coming off of RTCPeerConnection.

In all of your work with WebRTC so far, there has been exactly one self and one peer on each call. Multipeer by definition means that we need to anticipate setting up, maintaining, and tearing down connections to one or more remote peers, even if there is still just one self (thankfully). Unlike a one-to-one call, the number of connected peers in a multipeer call will change over time—and can change at any time: connected peers might leave, and new peers might join. Coordinated as members of a group might be, they're not going to all show up and connect to the call in the exact same instant.

Consider the $self object first: we need to get rid of all of its state properties. Each of them—isPolite, isMakingOffer, isIgnoringOffer, and isSettingRemoteAnswerPending—will be set instead on a per-peer basis. We'll soon see that the self side of a multipeer call might simultaneously be polite with one peer and impolite with another. For now, delight in the stress-relief of selecting all of that code and deleting it. There. Feel better? The few things that survived your wrath on $self are the timeless, reusable, and peer-independent configuration, media, and features properties:

```
demos/multipeer/js/main.js
const $self = {
  rtcConfig: null,
  mediaConstraints: { audio: true, video: true },
  mediaStream: new MediaStream(),
  mediaTracks: {},
  features: {
    audio: false,
  },
};
```

From here on out, "timeless, reusable, and peer-independent" are the must-have qualities for any value stored on $self.

Now it's the doomed $peer object's turn to witness the firepower of your armed and fully operational Delete key. Up to this point, you've optimistically created a new RTCPeerConnection on $peer as soon as your app loaded or the call was reset. With just one remote peer, that approach worked fine. Not so for multipeer. Let's obliterate the $peer object literal entirely. In its place, we'll create and assign a new JavaScrip `Map` object to a plural $peers variable, to reflect the possibility of multiple peers on the call:

demos/multipeer/js/main.js
```
const $peers = new Map();
```

You already saw briefly in Working with a Multipeer-Ready Signaling Channel, on page 136, that the signaling channel itself uses a JavaScript `Map` object. Maps are incredibly useful structures that share features of both arrays and object literals. We'll get into maps in greater detail in Initializing Peers as Needed, on page 150, where we'll write logic to create a reference to each remote peer as needed, behind a unique key on the $peers map.

All right. Deleting code is exhilarating. But perhaps now you're feeling a tinge of guilt or at least a nagging sense you have gone too far by gutting these fundamental objects you spent so much time setting up earlier in the book. It may seem drastic, but it's necessary: in a multipeer setting, we simply have no idea going in how many peers might join the call, or when. Two peers might be connected for several minutes, for example, before a third peer connects. That means holding off and not creating any instances of `RTCPeerConnection` until the local peer actually needs them.

But before we worry about that, let's get this app talking to the multipeer signaling channel's namespace.

Preparing the Multipeer Namespace

The next thing we need to do in the client-side code is revise the prepareName-space() function to handle the correct pattern for connecting to the multipeer signaling channel's namespace. Let's update the regular expression to match the one on the server (the three groups of four lowercase alpha characters, each group separated by a hyphen), and call a function that we'll write next to return a random string of alpha characters separated by hyphens:

demos/multipeer/js/main.js
```
function prepareNamespace(hash, set_location) {
  let ns = hash.replace(/^#/, ''); // remove # from the hash
  if (/^[a-z]{4}-[a-z]{4}-[a-z]{4}$/.test(ns)) {
    console.log(`Checked existing namespace '${ns}'`);
    return ns;
  }
  ns = generateRandomAlphaString('-', 4, 4, 4);
  console.log(`Created new namespace '${ns}'`);
  if (set_location) window.location.hash = ns;
  return ns;
}
```

Great. The prepareNamespace() function is testing hashes against the correct regular expression. That function now also calls generateRandomAlphaString(), which takes a separator argument—the hyphen, in this case—as well as integers indicating the length of each group. Let's define this function using rest-parameter syntax, which you first encountered back in Sharing Features as Needed, on page 114, to make the function capable of returning as many groups of letters of whatever length as we'd like:

demos/multipeer/js/main.js
```
function generateRandomAlphaString(separator, ...groups) {
  const alphabet = 'abcdefghijklmnopqrstuvwxyz';
  let ns = [];
  for (let group of groups) {
    let str = '';
    for (let i = 0; i < group; i++) {
      str += alphabet[Math.floor(Math.random() * alphabet.length)];
    }
    ns.push(str);
  }
  return ns.join(separator);
}
```

This function is pretty flexible, should you decide to work with a different alpha-namespace pattern in the future. The rest-parameter syntax (...groups) enables you pass in as many group arguments as you like, of whatever length you choose. For example, to generate a random Google Meet–style aaa-bbbb-ccc pattern, you'd call the function like this:

```
generateRandomAlphaString('-', 3, 4, 3);
```

That's pretty slick. But do note the risk of scandal that comes with including the entire alphabet when generating random alpha strings: you and your users will eventually discover that generateRandomAlphaString() can have a potty mouth. The quickest fix for this is an exercise I leave to you, dear reader: write down all the offensive words you know (*gosh, dang, gee whiz,* and so on) and remove their vowels and giveaway consonants from the alphabet string. Alternatively, if you prefer to have portions of your codebase read like the script for an episode of *Deadwood,* you can build yourself a profanity block list that triggers a fresh call to generateRandomAlphaString(). Whatever your approach, you'd also need to modify the signaling channel to disallow user-composed profanities on the namespace. (Not that your gentle, pious users would ever do anything so uncouth.)

Revising the Signaling Callbacks

Now that the client-side JavaScript is capable of connecting to the namespace for the multipeer signaling channel, let's return to the stack of signaling callbacks. Open up registerScCallbacks() and pass in a brand-new callback for the connected peers event:

demos/multipeer/js/main.js
```
function registerScCallbacks() {
  sc.on('connect', handleScConnect);
  sc.on('connected peers', handleScConnectedPeers);
  sc.on('connected peer', handleScConnectedPeer);
  sc.on('disconnected peer', handleScDisconnectedPeer);
  sc.on('signal', handleScSignal);
}
```

Onward to the callback definitions themselves. Start by revising the handleSc-Connect() callback. We'll strip it of the establishCallFeatures() function, which we'll have to call elsewhere in the signaling events, and capture the peer's own ID from the sc object and preserve it on a $self.id property. Let's also log the $self.id value to the console:

demos/multipeer/js/main.js
```
function handleScConnect() {
  console.log('Successfully connected to the signaling server!');
  $self.id = sc.id;
  console.log(`Self ID: ${$self.id}`);
}
```

Below that, you can create the new, skeletal handleScConnectedPeers() callback you registered above. It will need to receive the array of already-connected peers, here as the argument ids, that the signaling channel will send down with the connected peers event. All this function will do for now is log to the console a comma-separated list of connected peer IDs:

demos/multipeer/js/main.js
```
function handleScConnectedPeers(ids) {
  console.log(`Connected peer IDs: ${ids.join(', ')}`);
}
```

Now let's revisit the handleScConnectedPeer() callback. It also needs to work with data returned by the signaling channel: the ID of the newly connected peer, which we'll pass into the function as an id argument.

In the peer-to-peer logic, all the function body did was set self to polite. We can strike that line, and instead again temporarily log the ID of the connecting peer:

demos/multipeer/js/main.js
```
function handleScConnectedPeer(id) {
  console.log(`Newly connected peer ID: ${id}`);
}
```

Go ahead and make parallel revisions to the handleScDisconnectedPeer() function:

demos/multipeer/js/main.js
```
function handleScDisconnectedPeer(id) {
  console.log(`Disconnected peer ID: ${id}`);
}
```

That's it for the skeletal logic needed to work with the multipeer signaling channel's events and data. Fire up your server with npm run start and point a browser to https://localhost:3000/multipeer/. Watch your browser's address bar and on-page heading for a properly-formed random namespace containing three groups of four alpha characters, with each group of characters separated from the others by a hyphen.

Testing Out the Multipeer Namespace and Callbacks

Now for the preview of things to come: pop open a couple more browser windows, and copy and paste in the namespaced address from the first window. Be sure to open the console in each window, and observe what happens as you click the Join button in window after window. Keep in mind we're only working with the signaling channel at this point. There are no RTCPeerConnection objects being created yet, so all the action is in the console:

When a peer first joins the call, a list of the already-connected peer IDs will be logged to the console. As other peers join, each of their IDs will also be logged. Now try disconnecting a few of the peers: you'll also see the IDs logged in all the other windows for the disconnecting peer. Rejoin, and note that a brand-new ID is logged in each of the windows still connected to the call. The rejoining peer will also receive a fresh list of all the IDs for everyone already on the call.

Awesome. You've now got your fundamental signaling callbacks in place to support establishing multipeer WebRTC calls. You're observing data logged to the console from the connected peers, connected peer, and disconnected peer events, which means you're correctly handling the data payloads the signaling channel sends down now, too.

Plenty of revisions remain, of course. We'll need to do way more with those peer ID values than log them. We'll also need to think about which signaling callbacks should call the establishCallFeatures() function that you removed from the handleScConnect() callback. And we'll even need to decide where and when all the various state properties formerly on $self get set, too, including the politeness value that you struck from handleScConnectedPeer().

Honestly, is it any wonder that so many developer-help forums have unanswered questions on how to connect more than two peers over WebRTC? You'll soon be able to go through and respond to all of those posts, and dazzle the world with your expertise.

All right. Before you put on your cape and fly off to be a multipeer superhero for the whole Q&A internet, there's still a lot of work to do. Let's hold off on pushing further ahead with the negotiation aspects of the client-side JavaScript, and return instead to the HTML. (You knew *that* was coming, didn't you?) There you'll pave the way for JavaScript to generate video elements to handle the incoming streams from each remote peer. We should also rework the CSS to display an ever-changing number of video elements on screen. By attending to these tasks now, you'll be able to whip up fresh video elements to go to prove your multipeer WebRTC code works, when the time comes. Those'll be a welcome improvement over convincing yourself you're having the time of your life squinting at some crummy console output.

Generating Video Structures on the Fly

The peer-to-peer HTML has its own hard-coded values, just like the JavaScript did on $self and $peer. A single <video id="peer"> element worked fine in a peer-to-peer call, but it's not suited to multipeer. Let's resume our code-deletion therapy regimen, and remove the peer video-element completely from the HTML. And while we're in the HTML, let's beef up the semantics for the self video and structure it in a <figure> element:

```
<article id="videos">
  <h2 class="preserve-access">Streaming Videos</h2>
➤ <figure id="self">
    <video
      autoplay
      muted
      playsinline
      poster="img/placeholder.png">
    </video>
➤   <figcaption>
➤     You
➤   </figcaption>
➤ </figure>
</article>
```

The video element remains unchanged except that its id attribute shifts to a containing <figure> element, which is a solidly accessible structure for presenting media. Details about the media can be structured in an associated <figcaption> element. In a multipeer call, for example, keeping track of everyone's name can be a challenge. Later, in Sharing Features over Multipeer Data Channels, on page 165, we'll enable users to set their names for display on the screens of all remote peers. But for now, we're establishing the markup pattern and providing a hard-coded "You" in the <figcaption> element on the self side of the call.

With the peer video element removed from the HTML, flip back over to your JavaScript and define a new createVideoStructure() function to construct peer video elements on the fly. You can structure them just like the video element for self you wrote in the HTML, with a containing <figure>:

```
demos/multipeer/js/main.js
/**
 *  User-Media and Data-Channel Functions
 */

function createVideoStructure(id) {
  const figure = document.createElement('figure');
  const figcaption = document.createElement('figcaption');
  const video = document.createElement('video');
  const attributes = {
    autoplay: '',
    playsinline: '',
    poster: 'img/placeholder.png',
  };
  const attributes_list = Object.keys(attributes);
```

```
  // Set attributes
  figure.id = `peer-${id}`;
  figcaption.innerText = id;
  for (let attr of attributes_list) {
    video.setAttribute(attr, attributes[attr]);
  }
  // Append the video and figcaption elements
  figure.appendChild(video);
  figure.appendChild(figcaption);
  // Return the complete figure
  return figure;
}
```

The createVideoStructure() function takes a single argument, id. Just like you wrapped the #self video in a <figure> element in the HTML, createVideoStructure() creates new <figure> and <figcaption> elements along with a <video> element. The function also contains an object literal with the peer video's three attributes—autoplay, playsinline, and poster—that we'd previously set directly in HTML. Rather than call video.setAttribute() over and over, we iterate over a list of the attributes object's keys.[2] That's a convenient structure if you ever need additional attributes: just add them to the object literal.

Rounding out createVideoStructure(), we set the id value, prefixed with peer-, on the figure element's id attribute. The peer- prefix is useful in case any of the signaling-channel's ID values would make for an invalid HTML id, which would be the case for any ID whose first character is a digit. We also set the raw, unprefixed id as the text in <figcaption>, which will be a useful on-screen debugging feature until we improve the multipeer app to handle names that users choose for themselves. The function then appends the newly created <video> and <figcaption> elements to the <figure> element, which the function ultimately returns.

Because the createVideoStructure() only returns the figure element, we have to write logic to attach it to the DOM and set the video's srcObject value to the correct incoming peer stream. Let's tackle both of those issues next by revising the displayStream() function.

Setting Multipeer Video Streams

Previously, all the displayStream() function did was accept a stream and a selector, basically acting as a wrapper around document.querySelector(). But now that we're presenting dynamically generated video elements wrapped in <figure> elements,

---

2. https://developer.mozilla.org/en-US/docs/Web/JavaScript/Reference/Global_Objects/Object/keys

we need to build out this function a bit more—and put the createVideoStructure() function to work, too.

First off, let's modify the parameters on displayStream() to take a peer id. For occasions when displayStream() is used for self, we'll assign "self" as the default id (we'll update the code for such occasions next):

demos/multipeer/js/main.js
```
function displayStream(stream, id = 'self') {
  const selector = id === 'self' ? '#self' : `#peer-${id}`;
  let video_structure = document.querySelector(selector);
  if (!video_structure) {
    const videos = document.querySelector('#videos');
    video_structure = createVideoStructure(id);
    videos.appendChild(video_structure);
  }
  video_structure.querySelector('video').srcObject = stream;
}
```

Inside the function, we build a selector and then check whether it exists in the DOM. If the needed figure element is undefined because it doesn't yet exist, a small if block calls up createVideoStructure() and appends its returned element to the <article id="videos"> element in your HTML. The function then queries for the <video> element inside the <figure>, and sets its srcObject to the stream.

Take a minute now and hunt down the function definitions for toggleCam() and requestUserMedia(), and update their calls to displayStream() to remove the #self argument that you used to pass in:

demos/multipeer/js/main.js
```
function toggleCam(button) {

  // snip, snip

  if (enabled_state) {
    $self.mediaStream.addTrack($self.mediaTracks.video);
  } else {
    $self.mediaStream.removeTrack($self.mediaTracks.video);
    displayStream($self.mediaStream);
  }
}

// (elsewhere in your main.js file...)

async function requestUserMedia(media_constraints) {

  $self.media = await navigator.mediaDevices
    .getUserMedia(media_constraints);

  // snip, snip

  displayStream($self.mediaStream);
}
```

That completes the logic for generating and attaching video elements on a per-peer, as-needed basis. Self videos should now be displayed as expected, too. Now let's turn to displaying the videos optimally in whatever screen space is available, care of a little CSS.

Adding CSS to Display a Grid of Videos

We can't predict in advance how many videos will need to be presented on the screen. But we also want to make sure that we're maximizing the screen space allotted to videos—regardless of their number. Let's set up a highly flexible grid on the videos container:

```
demos/multipeer/css/screen.css
#videos {
  align-self: start;
  display: grid;
  grid-template-columns: repeat(auto-fit, minmax(200px, 1fr));
  gap: 11px;
}
```

That CSS is duded up in some surprisingly fancy pants. It sets the #videos element to display as a grid, with a gap of 11px between each column and row of videos. The real action is on grid-template-columns, which uses the CSS grid repeat() syntax to create as many columns as there are video elements.[3] The auto-fit value on repeat() means the grid will include as many columns as it can without any of them spilling over the <article id="videos"> element that contains them.

Specifically, rather than squeeze all of the videos onto one row, the minmax() function specifies that videos must be at least 200px wide,[4] but no wider than one fractional unit (1fr)—meaning that all videos will be sized equally. Thanks to auto-fit, as video elements are attached to the DOM, any empty 200px columns in the grid will collapse—allowing the columns that contain videos to uniformly expand and fill the space. That means that this grid will work responsively across any viewport size, without us having to fuss over media queries—a technique that Jen Simmons dubbed *intrinsic layout*.[5]

Let's also set up some styles for the <figcaption> elements. Remember each figure caption will contain the remote peer ID assigned by the signaling channel, or the hard-coded "You" value for self. This CSS will present that information in a slightly transparent overlay at the bottom of each video element:

---

3.   https://developer.mozilla.org/en-US/docs/Web/CSS/repeat()
4.   https://developer.mozilla.org/en-US/docs/Web/CSS/minmax()
5.   https://aneventapart.com/news/post/designing-intrinsic-layouts-aea-video

demos/multipeer/css/screen.css

```
figure {
  position: relative;
}
figcaption {
  color: #EEE;
  background: rgba(16,16,16,0.6);
  font-weight: normal;
  font-size: 14px;
  position: absolute;
  bottom: 0;
  left: 0;
  width: 100%;
  padding: 5.5px;
}
```

All right. With the createVideoStructure() and displayStream() functions set and some basic CSS in place to display all the video elements in an intrinsic grid, you've now prepared your UI to handle multiple videos as peers join the call. Let's get back to the JavaScript in earnest to address the major challenge that remains: enhancing and revising the call setup and negotiation logic to handle multiple connecting peers.

Initializing Peers as Needed

Let's create a new function to populate the $peers map that you created in Stripping Back Self and Peer, on page 140. The map will maintain per-peer instances of RTCPeerConnection and the state properties formerly on $self.

At the top of the stack of functions in the Call Features and Reset Functions part of your main.js file, open up a new function definition for initializePeer(). This function should take two parameters: id, for tracking the peer ID value returned by the signaling channel, and polite, for assigning a Boolean to indicate politeness:

demos/multipeer/js/main.js

```
/**
 *  Call Features & Reset Functions
 */

function initializePeer(id, polite) {
  $peers.set(id, {
    connection: new RTCPeerConnection($self.rtcConfig),
    mediaStream: new MediaStream(),
    mediaTracks: {},
    features: {},
    selfStates: {
      isPolite: polite,
      isMakingOffer: false,
```

```
      isIgnoringOffer: false,
      isSettingRemoteAnswerPending: false,
    },
  });
}
```

As promised, the body of the initializePeer() function resurrects everything we deleted earlier from the old $self and hard-coded $peer variables. The function uses a peer ID value to create a key on the JavaScript map object using the set() method.[6] The map's key takes as its value an object literal with numerous familiar properties, including connection and selfStates.

The RTCPeerConnection instance on connection receives the configuration value from $self: values in $self.rtcConfig will be identical for every peer connection (null for the time being). The new selfStates property maintains its own per-peer object literal for the state properties you previously stored on $self. In a multi-peer setup, it's convenient to track self states alongside their corresponding connection instance.

Behind the scenes, initializePeer() will structure entries in the $peers map to look something like this, here showing a get() call on the map with a specific peer ID:

```
$peers.get('W1MHdVPsbP3JgpwfAAAB');
// Returned value for an example 'W1MHdVPsbP3JgpwfAAAB' key ID:
Object {
  connection: RTCPeerConnection { }, // values omitted...
  features: Object { audio: false },
  mediaStream: MediaStream { }, // values omitted...
  mediaTracks: Object { }, // values omitted...
  selfStates: Object {
    isPolite: true, // or false, depending
    isMakingOffer: false,
    isIgnoringOffer: false,
    isSettingRemoteAnswerPending: false,
  }
}
```

That looks complicated, but it's meant to illustrate how each peer is structured as a key-value pair inside the $peers JavaScript map. Don't worry, though: you won't have to fuss over the ID keys manually. The logic you're writing will do everything needed to store and access the per-ID data, and you'll soon be retrieving those values in your signaling and WebRTC callbacks with the map's .get() method as in the example above.[7]

---

6. https://developer.mozilla.org/en-US/docs/Web/JavaScript/Reference/Global_Objects/Map/set
7. https://developer.mozilla.org/en-US/docs/Web/JavaScript/Reference/Global_Objects/Map/get

In addition to setting and getting peers, we'll also need to delete them when they leave the call. Let's look at how that's done by revising resetPeer() function, which must now play the role of the Grim Reaper.

Resetting Peers on Multipeer Calls

Have a look at the existing resetPeer() function definition. In a peer-to-peer context, it looked like this:

```
function resetPeer(peer) {
  displayStream(null, '#peer');
  document.querySelector('#mic-status')
    .setAttribute('aria-hidden', true);
  peer.connection.close();
  peer.connection = new RTCPeerConnection($self.rtcConfig);
  peer.mediaStream = new MediaStream();
  peer.mediaTracks = {};
  peer.features = {};
}
```

Its logic was all tied pretty closely to both the interface and the hard-coded $peer instance. For multipeer purposes, you can cut things back pretty hard. There is no need to continue setting up a new peer connection or any peer properties, nor to worry about the mic status—which is part of the video structures you're now creating on the fly as peers join:

demos/multipeer/js/main.js
```
function resetPeer(id) {
  const peer = $peers.get(id);
  displayStream(null, id);
  document.querySelector(`#peer-${id}`).remove();
  peer.connection.close();
  $peers.delete(id);
}
```

In its revised form, resetPeer() closes the existing peer connection for a particular ID, and nulls out the associated video stream (be sure you update the arguments on displayStream()). The function then removes the video structure from the DOM entirely and deletes the references to the now-defunct peer ID from both the $peers and $self objects.

Having built the initializePeer() function, and revised resetPeer(), we can move onto the signaling callbacks that actually call them.

Fleshing out the Skeletal Signaling Callbacks

We need to call initializePeer() from within two signaling callbacks, handleScConnectedPeer() and handleScConnectedPeers(), that fire in response to peer-connection events. Both callbacks must now process data payloads containing peer IDs from the signaling channel.

Let's start with handleScConnectedPeer(), which works with a single incoming ID. It should initialize a peer for that ID and establish the call features, too:

```
demos/multipeer/js/main.js
function handleScConnectedPeer(id) {
  console.log(`Newly connected peer ID: ${id}`);
  // be impolite with each newly connecting peer
  initializePeer(id, false);
  establishCallFeatures(id);
}
```

You might recall that handleScConnectedPeer() will be called by everyone already connected to the call. By passing in false as the polite argument to the new initializePeer() function, the peers already on the call will be impolite to each new connecting peer. (That's the opposite of what you did for basic peer-to-peer calls, where the later peer to join was impolite. See the sidebar *Changing Up Politeness in Multipeer Calls*, on page 154.)

While we have yet to revise establishCallFeatures(), for the moment, let's keep going and revise the handleScConnectedPeers() callback function first. This callback will require looping through an array of IDs for any peers already connected to the namespace:

```
demos/multipeer/js/main.js
function handleScConnectedPeers(ids) {
  console.log(`Connected peer IDs: ${ids.join(', ')}`);
  for (let id of ids) {
    if (id === $self.id) continue;
    // be polite with already-connected peers
    initializePeer(id, true);
    establishCallFeatures(id);
  }
}
```

The ids array contains the IDs of everyone connected on the namespace, including the newly connected peer. To keep things from getting weird, you need to filter out $self.id, which you captured inside the handleScConnect() callback. The handleScConnectedPeers() function uses a small conditional that, when true, quietly executes a continue statement to skip the current ID ($self's) and proceed to the next iteration through the for-loop.[8]

---

8. https://developer.mozilla.org/en-US/docs/Web/JavaScript/Reference/Statements/continue

For all the other peer IDs, handleScConnectedPeers() initializes each peer and establishes the call features. By setting polite to true on initializePeer(), the newly connected peer will be polite to everyone already on the call.

Changing Up Politeness in Multipeer Calls

Remember that perfect negotiation requires each connection to have a polite and impolite peer, as you saw in Establishing the Polite Peer, on page 45. Polite peers will be able to roll back any offer they've already sent in order to accept a clashing incoming offer from an impolite peer. In multipeer calls, any given peer will play the polite role with some peers and the impolite role with others.

In peer-to-peer calls, the second peer to join the call—the newbie—was impolite. The logic in the revised handleScConnectedPeers() function hints at why it's better to change things around and make newbies polite in a multipeer call: peers just joining the call might well receive a large payload of connected-peer IDs and begin acting on them immediately—before the connected peers are all notified of the newbie on the call. The newbie's own signaling logic might also start firing off offers before the connected peers are ready: the connected peers might not yet have created a new instance of RTCPeerConnection by the time the newbie starts signaling. Without a properly ID'd instance of RTCPeerConnection on $peers, there's nothing for the connected peers to do with any new incoming signals. The newbie therefore needs to be polite in order to ditch any offers it sent out eagerly but prematurely.

Establishing Call Features for Multiple Peers

All right. Let's update the establishCallFeatures() wrapper function that you're now calling within the handleScConnectedPeer() and handleScConnectedPeers() signaling callbacks. While it's not essential to update the establishCallFeatures() function, your code will read more sensibly if you change the old peer parameter to id, which clarifies that it's peer ID and not a $peer instance the function expects:

demos/multipeer/js/main.js
```
function establishCallFeatures(id) {
  registerRtcCallbacks(id);
  addFeaturesChannel(id);
  addStreamingMedia(id);
}
```

The change from peer to id is cosmetic in that case. But the three functions called from within establishCallFeatures() each need to be reworked to accept ID values rather than peer instances. We'll look at registerRtcCallbacks() shortly, in Restructuring WebRTC Callbacks with Closures, on page 159. But we can go ahead right now and fix up the other two.

First up, let's update addStreamingMedia() with a single new line:

demos/multipeer/js/main.js

```
function addStreamingMedia(id) {
  const peer = $peers.get(id);
  const tracks_list = Object.keys($self.mediaTracks);
  for (let track of tracks_list) {
    peer.connection.addTrack($self.mediaTracks[track]);
  }
}
```

Here you're again renaming the peer parameter to id. But a peer variable scoped to the function restores your existing references to peer by grabbing a specific peer record from the $peers map. (Get used to that const peer = $peers.get(id); line—you'll be writing it a lot.) The rest of the function adds media tracks to the connection, as before, but now it adds them to a specific peer connection.

The addFeaturesChannel() function will take a pair of fixes. Again, the function body kicks off by accessing the correct peer from the $peers map. The only other change you need to address is in the feature-function callbacks: you need to call displayStream() and pass in the id argument for the video feature:

demos/multipeer/js/main.js

```
function addFeaturesChannel(id) {
  const peer = $peers.get(id);

  const featureFunctions = {

    // snip, snip

    video: function() {
      // This is all just to display the poster image,
      // rather than a black frame
      if (peer.mediaTracks.video) {
        if (peer.features.video) {
          peer.mediaStream.addTrack(peer.mediaTracks.video);
        } else {
          peer.mediaStream.removeTrack(peer.mediaTracks.video);
          displayStream(peer.mediaStream, id);
        }
      }
    },
  };

  // snip, snip

}
```

And with that, you've got all the necessary functions set up for building out peers as they connect. Let's shift now to do the opposite, and write logic to clean up after peers leave the call, too.

Managing Leaving Peers

You can get things started in the skeletal handleScDisconnectedPeer() callback, and drop in a call to the Grim Reaper version of the resetPeer() function that you worked on above, in Resetting Peers on Multipeer Calls, on page 152:

demos/multipeer/js/main.js
```
function handleScDisconnectedPeer(id) {
  console.log(`Disconnected peer ID: ${id}`);
  resetPeer(id);
}
```

That's literally it: just removing any trace that the peer was ever connected or even existed in the first place. The ID of the departed sleeps with the fishes.

Now onto the leaveCall() function that's triggered by clicks on the Leave Call button. Similar to the handleScConnectedPeers() callback, you need a loop so that the departing peer can completely obliterate all traces of any peers who were on the call:

demos/multipeer/js/main.js
```
function leaveCall() {
  sc.close();
  for (let id of $peers.keys()) {
    resetPeer(id);
  }
}
```

To build this loop, we use the for...of syntax for looping over the Map object's iterable keys.[9] Within the loop, resetPeer() will be called with a reference to each peer on the call at the time the departing peer chooses to leave. A real massacre.

All right. You've got your multipeer app's logic set up for initializing and removing peers. That leaves one more piece of signaling logic to attend to: processing the descriptions and candidates that come across the signaling channel and into the handleScSignal() callback.

Working with Peer IDs in the handleScSignal() Callback

The first order of business with the handleSCSignal() callback is to use a slightly more involved piece of destructuring assignment to work with the new values returned by the multipeer-capable signaling channel.

As you might've guessed back in Working with a Multipeer-Ready Signaling Channel, on page 136, you now need to access the sender and signal values

---

9. https://developer.mozilla.org/en-US/docs/Web/JavaScript/Reference/Statements/for...of

returned by the signaling channel, as well as the candidate and description values inside of signal. The parameters for handleScSignal() take on a slightly more complex look compared to the { description, candidate } destructured parameters for peer-to-peer signaling:

```
async function handleScSignal({ sender,
  signal: { candidate, description } }) {
```

What that does is destructure both sender and signal, as well as the familiar candidate and description that signal now contains. Remember the recipient value is used only by the signaling channel logic on the server, for routing the signal to the intended peer. The intended peer, of course, is the one actually calling handleScSignal(), so you can safely omit recipient from the destructuring syntax on the handleScSignal() callback definition. (That said, if you want to add an additional level of debugging, you could destructure recipient as well and compare its value against $self.id and see if they match—and call console.error with a message if they don't.)

With the destructured parameters ready for action, you can then set up three function-scoped variables inside the function:

- id: a reference to the sender value (as it's the peer behind the received signal whose ID you need)

- peer: the specific peer instance from the $peers JavaScript Map object

- self_state: the state values for the self side of the call on a peer instance

Put those together, and your handleScSignal() callback should open like this:

```
demos/multipeer/js/main.js
async function handleScSignal({ sender,
  signal: { candidate, description } }) {

  const id = sender;
  const peer = $peers.get(id);
  const self_state = peer.selfStates;

  if (description) {
    // snip, snip...
```

So far, so good. But you now have a bit of a tedious task that's better left to the find-and-replace feature on your editor of choice: correcting variable references.

Correcting Variable References

So long as we're thinking about variables, let's change all of the old peer-to-peer $self.is* references to self_state.is* inside of handleScSignal(). If your editor has a find-and-replace function that you can scope to a code selection, you can make very quick work of that. Similarly, the old references to $peer must be changed to reference the new function-scoped peer variable, which differs only in its lack of a dollar sign from the old $peer global. Run another find and replace for all instances of $peer inside of handleScSignal() and change them to peer, taking care not to mess up the dollar sign on the line where you assign $peers[id] to peer.

Another variable-oriented fix is to add routing to the one call to sc.emit() appearing inside handleScSignal(). You'll need to specify values for the recipient and sender, and tuck the description inside of an object literal assigned to signal:

demos/multipeer/js/main.js

```
    // still inside the handleScSignal callback()

    // snip, snip...

    if (self_state.isIgnoringOffer) {
      return;
    }

    self_state.isSettingRemoteAnswerPending = description.type === 'answer';

    await peer.connection.setRemoteDescription(description);

    self_state.isSettingRemoteAnswerPending = false;

    if (description.type === 'offer') {
      await peer.connection.setLocalDescription();
      sc.emit('signal', { recipient: id, sender: $self.id,
        signal: { description: peer.connection.localDescription } });
    }
  } else if (candidate) {
// snip, snip...
```

Note the lines of context in that example, showing the changes from references like $self.isIgnoringOffer to self_state.isIgnoringOffer.

Logging Peer IDs with Failed ICE Candidates

The final improvement to the handleScSignal() callback is diagnostic. Let's log the peer ID with any errors in adding ICE candidates when offers aren't being ignored. While that is not likely to happen, the presence of such errors can suggest there might be something the matter with your signaling logic—in which case you'll want to rework your way through the previous sections. But with any luck, you'll never see any such errors logged:

```
demos/multipeer/js/main.js
// still inside the handleScSignal callback()

// snip, snip...
  } else if (candidate) {
    // Handle ICE candidates
    try {
      await peer.connection.addIceCandidate(candidate);
    } catch(e) {
➤     // Log error unless state is ignoring offers
➤     // and candidate is not an empty string
➤     if (!self_state.isIgnoringOffer && candidate.candidate.length > 1) {
➤       console.error(`Unable to add ICE candidate for peer ID: ${id}.`, e);
➤     }
    }
  }
// snip, snip...
```

And that's it. You've revised all of your signaling callbacks. To review: your signaling logic is now capable of initializing and removing peers from the call as they come and go. You've also fixed up how call features are established, including the functions for adding streaming media to a connection and setting up a features channel with each peer. And now, you've also written the logic to ensure that any two peers are able to send and receive signals to establish an RTCPeerConnection with each other. That's the key to setting up a mesh network with WebRTC.

Take a deep, cleansing breath. Maybe go for a walk around the block. Once you're ready to proceed, let's get down to work on the WebRTC-callback logic, starting with the callback-registration function that establishCallFeatures() calls: registerRtcCallbacks().

Restructuring WebRTC Callbacks with Closures

So far, rewriting the peer-to-peer code to work on multipeer calls has been pretty straightforward. Well, fairly straightforward. Fine—*straightforwardish*, the way an alien abduction is straightforward. However you want to spin it, your work towards a multipeer WebRTC app has required shifting some logic around on the signaling callbacks and introducing a new id variable to a number of functions.

By contrast, the revisions you'll make to your WebRTC callbacks require rethinking your approach to callbacks entirely, especially how the callbacks themselves are registered.

Let's step back and think about peer IDs for a moment: each of your WebRTC callbacks needs to be associated with a specific peer ID's RTCPeerConnection instance. Accessing IDs wasn't a problem with signaling callbacks: peer IDs are included in all data returned by the signaling channel's events. But neither the RTCPeerConnection object nor the data returned by its events have any access to peer IDs. And that's a problem, because unique peer IDs are central to the way we're architecting multipeer, mesh-networked calls.

Providing the correct ID value to each WebRTC callback that needs it is a trickier proposition than it might sound. But it's not impossible. Let's start big-picture and open up the registerRtcCallbacks() function, modify it to take an id argument that will be passed into the function from within establishCallFeatures(), and prepare each of its event assignments so that we're passing in the ID for a specific peer. Remember that establishCallFeatures() is executed for each peer on a call, thanks to the logic you wrote a moment ago in Fleshing out the Skeletal Signaling Callbacks, on page 152:

```
demos/multipeer/js/main.js
/**
 *  WebRTC Functions and Callbacks
 */

function registerRtcCallbacks(id) {
  const peer = $peers.get(id);
  peer.connection
    .onconnectionstatechange = handleRtcConnectionStateChange(id);
  peer.connection
    .onnegotiationneeded = handleRtcConnectionNegotiation(id);
  peer.connection
    .onicecandidate = handleRtcIceCandidate(id);
  peer.connection
    .ontrack = handleRtcPeerTrack(id);
}
```

Just like you did with addStreamingMedia(), you're setting up a function-scoped peer variable inside registerRtcCallbacks(). But something probably looks off about those rewritten callback assignments. In Writing Named Functions as Callbacks, on page 22, you read about how it's a very big deal to make sure that callback functions are passed in or assigned by reference, without parentheses. But here, not only are you calling functions with parentheses, but you're even passing each of them an id value. That will blow up all of the peer-to-peer WebRTC callbacks you wrote previously, which destructured data returned by the WebRTC events that triggered them.

That's a big problem: the rules have not changed on callback assignments. The callbacks assigned to WebRTC events must still reference functions to be executed when each associated event fires—now with the added complexity of firing on a specific peer.connection instance, too.

What we need to do, then, is restructure all the peer-to-peer WebRTC callback functions to create closures.[10] In other words, each of the existing WebRTC callbacks must be rewritten so as to return a function when executed. When a WebRTC event fires, it will execute the returned function, which must be capable of receiving and acting on the WebRTC event's data.

Let's try expressing those abstract ideas as real code. Right below the registerRtcCallbacks() function definition, find the handleRtcPeerTrack() callback. Think back to how you wrote that function to display the media streaming in from a single remote peer:

```
// main.js, peer-to-peer logic
function handleRtcPeerTrack({ track }) {
  console.log(`Handle incoming ${track.kind} track...`)
  $peer.mediaTracks[track.kind] = track;
  $peer.mediaStream.addTrack(track);
  displayStream($peer.mediaStream, '#peer');
}
```

We must do two things to rewrite that callback to create a closure: first, we'll grab the ID argument that's being passed into handleRtcPeerTrack() from within registerRtcCallbacks(). And then we'll change the body of handleRtcPeerTrack() to return a function—an anonymous but otherwise identical version of the original callback that you wrote—which will be called when the track event actually fires the peer connection for that ID value:

```
demos/multipeer/js/main.js
function handleRtcPeerTrack(id) {
  return function({ track }) {
    const peer = $peers.get(id);
    console.log(`Handle incoming ${track.kind} track from peer ID: ${id}`);
    peer.mediaTracks[track.kind] = track;
    peer.mediaStream.addTrack(track);
    displayStream(peer.mediaStream, id);
  };
}
```

---

10. https://developer.mozilla.org/en-US/docs/Web/JavaScript/Closures

If you've not worked with closures before, the idea behind them is that the returned function is capable of holding onto the values of any variables, like id, from the scope of the outer function: in this case, handleRtcPeerTrack(). The anonymous function returned by handleRtcPeerTrack() is what's actually assigned to the peer.connection.ontrack event property. Note that the anonymous function is still neatly destructuring the track from the event, too.

In slightly more concrete terms: the new function returned by handleRtcPeerTrack() must fire on the track event for a specific remote peer. Preserving the reference to that peer's ID is made possible by the closure. The ID value makes it possible to continue to preserve the tracks and stream on the peer's record in the $peers map. The peer's ID itself must also be passed into the displayStream() function you wrote back on page 148.

In slightly more nerdy terms: the inner anonymous function has access to the outer function's lexical scope, including the id value, at the moment the anonymous function is defined. That's the magic of closures in JavaScript: we can preserve custom values for use inside a callback function without messing with the set structure of arguments passed into the callback at runtime.

Enough nerding out. Let's keep going. If you're still feeling uncertain about closures, that's okay. Their behavior should become clearer as you write a few more. Find the "Reusable WebRTC Functions and Callbacks" area of your main.js file and rewrite those three callbacks to use closures, too. You can go in order, and prove to yourself what a champ you are by starting with handleRtc-ConnectionNegotiation(), which also involves the signaling channel:

demos/multipeer/js/main.js

```
/**
 *   Reusable WebRTC Functions and Callbacks
 */
function handleRtcConnectionNegotiation(id) {
  return async function() {
    const peer = $peers.get(id);
    const self_state = peer.selfStates;
    self_state.isMakingOffer = true;
    await peer.connection.setLocalDescription();
    sc.emit('signal',
      { recipient: id, sender: $self.id,
        signal: { description: peer.connection.localDescription } });
    self_state.isMakingOffer = false;
  };
}
```

Here you're making use of the self states associated with a specific peer ID, which for the sake of brevity gets its own variable assignment (self_state) for use in the connection-negotiation callback's logic.

Beyond that adjustment in how you reference self states, the most significant change to handleRtcConnectionNegotiation() is on its call to the sc.emit() method. In the peer-to-peer code, that call looked like this:

```
// main.js
// snip, snip...
  sc.emit('signal',
    { description: $peer.connection.localDescription });
// snip, snip...
```

But in a multipeer setup, it's necessary to include the recipient and sender values for properly routing signals over the signaling channel whenever you call sc.emit()—just like you did for the handleScSignal() callback in Correcting Variable References, on page 157. The routing values are made accessible from the returned anonymous callback function, care of the closure around id.

See? You are indeed a closure champ. You can make quick work of rewriting the other two reusable WebRTC callbacks as closures, too. They're less complicated by comparison.

The ICE-candidate callback needs to reference an id for routing each candidate to the correct peer:

```
demos/multipeer/js/main.js
function handleRtcIceCandidate(id) {
  return function({ candidate }) {
    sc.emit('signal', { recipient: id, sender: $self.id,
      signal: { candidate } });
  };
}
```

We can also write a diagnostic closure on the connection state-change callback. It doesn't make sense to add a class to the body in a multipeer setting (all of the changes from multiple peers' connection states would clobber each other), but what we can do instead is reference an element and add the connection state there, assuming the element exists. Because this is meant to be reusable code, let's opt for a generic peer_element, so that it reads sensibly even if you build WebRTC applications that do not include video elements as part of the interface. The connectionstatechange event will first fire immediately, likely before the peer element has been added to the self side of the call. So we check for the element's existence before doing anything with it:

```
demos/multipeer/js/main.js
function handleRtcConnectionStateChange(id) {
  return function() {
    const peer = $peers.get(id);
➤   const connection_state = peer.connection.connectionState;
➤   // Assume *some* element will take a unique peer ID
➤   const peer_element = document.querySelector(`#peer-${id}`);
➤   if (peer_element) {
➤     peer_element.dataset.connectionState = connection_state;
➤   }
    console.log(`Connection state '${connection_state}' for Peer ID: ${id}`);
  };
}
```

When the element exists, the function preserves the connection state in a data-connection-state attribute, care of the dataset property.[11] The camelCased dataset.connectionState property will automatically convert to a dash-styled data-connection-state attribute in the DOM. The latest state will always replace any older state on the data-connection-state attribute.

And with that, all of your WebRTC callbacks are properly using closures to return id-backed anonymous functions.

Testing Out a Multipeer Call

Now comes the big moment. Go big and open a whole bunch of browser windows, and get them all pointed at the same multipeer namespace. Pull out your phone or tablet so you can connect an external device or two, too. Try willy-nilly connecting some of the browsers. Leave and rejoin the call. Listen to the fans roar on your laptop, an issue we'll return to in Chapter 7, Managing User Media, on page 173 soon enough. Watch how every browser window adds and removes video elements for each peer, as shown in the screenshot on page 165. Scan through the console messages across different windows to see what is happening behind the scenes.

Congratulations: this is a monumental achievement. A triumph. At this point, you have fully mastered your command of the RTCPeerConnection object in the browser. You're creating and destroying numerous instances of it at will, and capitalizing on targeted routes over the signaling channel to ensure that each peer on the call successfully negotiates a connection with every other peer.

---

11. https://developer.mozilla.org/en-US/docs/Web/API/HTMLElement/dataset

Sharing Features over Multipeer Data Channels

There's only one significant thing we've yet to address on a multipeer call: data channels. Let's remedy that. Instead of displaying the IDs returned by the signaling channel with each peer video, you're going to create a bit of interface that lets users enter a username that will be shared with all the other peers on the call—including those who join the call later.

Let's start by putting together a small form element in the HTML. The form will take the place of the hard-coded "You" value that you wrote in Generating Video Structures on the Fly, on page 145:

```
demos/multipeer/index.html
<article id="videos">
  <h2 class="preserve-access">Streaming Videos</h2>
  <figure id="self">
    <video
      autoplay
      muted
      playsinline
      poster="img/placeholder.png">
    </video>
    <figcaption>
➤     <form id="username-form" action="#null">
➤       <label for="username-input" class="preserve-access">Username</label>
➤       <input type="text" id="username-input" placeholder="Username" />
➤       <button type="submit" id="username-set-btn">Set Username</button>
➤     </form>
    </figcaption>
  </figure>
</article>
```

You can then write a set of styles to present the form and its child elements to respond to whatever size video elements are currently displaying:

```
demos/multipeer/css/screen.css
figcaption form {
  display: flex;
  flex-flow: row wrap;
  gap: 5.5px;
}
figcaption form > * {
  font-family: inherit;
  font-size: inherit;
  font-weight: inherit;
  flex: 1 0 auto;
}
#username-input {
  background-color: inherit;
  border: 1px solid #CCC;
  color: #EEE;
  display: block;
  padding: 5.5px;
  max-width: 100%;
}
#username-set-btn {
  background: rgba(64,64,64,0.8);
  color: #EEE;
  padding: 5.5px;
}
```

With the HTML and CSS set for the form, you'll have an interface that looks like this:

Now we can wire up the username form's logic in JavaScript. First, let's attach a callback to the username form's submit event. This will swap out the form and show the username instead on the self side of the call:

```
demos/multipeer/js/main.js
/**
 *   User-Interface Setup
 */
document.querySelector('#username-form')
  .addEventListener('submit', handleUsernameForm);

/**
 *   User-Interface Functions and Callbacks
 */
function handleUsernameForm(e) {
  e.preventDefault();
  const form = e.target;
  const username = form.querySelector('#username-input').value;
  const figcaption = document.querySelector('#self figcaption');
  figcaption.innerText = username;
}
```

Now for the awesome part. To send and receive usernames, we'll use the same features-channel logic that we built for toggling cameras and mics in Sharing Features over Data Channels, on page 112.

In fact, let's begin by fixing up how we're sharing toggle states for cameras and microphones. We need to couch the old peer-to-peer shareFeatures() call inside of a loop that goes through each peer ID:

demos/multipeer/js/main.js

```
function toggleMic(button) {
  const audio = $self.mediaTracks.audio;
  const enabled_state = audio.enabled = !audio.enabled;

  $self.features.audio = enabled_state;

  button.setAttribute('aria-checked', enabled_state);

  for (let id of $peers.keys()) {
    shareFeatures(id, 'audio');
  }
}

function toggleCam(button) {

  // snip, snip

  button.setAttribute('aria-checked', enabled_state);

  for (let id of $peers.keys()) {
    shareFeatures(id, 'video');
  }

  // snip, snip

}
```

Those loops might strike you as inefficient, but it's a little reminder that your multipeer call is, in fact, relying on a mesh network. Sending messages over data channels means sending the same message to each connected peer separately. (For that reason, some WebRTC developers will repurpose Socket.IO to serve not only as a signaling channel, but also as the backbone for group messaging.)

To make that loop work, of course, you'll need to add an id parameter along with a familiar line of code to the shareFeatures() function definition:

demos/multipeer/js/main.js

```
function shareFeatures(id, ...features) {
  const peer = $peers.get(id);

  const featuresToShare = {};

  if (!peer.featuresChannel) return;

  for (let f of features) {
    featuresToShare[f] = $self.features[f];
  }

  try {
    peer.featuresChannel.send(JSON.stringify(featuresToShare));
```

```
  } catch(e) {
    console.error('Error sending features:', e);
  }
}
```

Back to the muted status: instead of showing a ham-fisted "Peer is muted" message, let's instead show a parenthetical "(Muted)" message next to the peer's ID and, in a moment, the peer's username. We can handle that with a reusable function we'll define inside the addFeaturesChannel() function, so it properly references the correct peer—thanks to our old friend, the closure:

```
function addFeaturesChannel(id);
  const peer = $peers.get(id);

  // snip, snip

  function showUsernameAndMuteStatus(username) {
    const fc = document.querySelector(`#peer-${id} figcaption`);
    if (peer.features.audio) {
      fc.innerText = username;
    } else {
      fc.innerText = `${username} (Muted)`;
    }
  }

}
```

It selects the correct <figcaption> element for a peer and sets the username (or ID) along with a possible mute status as the caption's inner text. We can put this into action on the existing audio feature function, which will have some ternary-operator logic to use the peer's username if it's been set. Otherwise, it uses the ID:

```
function addFeaturesChannel(id) {
  const peer = $peers.get(id);

  const featureFunctions = {
    // snip, snip

    audio: function() {
      const username =
        peer.features.username ? peer.features.username : id;
      showUsernameAndMuteStatus(username);
    },

    // snip, snip
  }

// snip, snip

}
```

Now to handle the username case. Back in the handleUsernameForm() function, you should preserve the username on $self.features.username. Then, again within a small loop over the keys of all the currently connected peers, you'll call your shareFeatures() function with both an ID and the feature, 'username', that you need to share:

demos/multipeer/js/main.js
```
function handleUsernameForm(e) {
  e.preventDefault();
  const form = e.target;
  const username = form.querySelector('#username-input').value;
  const figcaption = document.querySelector('#self figcaption');
  figcaption.innerText = username;
➤
➤ $self.features.username = username;
➤
➤ for (let id of $peers.keys()) {
➤   shareFeatures(id, 'username');
➤ }

}
```

Coupled with the little loop inside the handleUsernameForm() callback, shareFeatures() now fires off the username to all connected peers, too.

Note that the logic that you wrote originally in Sharing Features over Data Channels, on page 112, particularly the onopen event for the features channel, ensures that any new peers on the call will receive the username along with any other features information from every single other peer on the call. You've gotta admit—that's pretty awesome.

With all the sending logic fixed up, all that's left is to register a username feature function for when a username shows up in a feature payload. It will also call the mute-status-aware showUsernameAndMuteStatus() function:

demos/multipeer/js/main.js
```
function addFeaturesChannel(id) {

  // snip, snip
  const featureFunctions = {

    // snip, snip

➤   username: function() {
➤     // Update the username
➤     showUsernameAndMuteStatus(peer.features.username);
➤   },

    // snip, snip

  };
}
```

And that's it! You've now built out a tightly constructed feature that shares media-toggle states and the username whenever possible, with all current and future peers who join the call.

Time to test the feature out. Do your multipeer routine and open up a bunch of browser windows, and go to town joining the call. Try muting and unmuting mics and toggling cameras. From there, try coming up with all kinds of different usernames. You can even set a username or toggle off the camera before joining a call, and boom—those features will be shared immediately. Join the call later in yet another browser window. Note how the usernames and toggled cameras have already been set appear almost immediately for each remote peer.

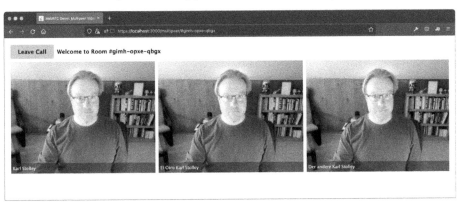

Next Steps

Your journey with WebRTC's core networking techniques and concepts is effectively complete. You're now able to do something quite difficult: support a multipeer call by orchestrating peer connections into a mesh network for streaming media and sharing arbitrary application data. Of course, the more connecting peers a call has (not to mention the more popular your WebRTC app gets), the wider the variety of available cameras and mics and responses to requests for media permissions your app's logic will encounter.

In the next chapter, you'll learn how to detect the availability of user media devices, which can change even over the life of a single call. You'll build logic to address some common device-availability edge cases—from systems that lack cameras or mics, to browsers that are denied user-media permissions— that a robust, fault-tolerant WebRTC app must handle. You'll also learn how to do some optimization of user media to be more efficient about the bandwidth and processing power each user-media stream consumes: you might already have wondered about that as your computer's fans began to roar in the middle of testing your multipeer app.

CHAPTER 7

Managing User Media

When it comes to requesting access to user media—cameras and mics—the code we've written so far has made some optimistic but naive assumptions: not only have we generally expected that users will grant our apps permission to access their media devices, but also that there will even be media devices available for users to grant access to in the first place.

Those assumptions suit us just fine in development. But the challenge in this chapter is to think about a wide range of far less ideal circumstances that any WebRTC app will face in the hands of real users. Much of your work along those lines will focus on the getUserMedia() method, which you haven't really touched since Adding Mic and Camera Toggles, on page 98. And even that was just to make a minor adjustment for requesting microphone access.

In this chapter, we'll look at how getUserMedia() and related MediaDevices methods behave under different conditions, including:

- When media devices aren't available, because there simply is no mic or camera attached—or because an overzealous system administrator has blocked access to them at the operating-system level

- When users deny access to media devices, either intentionally or accidentally, in the browser's media-permissions dialog box that appears after getUserMedia() has been called

Working in such close proximity to the MediaDevices interface on the Media Capture and Streams API,[1] you'll discover subtle differences in error states and messages and media-permissions models in different browsers. Those differences include how and even whether permissions persist for users returning to a WebRTC app that they've used previously.

---

1. https://developer.mozilla.org/en-US/docs/Web/API/Media_Capture_and_Streams_API

With logic in hand that addresses those types of conditions and browser differences, we'll then turn our attention to optimizing the media tracks returning data from user cameras and mics. You'll develop skills with specifying and applying media constraints objects. Those can be applied either to an initial call to getUserMedia(), or later, through the applyConstraints() method on a media track that's already been returned from getUserMedia().

Adjusting Low-Level WebRTC Objects

Beyond media constraints, it's possible to reach down to lower-level APIs like the RTCRtpTransceiver,[a] RTCRtpSender,[b] and RTCRtpReceiver[c] objects to do everything from try to force the use of a particular CODEC to scale video resolutions or bit rates up and down manually.

My advice is to avoid the temptation to do this. Your users' browsers already have highly tuned, well tested algorithms to respond to shifting network conditions and overtaxed CPUs. Any custom logic of your own won't be as good, and might well overlook certain conditions that will make for a degraded user experience with your apps.

---

a. https://developer.mozilla.org/en-US/docs/Web/API/RTCRtpTransceiver
b. https://developer.mozilla.org/en-US/docs/Web/API/RTCRtpSender
c. https://developer.mozilla.org/en-US/docs/Web/API/RTCRtpReceiver

The thing to remember throughout this chapter is that there's only so much you, as a developer, can do about suboptimal media availability or permissions, let alone limited bandwidth and computing power. Whether a user is missing a media device, or either can't or won't let your app access it, the result is the same: there'll be no video or audio (or both) streaming from that user. Your job is to develop an app that performs the best it can, given a wide and sometimes regrettable range of circumstances. But hey—that's the case for all forms of web development, not just WebRTC.

Determining Device Availability

Let's look at different possible device availability scenarios and write error-handling logic that addresses them. As you'll see, certain scenarios—like a missing camera, or users denying permission to access a microphone—throw different errors in Firefox, Chrome, and Safari. The sections below provide tables documenting browser-specific behavior and errors under different conditions.

The good news is the code you've written over all the previous chapters has avoided tying call-joining logic with media-device permissions and availability: those are separate code paths, and should remain that way. In other words, no app should demand that users grant device access as a pre-condition for joining a call. It's entirely possible some users might not even have a camera or mic to grant access to, anyway. So don't ice them out, if those users are still intent on joining.

Detecting Missing Media Devices

We can begin with the most clear-cut case: users without a camera or mic. They might simply not own one, or possibly they left a cable unplugged. They might also have a missing or misconfigured driver at the operating-system level. Whatever the case, it'll present the same problem to the browser—and your WebRTC apps.

If you have a device available to test that has no camera or mic, that's great. Regardless, you can start beefing up your trusty requestUserMedia() function with a try/catch statement around the call to getUserMedia(). As a basic diagnostic step, which will be useful for debugging your own apps, log both the error name and message to the console:

```
async function requestUserMedia(media_constraints) {
  try {
    $self.media = await navigator.mediaDevices
      .getUserMedia(media_constraints);
  } catch(e) {
    console.error(e.name, e.message);
  }

  // snip, snip

}
```

In the absence of an available camera and mic, no browser will display a permissions dialog on a call to getUserMedia(), which the apps you've built call when your app loads. Despite the lack of a dialog box, every browser's console still lights up with errors, as outlined in the following table.

	Error Name (e.name)	Error Message (e.message)
Firefox	NotFoundError	The object cannot be found here.
Chrome	NotFoundError	Requested device not found.
Safari	OverconstrainedError	Invalid constraint.

Table 1—Browser Error Names and Messages for Missing Media Devices

As you can see, Safari is the outlier here. Chrome and Firefox uniformly report a sensible-sounding NotFoundError. And while it's justifiable, as a general rule, to shake your fist at Safari, its OverconstrainedError actually provides an important clue that there might be more going on with these errors—however they're named—that we ought to investigate.

Recall the media constraints we have been passing to getUserMedia() since Adding Mic and Camera Toggles, on page 98: { audio: true, video: true }. That object requests access to both the mic and the camera. But even when a user has, say, a mic but not a camera, a NotFoundError will be thrown by getUserMedia(), and no permissions dialog will be shown! Boolean media constraints require users to have both device types available: browsers are not at liberty to pick and choose which parts of Boolean constraints they can satisfy. It's all or nothing.

So despite Safari's outlier OverconstrainedError here, there's a significant kernel of truth in it (one that we will see in action again under different circumstances later in this chapter): we're trying to constrain the media in ways that don't match against a system lacking a mic or a camera, or both.

Enumerating Available Devices

You can probably already see the problem: it's senseless to call getUserMedia() with constraints that reference a type of media device a user might not even have. But calling getUserMedia() and checking the errors it throws is the only way we've seen so far to detect missing devices. Catch-22 much?

Enter enumerateDevices(), another method on navigator.mediaDevices. With that method, we can figure out what types of devices, if any, are available before calling getUserMedia(). And using the information that enumerateDevices() returns, we can then adjust the media constraints that we pass to getUserMedia().

If we determine that there's no camera attached, for example, we shouldn't even bother passing anything other than video: false for the camera constraint. That means that we'll need to modify the media constraints we ultimately pass to getUserMedia(), based on our best understanding of the state of a given user's setup.

Let's express all of that in code. Start by adding a mediaDevices member to the $self object. You can use that to track available media devices for easy reference across your app's logic. Declare mediaDevices as an object, with audioinput and videoinput both initialized to empty arrays:

demos/user-media/js/main.js
```
const $self = {
  rtcConfig: null,
  mediaConstraints: { audio: true, video: true },
  mediaDevices: { audioinput: [], videoinput: [] },
  mediaStream: new MediaStream(),
  mediaTracks: {},
```

```
  features: {
    audio: false,
    video: true,
  },
};
```

Then, in the "User-Media and Data-Channel Functions" area of your JavaScript file, declare a new asynchronous function, detectAvailableMediaDevices(), that will await the output of navigator.mediaDevices.enumerateDevices(). Its promise resolves to an array of available devices, which might be empty if no devices are available.

Available Details on enumerateDevices()

Different browsers report different levels of detail on enumerateDevices(), especially before your app has secured media permissions. Firefox is the gabbiest browser, spilling a whole bunch of information without the need of permissions. For example, here are the members on a MediaDeviceInfo object for a microphone:

```
{
  deviceId: "6Wk1BAnyduwWD9bRlu7HooMPUiyQOM8lEDQhkbyfGhA=",
  groupId: "7FrL/njX5GZ8eUSFPdITWwpEMozdm8vzz53pOEBtTug=",
  kind: "audioinput",
  label: ""
}
```

After permissions have been granted, Firefox just fills in the label member: { label: "MacBook Pro Microphone"}.

Both Chrome and Safari are much more tight-lipped. That same microphone will be reported like this before media permissions have been granted:

```
{
  deviceId: ""
  groupId: ""
  kind: "audioinput"
  label: ""
}
```

And unlike Firefox, both Chrome and Safari return InputDeviceInfo objects. Firefox's MediaDeviceInfo object shows up in Chrome only for output devices, such as headphones and speakers. Safari does not appear to make use of MediaDeviceInfo objects at all. But since the structure of those objects is the same, you can reach into them without having to mind them.

One final difference worth noting: Chrome includes default input devices as separate but essentially redundant records returned from enumerateDevices. They're marked by a deviceId of "default" and a modified label prefixed with Default -, so something like { label: "Default - MacBook Pro Microphone"}.

We're only interested in devices whose kind value is audioinput or videoinput. Because Chrome also lists audiooutput for things like Bluetooth headphones, you'll need to do a little filtering here. When an audioinput or videoinput is detected, we push that device's MediaDeviceInfo object onto the end of the corresponding array for audio or video devices on $self.mediaDevices:

```
demos/user-media/js/main.js
/**
 *   User-Media and Data-Channel Functions
 */

async function detectAvailableMediaDevices() {
  // Assume there are no devices until we detect them
  $self.mediaDevices.audioinput = [];
  $self.mediaDevices.videoinput = [];

  const devices = await navigator.mediaDevices.enumerateDevices();

  for (let device of devices) {
    // Only interested in audio and video inputs
    const input_kinds = ['audioinput', 'videoinput'];
    if (input_kinds.includes(device.kind)) {
      $self.mediaDevices[device.kind].push(device);
    }
  }
}
```

With that logic written, call detectAvailableMediaDevices() from within the requestUser-Media() function, where we can now use its collection of detected devices to refine the original constraints object set on $self.mediaConstraints:

```
demos/user-media/js/main.js
async function requestUserMedia(media_constraints) {
➤   // Duplicate the media constraints so as to not affect
➤   // the original values on $self
➤   const refined_media_constraints =
➤     JSON.parse(JSON.stringify(media_constraints));
➤
➤   // See what devices are available
➤   await detectAvailableMediaDevices();
➤
➤   // Refine media constraints based on device availability
➤   if ($self.mediaDevices.audioinput.length === 0) {
➤     // There's no audio device, so ensure that constraint is false
➤     refined_media_constraints.audio = false;
➤   }
➤   if ($self.mediaDevices.videoinput.length === 0) {
➤     // There's no video device, so ensure that constraint is false
➤     refined_media_constraints.video = false;
➤   }
```

```
  if (!refined_media_constraints.audio &&
        !refined_media_constraints.video) {
    // If no media is available, we exit, as passing
    // { audio: false, video: false } as a constraint
    // results in a TypeError
    return;
  }

  try {
➤   $self.media = await navigator.mediaDevices
➤     .getUserMedia(refined_media_constraints);
    // Detect the devices again, now that permissions
    // have been granted; this helps capture a value
    // on the "label" field on MediaDeviceInfo for
    // easier inspection
    await detectAvailableMediaDevices();
  } catch(e) {
    console.error(e.name, e.message);
  }

    // snip, snip

}
```

Let's quickly walk through that new logic. It introduces a new refined_media_constraints object, which uses a one-two punch of JSON stringification and parsing to create a copy of the original constraints object. We create a copy so that the original constraints specified on $self.mediaConstraints remain unaltered (we'll see why below, in Detecting Device Changes, on page 182). A set of if conditions then step into action: If there's no camera detected, we'll set the video property to false on refined_media_constraints. Similarly, if there's no mic, we'll set audio to false. And if there's neither a video nor an audio input, we'll make an early exit from the requestUserMedia() function: there's no media to request access to, and there's nothing at the code level that we can do to change that. Passing { audio: false, video: false } to getUserMedia() will only end in a TypeError being thrown.

> ## Why Not Use structuredClone()?
>
> While modern JavaScript implementations have access to structuredClone() to duplicate objects like the media constraints,[a] that method doesn't enjoy broad support in older browsers that nonetheless support WebRTC. The JSON-serialization technique won't work for objects whose members aren't serializable,[b] but fortunately that's not the case for valid media-constraints objects. You are welcome to write detection and fallback logic for when structuredClone() isn't available, but that's beyond the scope of our work here.
>
> ───────────
>
> a. https://developer.mozilla.org/en-US/docs/Web/API/structuredClone
> b. https://developer.mozilla.org/en-US/docs/Web/JavaScript/Reference/Global_Objects/JSON/stringify#description

Finally, note it's useful to call detectAvailableMediaDevices() again after getUserMedia(). Once users grant permission to access media, the output of enumerateDevices will be much more complete, as you read about in Available Details on enumerateDevices(), on page 177. That includes filling out the label member, which will be useful in any user interface you might create around available devices.

Disabling the Mic and Camera Toggle Buttons

At this point, let's take a moment to update the buttons for toggling the mic and camera. There is no sense in presenting users with media toggles once we've detected that a particular kind of device isn't available.

Open up a new function definition for enableOrDisableMediaToggleButtons() near your other media-toggle functions, such as toggleCam():

```
demos/user-media/js/main.js
function enableOrDisableMediaToggleButtons() {
  const audio_button = document.querySelector('#toggle-mic');
  const video_button = document.querySelector('#toggle-cam');

  // Set the disabled attribute's value based on the
  // available media devices
  audio_button.disabled = $self.mediaDevices.audioinput.length === 0;
  video_button.disabled = $self.mediaDevices.videoinput.length === 0;
}
```

Inside that function, we reference the mic and camera toggles in the DOM, and then set the disabled attribute based on the refined constraints.

You can then call the toggle function inside of requestUserMedia(), before the early return that exits the function when there are no devices available:

```
async function requestUserMedia(media_constraints) {

  // snip, snip

  // Disable or re-enable toggle buttons
  enableOrDisableMediaToggleButtons();

  if (!refined_media_constraints.audio && !refined_media_constraints.video)  {
    // If no media is available, we exit, as passing
    // { audio: false, video: false } as a constraint
    // results in a TypeError
    return;
  }

  // snip, snip

}
```

You can then declare a small set of styles in your stylesheet to apply to disabled buttons, using the handy :disabled pseudo-class:

```
demos/user-media/css/screen.css
button[aria-checked="false"] {
  text-decoration: line-through;
  color: white;
  background: red;
}
button:disabled {
  cursor: not-allowed;
  text-decoration: unset;
  color: revert;
  background: revert;
}
```

Those styles show a not-allowed cursor (typically a circle with a diagonal crossbar through it). We unset the text-decoration property, if any, from the aria-checked ="false" selector, in case that has been set. And then we let the browser display its usual disabled background and text colors with the special CSS revert value.[2] You could, of course, define your own styles here—but the browser defaults are fine, too:

Conditionally Adding Tracks

With requestUserMedia() now robustly handling missing media devices prior to passing constraints to getUserMedia(), let's make parallel enhancements to the logic that adds tracks to the peer connection. No track will be returned for any media-constraint value of false, so trying to add those tracks will throw some errors behind the scenes:

---

2. https://developer.mozilla.org/en-US/docs/Web/CSS/revert

```
demos/user-media/js/main.js
async function requestUserMedia(media_constraints) {

  // snip, snip

  // Hold onto audio- and video-track references
  $self.mediaTracks.audio = $self.media.getAudioTracks()[0];
  $self.mediaTracks.video = $self.media.getVideoTracks()[0];

  if ($self.mediaTracks.audio) {
    // Mute the audio if `$self.features.audio` evaluates to `false`
    $self.mediaTracks.audio.enabled = !!$self.features.audio;
    // Add audio track to mediaStream
    $self.mediaStream.addTrack($self.mediaTracks.audio);
  }
  if ($self.mediaTracks.video) {
    // Toggle off the camera if `$self.features.video` evaluates to `false`
    $self.mediaTracks.video.enabled = !!$self.features.video;
    // Add video track to mediaStream
    $self.mediaStream.addTrack($self.mediaTracks.video);
  }

  displayStream($self.mediaStream);
}
```

All you need to do is see whether a track of a particular type has been returned from getUserMedia(). If it has, the usual feature-detection logic and call to addTrack() will run as expected.

Detecting Device Changes

Great. You have built a few solid mechanisms to act on what devices are available when your app loads, and you'll save your application from throwing TypeErrors by ensuring getUserMedia() is never called with a ham-fisted set of constraints when there's no mic or camera available. You're now also only adding tracks to $self.mediaStream when an available device has returned them.

But there are other cases of device ability to think about: external mics and cameras can have their cords unplugged by feral toddlers or vengeful cats, or be plugged back in if they were unplugged previously. Wireless media inputs can have their connections drop and reconnect, too.

Enter the devicechange event, which fires whenever a device is added to or removed from a system.[3] We can tap into devicechange and try to recover from a situation where a camera or mic is added to a system after a WebRTC app loads.

---

3. https://developer.mozilla.org/en-US/docs/Web/API/MediaDevices/devicechange_event

There's a whole lot you can do in response to devicechange events. But to keep things manageable while gaining exposure to some of the event's power and use, we are going to write callbacks to take action on this event only in two cases: when a device is added when no devices were previously available, or when the only device streaming media is removed.

Noting Browser-Specific Quirks with Device Changes

Some browser-specific quirks are worth noting up front with devicechange, however. It works in Firefox and Chrome pretty much as expected, firing when a camera or mic is connected or disconnected. The event will also seem to fire with a bit of a lag, likely owing to the underlying operating system's recognition of the device's availability. So don't expect to see a UI change or console message instantaneously after plugging a device in.

Firefox will not fire the devicechange event while the app's browser window isn't focused. That can be a little maddening if you've got the Firefox dev tools opened up in their own window, and you're waiting for a diagnostic line to log onto the console while plugging in or unplugging devices. The event will fire, though, once focus has returned to the browser window.

The most significant limitation to devicechange shows up in Safari, whose security policy prevents it from firing the event until after users grant media permissions. Users who load your app in Safari with neither a mic nor a camera connected initially will have no opportunity to grant the app media permissions. So regrettably for those users, even if they realize after loading your app they forgot to connect an input device, they'll need to reload your app in Safari for their newly connected devices to be recognized. Safari will fire the event on all changes as expected after media permissions have been granted.

Finally, in a rather useless turn of behavior, Firefox and Chrome will fire device-change events even if device permissions are blocked at the operating system or browser level. The reason that that behavior is useless is that once a user has denied access to your app, you can't ask for it again. We will look at denied media permissions in Programmatically Recognizing Denied Media Permissions, on page 190.

Registering and Debouncing a devicechange Callback

Let's get down to registering a callback function for devicechange. But we need to handle this with care. Given the lag noted above, it might seem surprising that we need to debounce calls to the devicechange callback. (You might recall that debouncing a function means holding off on executing it until after a certain period has passed after the last triggering event.)

The trick with devicechange is it will fire based on type of input. So, for example, a combination external mic and camera will actually cause devicechange to fire twice (once for audio, once for video), even if it's a single piece of hardware being plugged in.

I prefer a serviceable debounce function like this, which you can add to the other utility functions at the bottom of your JavaScript file:

demos/user-media/js/main.js
```
function debounce(callback_function, wait_in_milliseconds) {
  let timeout;
  return (...args) => {
    const context = this;
    clearTimeout(timeout);
    timeout = setTimeout(
      () => callback_function.apply(context, args),
      wait_in_milliseconds);
  };
}
```

With that in hand, you can register on the devicechange event a handleMediaDeviceChange() callback, which we'll write in a moment:

demos/user-media/js/main.js
```
/**
 *  User-Media Setup and Events
 */

requestUserMedia($self.mediaConstraints);

// These events can fire in rapid succession when,
// for example, a camera with built-in mic is connected.
// That's why it's necessary to debounce to 500ms before
// executing the callback. Otherwise, the callback might
// prompt users to access the camera, and then again to
// access the camera and the mic both.
navigator.mediaDevices.ondevicechange = debounce(handleMediaDeviceChange, 500);
```

I've opted for a healthy, 500-millisecond period for debouncing the callback. That might seem a little too generous, but on slower systems that might take a moment to register both a camera and mic from a single device, this will save users from being double-prompted by calling requestUserMedia() too soon. That'll become clearer once you've written your handleMediaDeviceChange() callback. Let's do that next.

Building a devicechange Callback

When it's complete, your handleMediaDeviceChange() callback will respond to two situations: when a device has been added with none previously available, and when a device has been removed with no other devices now available.

Let's start with the first case:

```
demos/user-media/js/main.js
async function handleMediaDeviceChange() {
  const previous_devices =
    $self.mediaDevices.audioinput.length > 0
      || $self.mediaDevices.videoinput.length > 0;

  // First things first: on any device change,
  // update the list of available media devices
  await detectAvailableMediaDevices();

  const available_devices =
    $self.mediaDevices.audioinput.length > 0
      || $self.mediaDevices.videoinput.length > 0;

  // Case One: A device has been plugged in and
  // no other devices were previously available
  if (!previous_devices && available_devices) {
    // Request user media as though the app had just been opened,
    // but await it so that we can ensure there's media available
    // before adding it to the connection
    await requestUserMedia($self.mediaConstraints);

    for (let id of $peers.keys()) {
      addStreamingMedia(id);
      shareFeatures(id, 'audio', 'video');
    }
  }

}
```

Here, you're reaching into your $self.mediaDevices object to look for the list of last-known available devices. As soon as you've captured that as a Boolean, on previous_devices, it's important to again call detectAvailableMediaDevices(). After all, devicechange fires whenever there's been some change in connected devices.

You can then set up a parallel Boolean on available_devices, for use in comparing the current state with the last known state. If no devices were previously available but there are devices now, you can make a call to requestUserMedia(). Remember that if your app loaded without any available devices, your improvements to requestUserMedia() would have exited the function before reaching the point of calling getUserMedia(), just as you set things up back in Enumerating Available Devices, on page 176.

However, it's that call to requestUserMedia() that's behind the need to debounce the callback the way you did in the previous section. If a single device registers first a mic, and then a camera and mic, users would be presented with and have to respond to two separate media-permissions modals. By debouncing, you increase the likelihood that a single device will produce a single request for media permissions, and save your users some annoyance in the process.

With this code in place, if you load your app without a camera attached, you can join the call without any streaming media. But very shortly after plugging a device in, you'll see your stream on the self side of the call, and then on any remote peers you've got connected, too. Sweet.

Responding to Removed Devices on the Callback

When going from no devices to available devices, things were pretty clear cut: you had to tap into some of the existing logic that you've already been using elsewhere in your app.

But responding to a system that goes from having a camera and mic to no camera and mic is going to be a little trickier—at least if you want to have some polish to your app. If you try unplugging a camera now, you will see the last frame the device captured at the moment of disconnection on both the self and remote sides of the call, for as long as the call continues to last. Suboptimal.

Ideally, in the event a device goes missing, there are two things we ought to do. First, we should null out the stream being displayed on the self side of the call. That will help suggest to users that their camera connection was lost, rather than the camera being frozen. And then we should do the same for any remote peers as well.

The remote case will be a bit trickier. While there is a handsome built-in track event on RTCPeerConnection, which you first worked with way back in Receiving Media Tracks, on page 59, that only fires when tracks are added to the peer connection. When tracks are removed, we need to write custom logic of our own to communicate that change to the remote peer.

Go ahead and open your handleMediaDeviceChange() function again, and let's start by defining the logic that will be needed there. To start with, you'll reference a removeStreamingMedia() function that you can define in just a bit:

```
demos/user-media/js/main.js
async function handleMediaDeviceChange() {
  // snip, snip

  // Case Two: The current device has been unplugged
```

```
    // and there are now no devices available
    if (!available_devices) {
      // Reset all the media properties
      $self.media = false;
      $self.mediaTracks = {};
      $self.mediaStream = new MediaStream();
      // Toggle off the media buttons, and null out
      // the self-side stream
      enableOrDisableMediaToggleButtons();
      displayStream(null);
      // Remove tracks from peer connections
      for (let id of $peers.keys()) {
        removeStreamingMedia(id);
      }
    }
  }
```

We're interested only in there being no devices available. Under that circumstance, it's useful to reset all the media properties and, perhaps optimistically, create a new MediaStream instance for later use. (Note that that is ordinarily instantiated when $self is initialized at the top of your JavaScript file.)

With no devices available, it's also sensible to disable the media-toggle buttons, and null out the video stream for the self side of the call.

Finally, it's necessary to loop through all the connected peers, and remove the streaming media from the now-defunct device from each of those connections. Let's look at writing that removeStreamingMedia() function alongside your trusty addStreamingMedia() function in your JavaScript file.

Removing User Media for Remote Peers

Removing streaming media from a peer connection takes a little finesse and creativity. Let's look at and then walk through the complete removeStreamingMedia() function—which we will follow up with a slight adjustment to how the shareFeatures() function works:

```
demos/user-media/js/main.js
function removeStreamingMedia(id) {
  const peer = $peers.get(id);
  // Detect the senders on the connection; we need
  // them to remove tracks from the peer connection
  const senders = peer.connection.getSenders();
  const senders_list = Object.keys(senders);
  // Loop through the senders, and pull the tracks
  // off them, one by one
  for (let sender of senders_list) {
    const track = senders[sender].track;
    if (track) {
```

```
        // Remove the track on its associated sender
        peer.connection.removeTrack(senders[sender]);
    }
  }
  // Send a 'removeAllTracks' feature to clean things up
  // on the receiving peer's side.
  shareFeatures(id, 'removeAllTracks');
}
```

We start, as always, by grabbing a reference to a specific peer by ID. Then it's necessary to determine all of the senders on the connection for that peer, care of the getSenders() method.[4] That method returns an array of senders, one for each type of track on the connection. So, for example, a connection carrying both audio and video will have two senders: one for audio, and one for video.

We need the sender's information because that's an essential argument for the removeTrack() method.[5] That clears tracks from the connections, leaving things a little cleaner.

But again, there's no event fired natively by WebRTC to alert remote peers of a removed track. We have to do that ourselves. At the bottom of the removeStreamingMedia() function, you can call up your trusty shareFeatures() function to build your own system for alerting remote peers that the tracks have been removed from the connection.

Improving the Feature-Sharing Function

When you wrote the shareFeatures() function back in Sharing Features as Needed, on page 114, the assumption was that a feature name would accompany data on a member on the $self.features object. However, for something like 'removeAllTracks', there's no real need to store that as data. We need to issue the feature as something like a custom event or command to all connected peers.

So let's make a quick adjustment to shareFeatures() that will send any $self.features data that it has, but also a simple 'true' string value for anything else, including 'removeAllTracks':

demos/user-media/js/main.js
```
function shareFeatures(id, ...features) {
  const peer = $peers.get(id);

  const featuresToShare = {};

  if (!peer.featuresChannel) return;
```

---

4. https://developer.mozilla.org/en-US/docs/Web/API/RTCPeerConnection/getSenders
5. https://developer.mozilla.org/en-US/docs/Web/API/RTCPeerConnection/removeTrack

```
  for (let f of features) {
➤    featuresToShare[f] =
➤      $self.features[f] ? $self.features[f] : 'true';
  }

  try {
    peer.featuresChannel.send(JSON.stringify(featuresToShare));
  } catch(e) {
    console.error('Error sending features:', e);
  }
}
```

That enhancement makes shareFeatures() a little more flexible. You can now open up your addFeaturesChannel() function, and add a new callback function to featureFunctions that works with removeAllTracks:

demos/user-media/js/main.js
```
function addFeaturesChannel(id) {
  const peer = $peers.get(id);

  const featureFunctions = {
    audio: function() {
      const username = peer.features.username ? peer.features.username : id;
      showUsernameAndMuteStatus(username);
    },
➤   removeAllTracks: function() {
➤     const tracks_list = Object.keys(peer.mediaTracks);
➤     for (let track of tracks_list) {
➤       peer.mediaStream.removeTrack(peer.mediaTracks[track]);
➤     }
➤     // Empty out the media tracks object
➤     peer.mediaTracks = {};
➤     // Create a brand-new media stream in case tracks
➤     // need to be added later
➤     peer.mediaStream = new MediaStream();
➤     // But null out the display of the media stream
➤     // for the time being
➤     displayStream(null, id);
➤   },

    // snip, snip

  };

  // snip, snip

}
```

The removeAllTracks callback loops through the track and stream records for the peer that has announced they've stopped sending media, much like that peer did on their own side of the call. Calling displayStream() then nulls out the video for the remote peer.

Excellent. You've now got an app that responds to some baseline media-device availability. As devices are added and removed, your app and the peer connections it's maintaining respond accordingly. However, we're still assuming that users will grant media permissions when asked.

Let's turn now to a code-free survey of the errors that are thrown when users deny those permissions.

Programmatically Recognizing Denied Media Permissions

Hard truth: when users, for whatever reason, deny your WebRTC app permission to access their mic or camera, there's little you can do in response. Some users may accidentally hit the Block button in the permissions dialog, or dismiss it without having explicitly granted or denied permission. Browsers generally do not make it easy to unblock requested media permissions, and will often save that as a preference tied to your app's domain.

Avoid the Permissions API

You may find yourself tempted to employ the Permissions API[a] to do a quick check for whether users have granted your app access previously to their media devices.

However, the camera permissions value on the name property is not implemented in Firefox, owing to some significant disagreements over privacy and the Permissions API generally. Unlike Chrome, Firefox does not implicitly grant permission to media devices on subsequent uses of a WebRTC app.[b]

At the code level, using the Permissions API will make it very tricky to know whether you're dealing with a user who has previously denied permissions, never visited before, or is simply using Firefox. The end result can end up being a double-nag: your code might toss up a modal that says, "You need to allow media permissions" at the same exact time as the permissions modal itself is showing. Great, two things now to respond to, instead of one.

For that reason, the only fail-safe way to know if someone has granted your app media permissions is to watch what happens as a result of calling getUserMedia(). In browsers like Firefox or Safari, that will mean a dialog box shown on every visit, whereas Chrome—for good or ill—will apply the same permissions response as a user made previously.

---

a. https://developer.mozilla.org/en-US/docs/Web/API/Permissions_API
b. https://bugzilla.mozilla.org/show_bug.cgi?id=1449783#c1

The purpose of this section, then, is to help you identify different error conditions your app might encounter. Whether and how you handle them is, of course, up to you. But note that denied permissions are generally a dead end: you cannot successfully call getUserMedia() again, and other APIs on the navigator.mediaDevices will become locked down or otherwise unavailable.

Yes, you could nag the user or try to walk them through how to change their minds and grant permission, but that's still going to require your app being reloaded once they make the switch. Additionally, if you do offer tips like that, they can become a maintenance headache if browsers move things around or otherwise change how previously denied permissions can be removed or reset.

Detecting Media Devices Blocked at the Operating-System Level

OS-level device restrictions are typically the result of actions by an overzealous sysadmin, or perhaps a paranoid user. Either way, specific, intentional actions have to be taken to configure the operating system to lock things down.

What is tricky about OS-blocked devices is that browsers may still offer up a media-permissions dialog box, even when the operating system itself will deny access, regardless of whether a user clicks Allow or Deny. (Ever the outlier, Safari has such no errors because macOS has no setting to deny device access to Safari.)

As you can see in the following table, different errors may be thrown from a doomed dialog box, depending on whether or not a user hits Allow or Block. If you compare this table with Table 3, Browser Error Names and Messages for User-Denied Permissions, on page 192, you'll see that the Block errors are identical.

	Error Name (e.name)	Error Message (e.message)
Firefox (Allow)	NotFoundError	The object cannot be found here.
Firefox (Block)	NotAllowedError	The request is not allowed by the user agent or the platform in the current context.
Chrome (Allow)	NotAllowedError	Permission denied by system.
Chrome (Deny)	NotAllowedError	Permission denied.
Safari	—	—

Table 2—Browser Error Names and Messages for OS-Level Device Blocking

Detecting Media Devices Blocked in the Browser

In contrast to the fairly intentional work required to deny media-device access at the OS level, the Block button is right there for users to hit—intentionally or accidentally—when your app requests device access. In what might be cold comfort to developers, the NotAllowedError is thrown from all browsers, even if the error messages differ somewhat.

Note that Chrome is the only browser that currently distinguishes between blocking a request for access and dismissing the modal entirely. But also note that dismissing the permissions modal (accomplished easily by hitting the Escape key) is functionally the same as hitting Block. Only by clicking Allow is device access allowed; anything else results in denied permissions.

	Error Name (e.name)	Error Message (e.message)
Firefox (Block)	NotAllowedError	The request is not allowed by the user agent or the platform in the current context.
Firefox (Dismiss)	NotAllowedError	The request is not allowed by the user agent or the platform in the current context.
Chrome (Block)	NotAllowedError	Permission denied.
Chrome (Dismiss)	NotAllowedError	Permission dismissed.
Safari (Block)	NotAllowedError	The request is not allowed by the user agent or the platform in the current context, possibly because the user denied permission.
Safari (Dismiss)	NotAllowedError	The request is not allowed by the user agent or the platform in the current context, possibly because the user denied permission.

Table 3—Browser Error Names and Messages for User-Denied Permissions

Armed with all of these different error names and messages, you can absolutely go to town in the try/catch statement inside your requestUserMedia() function. But note that your work there is essentially going to be limited to informing—and perhaps annoying—your users about the obvious: your app can't access their devices, so it will be impossible for them to be seen or heard by others on the call they're about to join.

But to address the needs of users who do grant access, let's turn our attention now to the media constraints object, and look at how we can refine permissions requests beyond the Boolean values of { audio: true, video: true }.

Setting and Applying Media Constraints Objects

When passing { audio: true, video: true } to getUserMedia(), you effectively defer to a given browser's default settings for audio and video. And it's quite possible that those sensible defaults are fine for your app.

But, if you know that you need, for example, videos that run at a smaller or larger size, or have reasons to adjust things like the frame rate of a video or the sample rate for audio, the MediaTrackConstraints dictionary is your friend.[6] Kind of.

If you look at the compatibility table for the different entries in the constraints dictionary,[7] you will discover that only a handful of properties—height, width, and frameRate for video, or echoCancellation for audio—are well supported across all browsers.

And while you can use MediaDevices.getSupportedConstraints() to determine whether a browser running your app supports a given constraint,[8] its reports are little more than trivia: presented with an unfamiliar constraint, browsers will ignore it. Note that that is very different behavior from what we saw at the start of this chapter, where a true value for video was a dealbreaker in the absence of a camera. That is only the case for Boolean values, not entries in the constraints dictionary.

So, for example, if you know your app's UI will never make use of videos larger than 320 by 240 pixels, you can specify so on $self.mediaConstraints (alternatively, you can apply constraints at some point in the future by calling applyConstraints() on a track that has been returned from getUserMedia()):[9]

```
const $self = {
  rtcConfig: null,
  mediaConstraints: {
    audio: true,
    video: {
      height: 240,
      width: 320
    }
  },
  mediaDevices: { audioinput: [], videoinput: [] },
  mediaStream: new MediaStream(),
  mediaTracks: {},
```

6. https://developer.mozilla.org/en-US/docs/Web/API/MediaTrackConstraints
7. https://developer.mozilla.org/en-US/docs/Web/API/MediaTrackConstraints#browser_compatibility
8. https://developer.mozilla.org/en-US/docs/Web/API/MediaDevices/getSupportedConstraints
9. https://developer.mozilla.org/en-US/docs/Web/API/MediaStreamTrack/applyConstraints

```
  features: {
    audio: false,
    video: true
  }
};
```

Note very well that those constraints do not at all guarantee that the video that comes back will be precisely 320 by 240 pixels. It means only that the browser applying that constraint will deliver on the closest value it can without going under what you've specified in relaxed constraints like these. We'll look in a moment at much more precise constraints, which are never a good idea, in Avoiding Overconstrained Media, on page 194.

Differing Constraints Between Browsers

If you spend some time playing around with a tool like Mozilla's Constraints Exerciser,[10] you can get a sense of what's possible for the given hardware, operating system, and browser you're running.

One thing you'll discover is even when the hardware and OS are the same, browsers honor constraints differently. For example, passing { video: { height: 200, width: 200 } } as a media constraint in Firefox will probably return a 4:3 aspect-ratio video of about 320 pixels wide. Chrome, by contrast, may scale and crop to return a true 200-by-200 image from the camera.

And that's an important thing to note: in some browsers, like Firefox, constraints are gravitational—meaning that the browser will come as close as possible to the value you pass in. So something like { video: { height: 1, width: 1 } } will prompt Firefox to return the smallest video it can, based on the hardware, camera drivers, and OS running.

But Chrome may very well return a 1-by-1 video, meaning that the constraint you're applying won't work out in the cross-browser fashion you might hope. So the best advice is to be honest and tolerant with your constraints, and trust browsers—and your own good code and UI—to do the right thing with whatever media a browser can deliver.

Avoiding Overconstrained Media

One parting word about media constraints: any constraint that includes min, max, or exact runs the risk of overconstraining the media you're trying to access with getUserMedia(). For example, { video: { width: { min: 1024, max: 1280 } } } will cause

---

10. https://developer.mozilla.org/en-US/docs/Web/API/Media_Capture_and_Streams_API/Constraints#example_con-straint_exerciser

an error for any camera that isn't capable of delivering at least 1024-pixel-wide frames of video.

And remember: just because a persnickety constraint works fine for you and your setup does not at all mean it will work for others. Overconstrained errors as listed in Table 4, Browser Error Names and Messages for Overconstrained Media, on page 195, are not easily recovered from without a lot of forking logic. So as you figure out the more specific needs of your app, make sure you use simple scalars like width: 800. Do the web thing, and let browsers adjust as they are able.

	Error Name (e.name)	Error Message (e.message)
Firefox	OverconstrainedError	Constraints could be not satisfied.
Chrome	OverconstrainedError	[empty string]
Safari	OverconstrainedError	Invalid constraint.

Table 4—Browser Error Names and Messages for Overconstrained Media

Next Steps

You've now got a firm grip on getUserMedia() and the types of media constraints that will give your app a better shot at suiting users' needs. You've learned how to detect and act on the availability of user media both once your app has loaded, and as conditions change for users over the life of a call. You've seen the limited options available for handling denied user permissions, but you are also now equipped with the knowledge needed for tuning your own apps to respond to those situations in a cross-browser fashion.

In short, your app is ready to make its debut on the open web. In the next chapter, you'll conclude your WebRTC journey by deploying your app for real-world use.

## CHAPTER 8

Deploying WebRTC Apps to Production

Deploying a WebRTC application requires two infrastructural components:

1. As with any web application, you need server space behind a domain you control. That's where you'll host the application's static files: HTML, CSS, and JavaScript. The server must also run whatever server-side scripts are powering your signaling channel.

2. You will also need a STUN server optionally paired with a TURN server for relaying peer media streams and data when a direct, peer-to-peer connection is not possible. You can configure your app to use a public STUN server, or you can run your own. You'll learn how to do both in this chapter. You'll also learn what the heck STUN and TURN even mean.

You can, of course, avoid much of the server setup outlined in this chapter and deploy your app to a cloud service capable of running your server-side scripts. The deployable app in this chapter, for example, uses Node.js. But because WebRTC needs only limited server-side capability to serve your app and power your signaling channel, you'll likely find you can do much of the setup yourself. So we'll keep things minimal and homespun in this chapter.

To make the advice here applicable to as many server setups as possible, this chapter assumes only that you're running your own server, on some flavor of Linux where you have root or sudo privileges. The server-side commands and configuration examples here use a stock LTS Debian Linux, but there's enough detail to help you locate documentation specific to whatever flavor of Linux you're running: Ubuntu, Arch, and so on. We'll take a very brief run through a checklist covering a few essential bits of preliminary server setup in Preparing a World-Ready Server: A Checklist, on page 203.

Prior to deployment, you'll need to make a few adjustments to your WebRTC app. You'll then need to somehow get the app's files onto your server. Although you can use plain old FTP or SFTP, you'll set up Git on your server and configure a post-receive Git hook that runs all the necessary tasks your app requires each time you deploy. And you'll deploy by running the git push command on your development machine.

You'll learn how to set up the Nginx web server (pronounced "engine ex") to serve your apps files, with an HTTPS assist from Let's Encrypt. Nginx shines at reverse proxying, which you'll configure to pass incoming requests—both for files and signaling—to the server-side scripts that power your WebRTC app. Tying all the server-side setup together, you'll install and set up pm2 so that you can start, monitor, and even automatically restart your WebRTC app on the server with each fresh deployment.

You'll finish off your deployment work by installing and configuring Coturn to power your own personal STUN/TURN server.[1] You'll then update your app to use your Coturn installation, deploy with another git push to your server, and ensure that everything is working correctly.

So let's get to it! We'll take all of this in manageable steps, and test things out as we go. To kick things off, you'll ready your WebRTC app for production. You're welcome to use any of the apps you've built so far, or follow along with the demo app in the /deploy/ directory in the book's companion source code.

Configuring a WebRTC App for Public Deployment

Ever since Setting Up the Peer Connection, on page 42, you've worked around a sad null value on $self's rtcConfig value. That's worked fine for developing and testing out WebRTC apps within the friendly confines of your local network. But any publicly deployed WebRTC app needs to connect to a STUN server, which enables a WebRTC app's users to discover routes to their locations on the internet (see Set Servers to STUN, on page 199). Users then share that information with each remote peer over the signaling channel in the form of additional ICE candidates.

Let's get things started by returning to the $self object and transform rtcConfig into an object literal with a single property, iceServers. That property will take an array of objects, each with information for connecting to a STUN/TURN server. You'll begin here by configuring your app's instances of RTCPeerConnection

---

1. https://github.com/coturn/coturn

Set Servers to STUN

It's time to expand a few acronyms: STUN stands for Session Traversal Utilities for NAT—with NAT being yet another acronym (YAA, of course) for Network Address Translation. NAT is a fundamental networking building-block for routing packets over complex network topographies. Simplifying a bit, NAT enables all devices on a private network to share a public IP address, while assigning each device its own private address behind the network's NAT gateway. A STUN server makes it possible to discover routes for network traffic to make its way over the public network and into the private network, care of NAT, right down to a specific device—a phone, a laptop, or whatever. That's essential for WebRTC's peer-to-peer architecture, where data must not only move to and from your public IP, but also your private IP.

When a direct peer-to-peer connection isn't possible, your app will need access to a TURN server. TURN expands to Traversal Using Relay around NAT: TURN passes media streams and data-channel traffic from one peer to another over a third-party server. TURN is often necessary to reach users on networks behind highly restrictive firewalls.

In quick summary: STUN discovers and describes possible network routes to a device, and TURN provides a server relay between two devices whenever STUN comes up short and cannot deliver on a usable peer-to-peer route.

to use a publicly available STUN server (in Setting Up Your Own STUN/TURN Server, on page 214, you'll configure your app to use your private STUN server):

```
$self = {
  rtcConfig: {
    iceServers: [
      // array of STUN/TURN servers
    ]
  },
  mediaConstraints: { audio: true, video: true },

  // snip, snip

}
```

A STUN server functions something like a GPS satellite. Just like your phone or other GPS-capable device uses satellites to determine your position on the planet, your web browser sends a request to a STUN server to determine your network's and device's location on the internet. STUN even includes routing information to your location: how—and even if—your device can be reached from beyond your network's firewall. The STUN server returns some basic information—like an IP address and port—that assists the browser in gathering ICE candidates for sharing with a remote peer as part of RTC connection negotiation, which you first encountered in Building Connection Logic to the "Perfect Negotiation" Pattern, on page 51.

Referencing STUN Servers on the RTC Configuration Object

To start, try configuring your WebRTC app to use one of a handful of established public STUN servers. A quick web search will turn up lists of such servers, all of varying quality (the servers and the lists). Google's public STUN servers are among the more stable ones available: stun:stun.l.google.com:19302, with redundant servers at stun1.l.google.com, stun2.l.google.com, stun3.l.google.com—all prefixed with stun: and suffixed with :19302, for port 19302.

Here is how you can configure $self to use Google's public STUN servers:

```
deploy/www/js/main.js
const $self = {
  rtcConfig: {
    iceServers: [
      { urls: 'stun:stun.l.google.com:19302' },
      { urls: 'stun:stun1.l.google.com:19302' },
    ],
  },
  mediaConstraints: { audio: true, video: true },
  mediaDevices: { audioinput: [], videoinput: [] },
  mediaStream: new MediaStream(),
  mediaTracks: {},
  features: {
    audio: false,
    video: true,
  },
};
```

The urls property accepts either a string, as in the example above, or an array of strings, each referencing a URL. An array of URLs is more convenient when you have multiple URLs that share the same credentials, such as for a TURN server that can be reached from more than one URL (see Configuring and Enabling Coturn's TURN Server, on page 217).

Note that the example above includes only the first two STUN addresses that Google hosts (see Deciding How Many STUN Servers to List, on page 201). As with any public server, there's no guarantee these will be available when your app's users need to use them. That's why it's advantageous to set up and run your own STUN server, which you'll learn how to do in Setting Up Your Own STUN/TURN Server, on page 214. But to deploy and test out your app for the first time, a public STUN server will do fine. Probably.

Your WebRTC app will now use responses from those STUN servers to help the browser gather ICE candidates, even in a local development environment. To prove that point, and to help ensure your app will work in production, you can log to the console the type of each ICE candidate your handleRtcIceCandidate()

Deciding How Many STUN Servers to List

Don't be tempted to put forward a huge stack of STUN servers in your configuration object. They're not like nameservers for DNS lookups, where redundancy can help ensure a successful lookup: a web browser will reach out to each STUN server that you've listed in your iceServers array. The more servers you list, the longer it will take for your browser to finish gathering ICE candidates. That can slow down the establishment of your WebRTC connections.

However, some public STUN servers are reachable on both port 80 and 443. It's useful in that case to include both ports in your iceServers array, because extremely restrictive firewalls might only allow traffic over 443, normally used for HTTPS.

callback encounters—including the STUN server's server-reflexive ICE candidates, which will have a type of srflx. Candidates gathered by your browser will have a type of host:

deploy/www/js/main.js
```
function handleRtcIceCandidate(id) {
  return function({ candidate }) {
    if (candidate) {
      console.log(`Handling ICE candidate, type '${ candidate.type }'...`);
    }
    sc.emit('signal', { recipient: id, sender: $self.id,
      signal: { candidate } });
  };
}
```

If you filter your console output for candidate, you should see something like this:

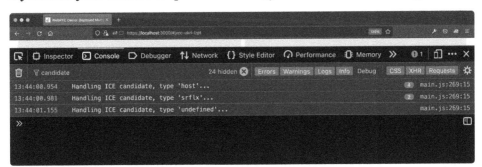

That output indicates four host candidates, generated by the browser independently, plus two srflx candidates, care of Google's STUN servers. The undefined candidate represents the empty candidate that indicates no more ICE candidates are available, which you read about way back in Handling Incoming ICE Candidates, on page 57.

If you're also seeing one or more candidates of type srflx in your console, that's confirmation enough that your app is correctly using the public STUN server you specified. If you run into trouble, try examining the output of the STUN servers you've listed in your config with the web-based TrickleICE tool.[2]

Having configured rtcConfig to contact a public STUN server, you've done your best to make sure your app is ready to venture out, seek its fortunes, and make its way in the world. Your task now is to take some time and trick out a server to host it.

Configuring a Server to Host Your WebRTC App

As promised in this book's opening chapters, you've not had to do any server-side work to speak of. Whenever you've run npm start or npm start:demos, however, you've been using a small bundle of server-side scripts in development. They are minimal, but let's talk about them briefly, so there's a little less mystery surrounding this chapter's sudden talk of server-side scripting.

Understanding Your App's Server Requirements

There are a few files to check out in the deploy/ directory. The first is the package.json file, which includes four dependencies:

```
"dependencies": {
  "express": "^4.18.2",
  "http-errors": "~1.6",
  "morgan": "~1.9",
  "socket.io": "^4.6.1"
}
```

Just like you've run npm install to install those dependencies for working with the code in this book, you'll need to do the same on your server.

The other two files to note are server.js and a companion script, scripts/start-server, which actually fires up the contents of server.js and starts your app listening on port 3000. You'll see several require statements at the top of server.js, four of which reflect the dependencies listed in package.json. Two others require the native Node.js path and crypto libraries, the latter of which you will read about in Generating Time-Limited Credentials with your Signaling Server, on page 219.

What you'll need to do on the server is very similar to what you've already done on your development machine back in Chapter 1, Preparing a WebRTC Development Environment, on page 1. But in addition, you'll need to get a

---

2.   https://webrtc.github.io/samples/src/content/peerconnection/trickle-ice/

fully-featured web server configured and running, and make sure that it serves HTTPS using certificates that don't send browsers into a panic. Let's tackle that setup next.

Preparing a World-Ready Server: A Checklist

There's not enough space to walk through an entire server setup. So consider this sidebar something like DevOps lite: it points out the essential steps and technologies, but you'll need to hunt down the particulars in the documentation for your specific flavor of Linux.

1. Configure a firewall and fail2ban: If you're like me, you want to mitigate as many security risks to your server as possible. As soon as I spin up a new server, I prefer to lock all its ports down except for 22, for SSH, with something like Uncomplicated Firewall, ufw.[a] You might also want to set up something like fail2ban,[b] which will automatically build a restricted list of IP addresses belonging to malicious users and bots that are standing by 24/7 to hammer away at your server, looking for a weakness to exploit.

2. Button down SSH: To keep access to your server more secure, it's a good idea to set yourself up with a pair of SSH keys. One key is public, which you can share with the whole world—including your server—and one is private, which you keep on your development machine and must guard with your life. Or at least a strong password. The idea is that the password unlocks your key—granting you access to your server. Read up on how to configure SSHD to allow only key-based authentication to your server, too.[c]

3. Install Nginx: You can install Nginx from your Linux's package manager's default sources, or you can get a little fancier and configure your package manager to read from the package sources that Nginx provides.[d] While you can opt instead to use Apache or another web server, Nginx quickly sets up a reverse proxy, including for WebSocket traffic. We'll look at setting up a reverse proxy in detail, later in Configuring Nginx for Reverse Proxies, on page 212.

4. Install Node.js: Your Linux's package manager probably has an older but serviceable version of Node.js that you can install, but there are other options for installing more up-to-date versions of Node.js on most Linux distributions.[e]

---

a.   https://wiki.debian.org/Uncomplicated%20Firewall%20%28ufw%29
b.   https://www.fail2ban.org/
c.   https://www.ssh.com/academy/ssh/sshd_config
d.   https://nginx.org/en/linux_packages.html
e.   https://nodejs.org/en/download/package-manager/

Configuring Nginx for Your App's Domain

Let's assume you've addressed all of the matters in Preparing a World-Ready Server: A Checklist, on page 203. That list includes having a base Nginx installation. We're going to customize Nginx with a per-domain configuration file and ensure that it works by serving a placeholder HTML file. Having tested that out, we'll use Let's Encrypt to generate the keys and certificates necessary to serve your app over HTTPS. Finally, we'll configure Nginx to work as a reverse proxy—taking HTTPS requests on port 443 and proxying them to the Express and Socket scripts that power your deployed app on the server.

On most stock installations, Nginx automatically loads any additional configuration files it finds in the /etc/nginx/conf.d/ directory. Confirm that you have a line like this in the default nginx.conf:

```
include /etc/nginx/conf.d/*.conf;
```

If that line's missing, you can add it to nginx.conf yourself, inside the http{} block—and of course create a conf.d directory adjacent your nginx.conf file.

To keep your per-domain configuration files easily identifiable at a glance, always name them after your domain. Here I'm creating a configuration file for a subdomain I control, prag.webrtc.gallery:

```
$ cd /etc/nginx/conf.d
$ sudo touch prag.webrtc.gallery.conf
```

Open that new configuration file on your server with a command-line editor that you're comfortable with, such as pico or vim, and edit it to look something like this (be sure to replace the references to prag.webrtc.gallery with your own domain or subdomain):

```
server {
  server_name prag.webrtc.gallery;

  listen [::]:80;
  listen 80;

  root /var/www/prag.webrtc.gallery/html;
  index index.html index.htm;

  location / {
    try_files $uri $uri/ =404;
  }
}
```

I prefer the old-school comfort of /var/www/ as the shared root path to any content that's web available, but choose a location that works for you. Within your chosen shared root path, be sure to create the path to the /<domain>/html/

directory you specified in your per-domain Nginx config file. Once you've created the entire path, run chown -R to give your server login ownership of it. Here, I'm referencing the common shell variable $USER, which should hold the value of your logged-in username on the server:

```
$ sudo mkdir -p /var/www/prag.webrtc.gallery/html
$ sudo chown -R "$USER" /var/www/prag.webrtc.gallery
```

Finally, drop in a temporary index.html file. Its contents will help you to verify that you're serving from the correct location:

```
$ touch /var/www/prag.webrtc.gallery/html/index.html
$ echo "Hello from Nginx" >> /var/www/prag.webrtc.gallery/html/index.html
```

With that all in place, you'll need to restart Nginx so that it reads and loads your domain's configuration from within /etc/nginx/conf.d/. The command to restart Nginx will depend on your operating system, but this is the command on Debian:

```
$ sudo systemctl restart nginx
```

Assuming you see no error messages upon restarting (check your log files if you do), point your browser to your newly configured domain. Again, in my case, that's going to be http://prag.webrtc.gallery. You should see your sad little "Hello from Nginx" message in the browser window. It'll be identical to whatever you echoed out to the placeholder index.html file.

Setting Up Let's Encrypt Certs

With Nginx properly configured to handle requests on your domain, you can now set up certificates to serve your app over HTTPS. Let's Encrypt provides a tool called Certbot that will do this for you. Certbot provides an interface with tailored instructions for your web server and Linux distribution.[3] They change somewhat frequently, so I won't attempt to replicate them here.

Once Certbot's scripts have run and done their thing, your per-domain Nginx configuration file will look something like this. The changes that Certbot makes are highlighted below:

```
server {
  server_name prag.webrtc.gallery;

  root /var/www/prag.webrtc.gallery/html;
  index index.html index.htm;
  error_page 404 /404.html;
```

---

3.   https://certbot.eff.org/instructions

```
    location / {
      try_files $uri $uri/ =404;
    }

    error_log  /var/log/nginx/prag.webrtc.gallery.error.log notice;
    access_log  /var/log/nginx/prag.webrtc.gallery.access.log  main;
➤   listen [::]:443 ssl ipv6only=on;
➤      # managed by Certbot
➤   listen 443 ssl;
➤      # managed by Certbot
➤   ssl_certificate /etc/letsencrypt/live/prag.webrtc.gallery/fullchain.pem;
➤      # managed by Certbot
➤   ssl_certificate_key /etc/letsencrypt/live/prag.webrtc.gallery/privkey.pem;
➤      # managed by Certbot
➤   include /etc/letsencrypt/options-ssl-nginx.conf;
➤      # managed by Certbot
➤   ssl_dhparam /etc/letsencrypt/ssl-dhparams.pem;
➤      # managed by Certbot
  }
➤ server {
➤
➤   if ($host = prag.webrtc.gallery) {
➤     return 301 https://$host$request_uri;
➤   } # managed by Certbot
➤
➤   listen 80;
➤   listen [::]:80;
➤
➤   server_name prag.webrtc.gallery;
➤   return 404; # managed by Certbot
➤ }
```

Certbot should have restarted Nginx for you, but there's no harm in restarting it manually yourself, just to be sure. Again, on Debian distributions, that command will be sudo systemctl restart nginx.

You should now be able to return to your browser and hit your domain from an https:// address—and again see the "Hello from Nginx" message in the browser window. If you try to reach the http:// address, that should also open to https://—care of the second server block that Certbot adds for redirecting HTTP requests on your domain to HTTPS.

We'll have some more work to do with the per-domain Nginx configuration file, but let's turn now to the task of deploying your app to the server a modern fancy-pants way, using git push and your own custom remote repository.

Deploying Your App with Git

If you've interacted with a Git repo hosted on GitHub or GitLab, you've already worked with remote repositories. Here you're going to set up a remote Git repository on your own server, which you can push to or pull from just like any other remote. All you need is the ability to SSH into your server, which should have Git installed (see the sidebar Installing and Configuring Git, Server Side, on page 207).

For anyone new to Git and looking for a complete education, check out Travis Swicegood's classic *Pragmatic Version Control Using Git [Swi08]*.

Installing and Configuring Git, Server Side

If your server doesn't have Git, you'll need to compile it or install it with your server's operating system's package manager. Aim to install Git version 2.28 or higher.

Once you've got Git installed on your server, you should configure your login with some essential values so that Git doesn't scream error messages at you. At a minimum, configure Git on your server by running a set of commands like this, much like you probably have done on your local development machine:

```
$ git config --global user.name "Your Name"
$ git config --global user.email "your.email@example.com"
$ git config --global init.defaultBranch "main"
```

Replace, of course, the values for user.name and user.email with your own name and email address. The init.defaultBranch property is new as of Git 2.28, and main is now widely preferred as the default branch name, including on GitHub and GitLab.

Initializing a Bare Repository on Your Server

No need to avert your eyes: a bare repository is a Git repo without a working tree, meaning you won't see your files listed in a bare repository. It's the same kind of thing you push your work to on GitHub or GitLab.

You can host bare repositories on your server and store them right in your home directory, perhaps in ~/repos/. It's convention to create each bare repo in a subdirectory whose name ends in .git, which gives a false sense that it's a file you're interacting with when you push or pull. To get started, you can run some commands like this—again using the values for your own custom domain or subdomain:

```
# On the server...
$ mkdir -p ~/repos/prag.webrtc.gallery.git
$ cd ~/repos/prag.webrtc.gallery.git
$ git init --bare
```

With your bare repo in place on the server, switch back to your project's directory on your development machine. Initialize Git if you've not already done so, and commit all your work. Then you can add your new bare repo as a remote. You will reach it via an SSH URL, which has the form ofs login@domain:repos/bare-repo-name.git. Name the remote something like live or deploy, if you'd like—especially if you've already got another repo called origin at GitHub or GitLab:

```
# On your local development machine...
$ git remote add deploy \
    ksrtc@prag.webrtc.gallery:repos/prag.webrtc.gallery.git
```

Again, be sure to use your own login, domain, and path to your bare repository.

You might be tempted to push at this point, but before you do, head back to your server to configure your bare repository to do a bit more than accept the contents of your repo when you push.

Setting up a Post-Receive Hook

While you can push your repository to your new remote immediately, take a few minutes first to set up a post-receive hook in Git on your server. Git supports numerous hooks, each of which can be triggered during the lifecycle of different Git operations, such as making commits or—in this case— receiving a push.[4]

On your server in your bare repository, change into the hooks subdirectory. You'll see a whole bunch of files, suffixed with .sample. Any executable script, written in pretty much any language you like, can be run as a Git hook, so long as the script's filename matches Git's naming conventions. With that in mind, you'll need to create a new hook called post-receive, which will be a shell script executed on the server after a push event. Be sure to change the permissions on the post-receive file to make it executable, too:

```
$ cd ~/repos/prag.webrtc.gallery.git/hooks
$ touch post-receive
$ chmod 755 post-receive
```

---

4. https://git-scm.com/book/en/v2/Customizing-Git-Git-Hooks

Again using vim or whatever command-line editor you prefer, open the post-receive file on the server and edit it to look like this example from the book's companion source code:

```
deploy/scripts/post-receive
#! /usr/bin/env zsh

WEB_ROOT=/var/www
APP_DOMAIN=prag.webrtc.gallery

GIT_REPO=$HOME/repos/$APP_DOMAIN.git
TMP_GIT_CLONE=/tmp/$APP_DOMAIN
DEPLOYED_APP=$WEB_ROOT/$APP_DOMAIN/app

git clone $GIT_REPO $TMP_GIT_CLONE
cd $TMP_GIT_CLONE
npm install
rm -rf $DEPLOYED_APP
mv $TMP_GIT_CLONE $DEPLOYED_APP
exit
```

Be sure to set both the WEB_ROOT and APP_DOMAIN variables to match what you've set up on your server and included in your Nginx per-domain configuration file.

After initializing a set of variables, the script clones the bare repository into a temporary location on your server, runs npm install to install the packages and dependencies referenced in package.json, and then removes the existing copy of the deployed app before moving the new copy into place. In short, it's all the commands you'd otherwise manually run to install your dependencies and move the app into place.

Testing Out Your Post-Receive Hook

With the script in place, return to your local machine and run git push deploy main, assuming you have used deploy as the name for your remote. You'll see output in your terminal similar to this:

```
$ git push deploy main
Enumerating objects: 22, done.
Counting objects: 100% (22/22), done.
Delta compression using up to 8 threads
Compressing objects: 100% (16/16), done.
Writing objects: 100% (22/22), 39.27 KiB | 13.09 MiB/s, done.
Total 22 (delta 2), reused 0 (delta 0), pack-reused 0
remote: Cloning into '/tmp/prag.webrtc.gallery'...
remote: done.
remote:
remote: added 72 packages, and audited 73 packages in 6s
remote:
```

```
remote: found 0 vulnerabilities
To prag.webrtc.gallery:repos/prag.webrtc.gallery.git
 * [new branch]      main -> main
```

Back on the server, look at your application's deployed location. You should see your app's files there, all ready to go.

The only thing the post-receive script doesn't do is start your app, the way that npm start has done for you when you're in development. But rather than manually change directories to your app and run npm start, let's automate that process with pm2, which will start and monitor your app—and even restart it automatically on fresh deploys.

Monitoring Your App with PM2

PM2 is a process manager written using Node.js.[5] To install it on your server, you'll need to run this command, possibly prefixed with sudo (see the sidebar Installing Global NPM Packages without Sudo, on page 210):

```
$ npm install -g pm2
```

Installing Global NPM Packages without Sudo

If you're like me, you probably get a little nervous thinking about invoking sudo along with a language's package manager. Who knows what evil lurks in those dependencies?

Fortunately, it's possible to configure npm to use a different, non-privileged location for storing global packages (the -g flag on npm install triggers a global installation).

For example, you can run:

```
$ mkdir ~/.npm-packages
$ npm config set prefix $HOME/.npm-packages
```

You'll then need to add the location $HOME/.npm-packages/bin to the $PATH variable in your shell's startup scripts, which are in a file like .bashrc or .zshrc. Adding these lines to the bottom of your startup file should do the trick:

```
# Add global npm packages to PATH
NPM_PACKAGES="$HOME/.npm-packages/bin"
export PATH="$NPM_PACKAGES:$PATH"
```

After you add those lines, don't forget either to exit and restart your terminal session or run source with the path to your startup file, something like source ~/.zshrc. Then you can install and execute global npm packages like PM2 without sudo.

---

5.   https://pm2.keymetrics.io/

Double check that PM2 is installed and available by asking for its version:

```
$ pm2 --version
5.2.0
```

Go ahead now and change directories to where your app has been deployed. In my case, that's /var/www/prag.webrtc.gallery/app. We'll pass the name webrtc to the PM2 --name option to make it a little easier to reference this specific app in subsequent PM2 commands:

```
$ cd /var/www/prag.webrtc.gallery/app
$ pm2 start ./scripts/start-server --name "webrtc" --watch
[PM2] Starting /var/www/prag.webrtc.gallery/app/scripts/start-server
[PM2] in fork_mode (1 instance)
[PM2] Done.

------------------------------------------------------------
| id | name    | mode  | ⊚ | status | cpu | memory  |
------------------------------------------------------------
| 0  | webrtc  | fork  | 0 | online | 0%  | 6.2mb   |
------------------------------------------------------------
```

Each row of boxes reveals information about your running apps. You can check on the status of your apps again later by running pm2 status. For more detailed information, use the name of your app with the show subcommand, like pm2 show webrtc. That will even tell you the Git commit hash for your app as currently deployed. Fancy!

With your app now running, try using curl with the -I flag on your server to hit the local URL http://127.0.0.1:3000 and print the response headers:

```
$ curl -I http://127.0.0.1:3000/
HTTP/1.1 200 OK
X-Powered-By: Express
Accept-Ranges: bytes
Cache-Control: public, max-age=0
Last-Modified: Thu, 21 Apr 2022 18:42:09 GMT
ETag: W/"4bc-1804d6e8398"
Content-Type: text/html; charset=UTF-8
Content-Length: 1212
Date: Sun, 22 May 2022 17:01:25 GMT
Connection: keep-alive
Keep-Alive: timeout=5
```

Great. Now that you've proved the app is running at http://127.0.0.1:3000/ on your server, we need to return to the per-domain Nginx configuration file for your app's domain and set up a reverse proxy.

Configuring Nginx for Reverse Proxies

The output from curl suggests that requests seem to be working fine. But to avoid forcing your users to pass high-numbered ports around with your chosen domain, like webrtc.example.com:3000, it's time to put Nginx to work as a reverse proxy.

Historically, web proxies work on the user's side, taking a web request and passing it along to a standard port on another web server. Nginx functions as a "reverse" proxy because it moves in the opposite direction on the server's side. That is, a reverse proxy processes requests coming in over HTTPS/port 443 on your domain and routes them on your server to a private address like localhost:3000.

Open up your per-domain configuration file inside of /etc/nginx/conf.d/. You can comment out the current location directive or modify it in place to look like this:

```
server {

  # Listening, SSL things (snipped)

  location / {
    proxy_pass              http://127.0.0.1:3000;
    proxy_http_version      1.1;
    proxy_set_header        Host $host;
    proxy_set_header        Upgrade $http_upgrade;
    proxy_set_header        Connection 'upgrade';
    proxy_cache_bypass      $http_upgrade;
  }
}
```

What all that does is take incoming requests on HTTPS/port 443 and pass them, using proxy_pass, to your app's localhost URL on port 3000. The proxy takes place over HTTP 1.1, with the host for the original request getting passed along, too. The last three lines, which set two headers (Upgrade and Connection) and bypass the proxy cache, make it possible for users to hit your signaling channel using the wss:// protocol over WebSockets.[6] Importantly, proxy_cache_bypass ensures that upgraded requests will not be served from a cache—which is precisely what you want for users interacting with your signaling channel.

Once you restart Nginx, all requests coming into your domain should now be passed along to your app running on port 3000. You can again use curl -I. But this time, reference the actual domain where you expect to be serving your app:

---

6.   http://nginx.org/en/docs/http/websocket.html

```
$ curl -I https://prag.webrtc.gallery/
HTTP/1.1 200 OK
Server: nginx
Date: Sun, 22 May 2022 17:30:52 GMT
Content-Type: text/html; charset=UTF-8
Content-Length: 1212
Connection: keep-alive
X-Powered-By: Express
Accept-Ranges: bytes
Cache-Control: public, max-age=0
Last-Modified: Thu, 21 Apr 2022 18:42:09 GMT
ETag: W/"4bc-1804d6e8398"
```

That doesn't look terribly impressive, given what you've actually accomplished, but the X-Powered-By: Express header proves you're now serving responses to reverse-proxied requests from your deployed WebRTC app.

You can now confidently open your web browser of choice, and hit your same public URL again (note that your browser might have cached your test index.html page, so you might need to do a hard refresh):

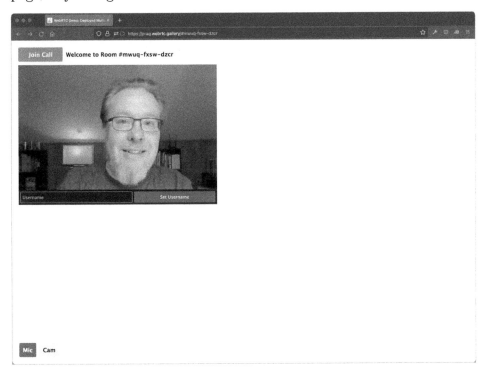

Go ahead now and try to establish a connection with yourself. If you have a phone or other device, try switching off Wi-Fi and joining the connection from your provider's cell network. Better yet, if you have any friends around to test this with you, send along your URL and have a nice little chat about how awesome you are for building and deploying the very app you're talking through!

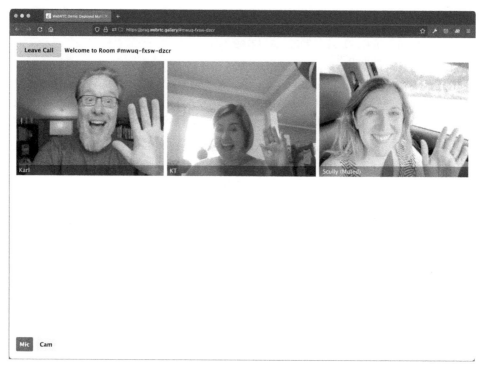

Fantastic. This is another major accomplishment. Once you're done with your call, come on back and we'll get to the last major remaining task in the book: setting up your own STUN/TURN server, so that your deployed app doesn't rely on a public STUN server to function.

Setting Up Your Own STUN/TURN Server

With your deployed app now working as expected, let's turn to one more task (pun intended): installing and configuring Coturn to power your own STUN/TURN server.[7] Coturn is the most prominent open-source STUN/TURN server, being descended from the TURN server project that accompanied the TURN

---

7.   https://github.com/coturn/coturn

specification, RFC 5766.[8] Adventurous readers might also want to have a look at the newer eturnal project,[9] but we'll stick with the tried-and-true Coturn project here.

Coturn packages are available for Debian[10] and Arch Linux.[11] The Coturn install guide will walk you through compiling Coturn for other distributions.[12]

On systems like Debian, Coturn's installation is no different from any other package. Take the time to first update and upgrade your system before installing Coturn:

```
$ sudo apt update
$ sudo apt upgrade
$ sudo apt install coturn
```

When you install Coturn, you'll likely see a few noteworthy lines appear in your terminal:

```
Adding group `turnserver' (GID 112) ...
Done.
Adding system user `turnserver' (UID 106) ...
Adding new user `turnserver' (UID 106) with group `turnserver' ...
Not creating home directory `/'.
# snip, snip
Processing triggers for ufw (0.36-7.1) ...
Rules updated for profile 'WWW Full'
Skipped reloading firewall
```

Coturn creates its own user and group, turnserver, to run the Coturn process. Debian will start the Coturn process automatically after a successful installation, care of systemctl. Check your own Linux distribution to see whether you need to start Coturn manually.

If you're running ufw, the Uncomplicated Firewall, you'll see post-installation lines about updates to the WWW Full profile. In addition to that, Coturn also adds its own profile in /etc/ufw/applications.d/turnserver. That file contains these lines:

```
[Turnserver]
title=Coturn Turnserver
description=Free open source implementation of TURN and STUN Server
ports=3478,3479,5349,5350,49152:65535/tcp| \
  3478,3479,5349,5350,49152:65535/udp
```

---

8. https://datatracker.ietf.org/doc/html/rfc5766
9. https://eturnal.net/
10. https://tracker.debian.org/pkg/coturn
11. https://archlinux.org/packages/community/x86_64/coturn/
12. https://github.com/coturn/coturn/blob/master/INSTALL

Those are the ports and ranges that must be open for Coturn to run properly under its default configuration. If you use iptables or another firewall, be sure to open access to the ports and ranges listed in the Turnserver group above. If your server runs ufw, you can allow everything in the Turnserver group by running:

```
$ sudo ufw allow "Turnserver"
```

Just to ensure that the new Turnserver rules are in effect, you can reload ufw manually by running sudo ufw reload.

Testing Out the Coturn STUN Server

You can test out your Coturn installation on your app running in development, just like you did with the public STUN servers in Referencing STUN Servers on the RTC Configuration Object, on page 200. Alternatively, you can open up the Trickle ICE test page, and enter your server's information. Don't forget to include both the stun protocol and the default STUN port, 3478. Here is an example of output returned by the STUN server I set up at a separate subdomain, coturn.webrtc.gallery:

At the bottom of that image are server-reflexive candidates, type srflx, indicating that the STUN server is doing its job. Note that that image was captured while I was connected to a VPN, not only to keep my actual IP address out of the screenshot—but also to show that STUN can work even in a properly configured VPN environment.

If you're seeing similar server-reflexive candidates in your test, congratulations! You've now got your STUN server configured and running properly. That will enable most users to successfully connect over your app. But to ensure the same for all users, including those behind restrictive firewalls, let's look at how to go about setting up Coturn to act as a TURN server.

Configuring and Enabling Coturn's TURN Server

Two steps are required to enable Coturn's TURN server functionality. First, the TURN server must be enabled in the system startup scripts that accompany Coturn. On Debian systems, you accomplish that by modifying the file at /etc/default/coturn and uncommenting the line that reads TURNSERVER_ENABLED=1, making the file look like this:

```
#
# Uncomment it if you want to have the turnserver running as
# an automatic system service daemon
#
TURNSERVER_ENABLED=1
```

The second step is to provide some kind of credential mechanism. STUN works reliably without any username or password. TURN servers are a different matter: unlike the simple requests and responses from STUN servers, TURN relays all peer-to-peer traffic, including user-media streams. That means that TURN servers can also intercept streaming media. So even if you're cool with skipping credentials (please don't be), browsers will refuse to connect to a TURN server unless you supply credentials for it.

Coturn supplies a number of different credential mechanisms, including long-term and time-limited credentials. It also offers database-backed solutions that are useful if you already have a means for providing user accounts and authentication. But that's not the case here.

Long-term credentials are easiest to set up, as they require nothing more than setting a user= option in the /etc/turnserver.conf file to a USERNAME:PASSWORD value. Go ahead and add one. While you're there, add a fingerprint line, which configures Coturn to play nicely with WebRTC by fingerprinting all STUN and TURN messages:

```
# in /etc/turnserver.conf
user=testingonly:topsecret
fingerprint
```

That sets a testingonly user with a password of topsecret. That will be enough to ensure your TURN server is running properly, but note that long-term credentials are terrible for security. Anyone clever enough to look at your WebRTC app's JavaScript file would see your long-term credentials, plain as day:

```
$self = {
  rtcConfig: {
    iceServers: [
      {
        urls: 'stun:coturn.webrtc.gallery:3478',
      },
      {
        urls: 'turn:coturn.webrtc.gallery:3478',
        username: 'testingonly',
        credential: 'topsecret'
      }
    ]
  },
  mediaConstraints: { audio: true, video: true }
}
```

That's all someone would need to run wild using your TURN server and hike up your bandwidth bill to a level that would eclipse the national debt. But for testing purposes, this is still enough to give things a spin. We'll improve this in a bit using your signaling channel in conjunction with the time-limited credentials mechanism in Coturn.

Testing Out the Coturn TURN Server

You can test out your Coturn TURN server on your app running in development, just like you did with the public STUN servers in Referencing STUN Servers on the RTC Configuration Object, on page 200, or you could again revisit the Trickle ICE test. In either case, be sure to prefix your URL with turn:, like turn:coturn .webrtc.gallery. This time, you're going to be looking for candidates of type relay. Here is a capture of the candidate portions of the Trickle ICE test page, showing the TURN server's relay candidates as well as the srflx candidates, from STUN:

Time	Component	Type	Foundation	Protocol Address	Port	Priority	Mid	MLine Index	Username Fragment
0.001	rtp host		0	udp 6361ec66-c953-4654-9f7f-2d055b3019b3 local	54192	126 | 32512 | 255	0	0	84a1f37d
0.001	rtp host		3	tcp 6361ec66-c953-4654-9f7f-2d055b3019b3 local	9	125 | 32704 | 255	0	0	84a1f37d
0.001	rtcp host		0	udp 6361ec66-c953-4654-9f7f-2d055b3019b3 local	51588	126 | 32512 | 254	0	0	84a1f37d
0.001	rtcp host		3	tcp 6361ec66-c953-4654-9f7f-2d055b3019b3 local	9	125 | 32704 | 254	0	0	84a1f37d
0.018	rtp srflx		1	udp 94.140.9.139	54192	100 | 32543 | 255	0	0	84a1f37d
0.055	rtp relay		2	udp 139.177.199.66	49204	5 | 32541 | 255	0	0	84a1f37d
0.056	rtcp srflx		1	udp 94.140.9.139	51588	100 | 32543 | 254	0	0	84a1f37d
0.091	rtcp relay		2	udp 139.177.199.66	55741	5 | 32541 | 254	0	0	84a1f37d
0.091						Done			

Excellent. That proves the TURN server is set up and doing its job. But let's take things a step further and set up time-limited credentials to better protect your TURN server.

Generating Time-Limited Credentials with your Signaling Server

Instead of relying on Coturn's long-term credentials (a hardcoded username and password that would end up exposed to the world), we can configure Coturn to use time-limited credentials. Those will require you to create a shared secret, which you'll need to include in the turnserver.conf file and also provide to your WebRTC app's server scripts.

Once your shared secret is set, we'll add logic to the signaling channel to push down automatically generated, time-limited credentials to users. Users already have to connect to the signaling channel, of course, so this won't do much at all to complicate the way a call is set up. Users will be completely unaware that all of this is happening.

Note that time-limited credentials will still be discoverable by people who might want to hijack your TURN server. But by restricting your credentials to be usable for only a certain period of time, your TURN server becomes a much less attractive target.

Open your turnserver.conf file again. At this point, you can remove or comment out the user=testingonly:topsecret line (or whatever username and password you chose for long-term credentials). In its place, add a new static-auth-secret line with a value of your choosing:

```
# in /etc/turnserver.conf
# user=testingonly:topsecret
static-auth-secret=someComplicatedSecretGoesHere
fingerprint
```

With that set, you can restart Coturn with sudo systemctl restart coturn or whatever command your operating system uses.

Back in your WebRTC app, like the one in the deploy/ directory, have a look at the server.js file. At the very top, server.js requires the Node.js crypto library,[13] which makes an appearance at the bottom of the file in a createCoturnCredentials() function:

```
deploy/server.js
// Load up necessary modules
const crypto = require('crypto');

// snip, snip...
```

_____

13. https://nodejs.org/api/crypto.html

```javascript
function createCoturnCredentials(expiry_in_hours, secret) {
  // JavaScript timestamps are in milliseconds, so divide by 1000
  const now = Math.round(Date.now() / 1000);
  const expiry = (now + (expiry_in_hours * 60 * 60)).toString();
  const hmac = crypto.createHmac('sha1', secret);
  hmac.setEncoding('base64');
  hmac.write(expiry);
  hmac.end();
  return {
    username: expiry,
    password: hmac.read()
  };
}
```

The createCoturnCredentials() function takes two arguments: expiry_in_hours, which is the number of hours the credentials should last once they've been generated, and secret, which will ultimately be the same value you set on static-auth-secret in turnserver.conf. The body of the function generates a Unix timestamp (the number of seconds since January 1, 1970) for the current time, to which it adds the number of seconds representing the hours set on expiry_in_hours. Note that JavaScript returns Unix timestamps in milliseconds, which is why it's necessary to divide by 1000. Without that division, your time-limited credentials would last for centuries.

The createHmac() crypto method then creates hash-based message authentication code (HMAC) based on a SHA-1 hash using the shared secret. Remember that this is all server-side logic, so that secret will not be exposed to end users. Two more methods, setEncoding() and write(), take the expiry value to create a hashed, base-64 time-limited password. The function then returns an object literal using the expiry as a username, and the hashed password.

It's that combination of the expiry-based username and hashed password that limits the time your credentials can be used: once the current Unix timestamp is greater than your set expiry, Coturn will no longer honor those credentials. Keep in mind that Coturn is able to make these same hashing calculations on its own end, which is why we're able to create this time-limited set of credentials without touching Coturn itself. It's pretty awesome.

Sharing Time-Limited Credentials with Users

Whether you agree that this crypto-wizardry is awesome or not, you'll nevertheless need to share the time-limited credentials with users. That happens inside of the anonymous callback attached to the signaling channel's connect event on your namespace:

```
deploy/server.js
mp_namespaces.on('connect', function(socket) {

  const namespace = socket.nsp;

➤  const expiry_in_hours = 4; // credentials last for four hours
➤  const secret = process.env.TURNSECRET || 'your secret goes here';
➤  const credentials = createCoturnCredentials(expiry_in_hours, secret);

  const peers = [];

  for (let peer of namespace.sockets.keys()) {
    peers.push(peer);
  }
  console.log(`   Socket namespace: ${namespace.name}`);

  // Send the array of connected-peer IDs and the TURN credentials
  // to the connecting peer
➤  socket.emit('connected peers', { peers, credentials });

  // Send the connecting peer ID to all connected peers
  socket.broadcast.emit('connected peer', socket.id);

  socket.on('signal', function({ recipient, sender, signal }) {
    socket.to(recipient).emit('signal', { recipient, sender, signal });
  });

  socket.on('disconnect', function() {
    namespace.emit('disconnected peer', socket.id);
  });

});
```

The expiry_in_hours value is set to 4 hours. Any value slightly longer than the longest call you can imagine on your app is a good one. Should the call last longer than the expiry, and should a user need to reconnect to the TURN server, but not the signaling server, the original credentials might no longer be valid. You could also, of course, write logic to generate and share credentials at shorter, regular intervals, if that's a concern or if you don't want to guess how long a call might last.

In addition to the expiry, the signaling channel needs access to the secret shared with Coturn. There are two ways to share your secret with your server.js file. One is to paste it in the 'your secret goes here' string. The other is to set on your server a TURNSECRET environment variable that contains the shared secret. The advantage to the environment variable is that you could conceivably automatically generate and frequently rotate the shared secret (say, every 24 hours), provided you script some mechanism to update the turnserver.conf file with it and restart Coturn programmatically. Additionally, by setting the TURNSECRET environment variable, there's no risk that your shared secret ends up on GitHub or GitLab, if you're keeping a copy of your repo on a public site like that.

However you choose to share your secret, the connected peers event now passes down an object containing both the peers array and the new credentials object literal. To make use of credentials, adjustments need to be made to the client-side JavaScript. Let's take a look at them, starting with a revised handleScConnectedPeers() callback:

deploy/www/js/main.js

```javascript
function handleScConnectedPeers({ peers, credentials }) {
  const ids = peers;
  console.log(`Connected peer IDs: ${ids.join(', ')}`);

  console.log(`TURN Credentials: ${JSON.stringify(credentials)}`);
  // addCredentialedTurnServer('turn:coturn.example.com:3478', credentials);

    for (let id of ids) {
      if (id === $self.id) continue;
      // be polite with already-connected peers
      initializePeer(id, true);
      establishCallFeatures(id);
    }
}
```

There, again, you see our old friend destructuring assignment pulling out the peers and credentials values the signaling server pushes down on the connected peers event. A quick assignment on ids keeps the rest of the function intact. The function logs the TURN credentials to the console, just in case you want to inspect them. Then there is a line that has been left commented out for you to add your TURN server URL, which will be appended to the $self.rtcConfig.ice-Servers array along with the credentials now coming down from the signaling channel. All of that happens right before users begin to build connections with any peers already connected on the call.

The addCredentialedTurnServer() function responsible for that looks like this:

deploy/www/js/main.js

```javascript
function addCredentialedTurnServer(server_string, { username, password }) {
  // Add TURN server and credentials to iceServers array
  $self.rtcConfig.iceServers.push({
    urls: server_string,
    username: username,
    password: password,
  });
}
```

All it's doing is taking your TURN server string, something like turn:coturn .example.com:3478, along with the time-limited credentials received via the signaling channel, and pushing those values onto the end of the iceServers array.

Go ahead once more and redeploy your app with those changes. Inspect the console output, or invite another group of friends to test out the app with you. If you really want to put the TURN server to work, you can modify your $self.rtcConfig object to include the iceTransportPolicy property set to 'relay'. If you opt to test that out, just remember to deploy your app again with that line removed or set to the default value of 'all'.[14]

Next Steps

The next steps are all up to you! You've developed a robust familiarity with WebRTC, and you've now even deployed your work to production. You've even set up your own STUN/TURN server with Coturn, and configured your app to use it securely in a production environment. That means you've now got the knowledge you need to begin building apps entirely of your own design. I hope you'll stay in touch on the book's forum,[15] and report any errors you might have found.[16]

---

14. https://developer.mozilla.org/en-US/docs/Web/API/RTCPeerConnection/RTCPeerConnection#parameters
15. https://forum.devtalk.com/t/programming-webrtc-pragprog/20203
16. https://forum.devtalk.com/c/community/pragprog-customers/85?tags=book-programming-webrtc

Connection Negotiation
in Legacy Browsers

Two types of fixes are required to achieve backward compatibility in browsers with older WebRTC implementations. The first type of fix involves manually creating offers and answers—a fix for the very oldest browsers that implement WebRTC. The second type of fix addresses glare. Glare is a state where both peers each have offers out and expect an answer from the other. But neither polite peers on older browsers nor impolite peers on any browser are capable of generating an answer when they have their own offers out. Glare represents a stalemate that cannot be recovered from—unless you step in with a fix yourself.

Implementing Backward-Compatible Fixes

All the examples in this appendix represent modifications to the signaling- and WebRTC-callback logic from a basic peer-to-peer application. To see these fixes as applied to a multipeer application, have a look at the example in the book's companion source code in the deploy/ directory.

Let's look at these fixes in source-code order.

Adding a New State Property

The first fix is to add a new isSuppressingInitialOffer state property to $self:

```
const $self = {
  rtcConfig: null,
  isPolite: false,
  isMakingOffer: false,
  isIgnoringOffer: false,
  isSettingRemoteAnswerPending: false,
```

```
    isSuppressingInitialOffer: false,
    mediaConstraints: { audio: true, video: true },
    mediaStream: new MediaStream(),
    mediaTracks: {},
    features: {
      audio: false
    }
};
```

That state, once set to true by logic you'll write below, will ensure that one peer does not produce an offer when connection negotiation starts over again.

Updating the negotiationneeded Callback

We can see that in the second fix, which is to update the handleRtcConnectionNegotiation() callback on the onnegotiationneeded event. The first thing to do is just exit the function when $self.isSuppressingInitialOffer evaluates to true.

The first set of adjustments is for very old browsers that do not create an offer when setLocalDescription() is called, as modern browsers do. A try/catch/finally statement will try the modern method. If it fails, the catch block manually creates the offer with createOffer(), and passes it into setLocalDescription(). Finally, however the offer was generated—automatically or manually—the finally block sends the local description over the signaling channel:

```
async function handleRtcConnectionNegotiation() {
  // peers suppressing initial offers should do nothing but exit
  if ($self.isSuppressingInitialOffer) return;

  // older browsers do not automatically create an offer when they
  // call `setLocalDescription`
  try {
    $self.isMakingOffer = true;
    await $peer.connection.setLocalDescription();
  } catch(e) {
    // manually create the offer with the automatic version fails
    const offer = await $peer.connection.createOffer();
    await $peer.connection.setLocalDescription(offer);
  } finally {
    // however the local description is set, send it over the
    // signaling channel
    sc.emit('signal',
      { description: $peer.connection.localDescription });
    $self.isMakingOffer = false;
  }
}
```

Adding a New Reset-and-Retry Function

The remaining adjustments are to how signals are processed with offers and answers. But before we get to those, write a brand-new function that handleSc-Signal() can call to reset and retry the peer connection under glare conditions:

```
function resetAndRetryConnection(peer) {

  // Reset all initial $self state-properties except isPolite
  $self.isMakingOffer = false;
  $self.isIgnoringOffer = false;
  $self.isSettingRemoteAnswerPending = false;

  // Set the offer-suppression state property to `true` for the
  // polite peer
  $self.isSuppressingInitialOffer = $self.isPolite;

  // Reset the peer and reestablish the call, which triggers
  // the `negotiationneeded` event and its callback again
  resetPeer(peer);
  establishCallFeatures(peer);

  // Inform the impolite peer to reset, too:
  if ($self.isPolite) {
    sc.emit('signal', { description: { type: '_reset' } });
  }

}
```

What that function does is reset the state properties on $self to false, with the exception of your new isSuppressingInitialOffer state. That now takes the value of isPolite—meaning that the polite peer from the original, failed attempt to connect will not create an offer but sit in silence and await an offer from the impolite peer.

The resetAndRetryConnection() function also calls the resetPeer() and establishCallFeatures() functions to start fresh. The call to establishCallFeatures() will trigger the negotiationneeded event anew, but only the non-suppressing peer can send out an offer now.

To wrap this function up, it will be the polite peer who determines that a glare state has been reached. So the polite peer will use the signaling channel to transmit a description of type '_reset' to the impolite peer. The reset type takes an underscore in the outside chance an official 'reset' description is added to the WebRTC spec in the future.

Updating the handleScSignal Callback

Now you can turn to the handleScSignal() function itself. First off, check for the new '_reset' description type. If that's what's come in, call resetAndRetryConnection() and exit the handleScSignal() function with a return statement:

```
async function handleScSignal({ description, candidate }) {
  if (description) {

➤     if (description.type === '_reset') {
➤       // Reset and retry the connection, and exit the `handleScSignal()`
➤       // function
➤       resetAndRetryConnection($peer);
➤       return;
➤     }

    // snip, snip

  }

  // snip, snip
}
```

Further down the function, you'll need to add a try/catch statement around the setRemoteDescription() call. Polite peers with modern browsers who have an offer out are able to roll back their own offer and accept the impolite peer's offer. But polite peers with older browsers will now put resetAndRetryConnection() in motion:

```
async function handleScSignal({ description, candidate }) {
  if (description) {

    // snip, snip

    if ($self.isIgnoringOffer) {
      return;
    }

    $self.isSettingRemoteAnswerPending = description.type === 'answer';
➤   try {
➤     // If this throws an error, as it will for polite peers on
➤     // older browsers, the connection must be reset and retried
➤     await $peer.connection.setRemoteDescription(description);
➤   } catch(e) {
➤     // Reset and retry the connection, and exit the `handleScSignal()`
➤     // function
➤     resetAndRetryConnection($peer);
➤     return;
➤   }
```

```
      $self.isSettingRemoteAnswerPending = false;

    // snip, snip

  }

  // snip, snip

}
```

That now completes all of the logic needed to recover from a glare state.

Your final adjustment to handleScSignal() is similar to the one that you made on handleRtcConnectionNegotiation(). This time, though, you will implement a try/catch/ finally statement to manually create an answer in response to an incoming offer, and send it over the signaling channel:

```
async function handleScSignal({ description, candidate }) {
  if (description) {

    // snip, snip

    $self.isSettingRemoteAnswerPending = false;

    if (description.type === 'offer') {
➤      try {
➤        await $peer.connection.setLocalDescription();
➤      } catch(e) {
➤        const answer = await $peer.connection.createAnswer();
➤        await $peer.connection.setLocalDescription(answer);
➤      } finally {
➤        sc.emit('signal',
➤          { description: $peer.connection.localDescription });
➤        $self.isSuppressingInitialOffer = false;
➤      }
    }

  } else if (candidate) {

  // snip, snip

  }

}
```

As one last fix for glare states, the finally block sets isSuppressingInitialOffer back to false. That will ensure polite peers who have been suppressing offers will be able to create additional offers, as can happen when additional media or a data channel gets added for the first time after a call has been established.

Bibliography

[Kel21]   Faraz K. Kelhini. *Modern Asynchronous JavaScript*. The Pragmatic Book-
            shelf, Dallas, TX, 2021.

[Swi08]   Travis Swicegood. *Pragmatic Version Control Using Git*. The Pragmatic
            Bookshelf, Dallas, TX, 2008.

Index

Thank you!

We hope you enjoyed this book and that you're already thinking about what you want to learn next. To help make that decision easier, we're offering you this gift.

Head on over to https://pragprog.com right now, and use the coupon code BUYANOTHER2024 to save 30% on your next ebook. Offer is void where prohibited or restricted. This offer does not apply to any edition of *The Pragmatic Programmer* ebook.

And if you'd like to share your own expertise with the world, why not propose a writing idea to us? After all, many of our best authors started off as our readers, just like you. With up to a 50% royalty, world-class editorial services, and a name you trust, there's nothing to lose. Visit https://pragprog.com/become-an-author/ today to learn more and to get started.

Thank you for your continued support. We hope to hear from you again soon!

The Pragmatic Bookshelf

SAVE 30%!
Use coupon code
BUYANOTHER2024

Rediscovering JavaScript

JavaScript is no longer to be feared or loathed—the world's most popular and ubiquitous language has evolved into a respectable language. Whether you're writing front-end applications or server-side code, the phenomenal features from ES6 and beyond—like the rest operator, generators, destructuring, object literals, arrow functions, modern classes, promises, async, and metaprogramming capabilities—will get you excited and eager to program with JavaScript. You've found the right book to get started quickly and dive deep into the essence of modern JavaScript. Learn practical tips to apply the elegant parts of the language and the gotchas to avoid.

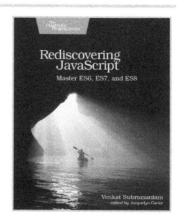

Venkat Subramaniam
(286 pages) ISBN: 9781680505467. $45.95
https://pragprog.com/book/ves6

Simplifying JavaScript

The best modern JavaScript is simple, readable, and predictable. Learn to write modern JavaScript not by memorizing a list of new syntax, but with practical examples of how syntax changes can make code more expressive. Starting from variable declarations that communicate intention clearly, see how modern principles can improve all parts of code. Incorporate ideas with curried functions, array methods, classes, and more to create code that does more with less while yielding fewer bugs.

Joe Morgan
(282 pages) ISBN: 9781680502886. $47.95
https://pragprog.com/book/es6tips

Node.js 8 the Right Way

Node.js is the platform of choice for creating modern
web services. This fast-paced book gets you up to speed
on server-side programming with Node.js 8, as you
develop real programs that are small, fast, low-profile,
and useful. Take JavaScript beyond the browser, explore dynamic language features, and embrace evented
programming. Harness the power of the event loop and
non-blocking I/O to create highly parallel microservices
and applications. This expanded and updated second
edition showcases the latest ECMAScript features,
current best practices, and modern development
techniques.

Jim R. Wilson
(334 pages) ISBN: 9781680501957. $33.95
https://pragprog.com/book/jwnode2

Async JavaScript

With the advent of HTML5, front-end MVC, and
Node.js, JavaScript is ubiquitous—and still messy.
This book will give you a solid foundation for managing
async tasks without losing your sanity in a tangle of
callbacks. It's a fast-paced guide to the most essential
techniques for dealing with async behavior, including
PubSub, evented models, and Promises. With these
tricks up your sleeve, you'll be better prepared to
manage the complexity of large web apps and deliver
responsive code.

Trevor Burnham
(104 pages) ISBN: 9781937785277. $17
https://pragprog.com/book/tbajs

Design and Build Great Web APIs

APIs are transforming the business world at an increasing pace. Gain the essential skills needed to quickly design, build, and deploy quality web APIs that are robust, reliable, and resilient. Go from initial design through prototyping and implementation to deployment of mission-critical APIs for your organization. Test, secure, and deploy your API with confidence and avoid the "release into production" panic. Tackle just about any API challenge with more than a dozen open-source utilities and common programming patterns you can apply right away.

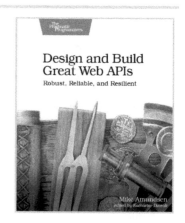

Mike Amundsen
(330 pages) ISBN: 9781680506808. $45.95
https://pragprog.com/book/maapis

Design It!

Don't engineer by coincidence—design it like you mean it! Grounded by fundamentals and filled with practical design methods, this is the perfect introduction to software architecture for programmers who are ready to grow their design skills. Ask the right stakeholders the right questions, explore design options, share your design decisions, and facilitate collaborative workshops that are fast, effective, and fun. Become a better programmer, leader, and designer. Use your new skills to lead your team in implementing software with the right capabilities—and develop awesome software!

Michael Keeling
(358 pages) ISBN: 9781680502091. $41.95
https://pragprog.com/book/mkdsa

The Way of the Web Tester

This book is for everyone who needs to test the web. As a tester, you'll automate your tests. As a developer, you'll build more robust solutions. And as a team, you'll gain a vocabulary and a means to coordinate how to write and organize automated tests for the web. Follow the testing pyramid and level up your skills in user interface testing, integration testing, and unit testing. Your new skills will free you up to do other, more important things while letting the computer do the one thing it's really good at: quickly running thousands of repetitive tasks.

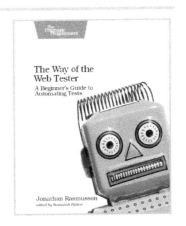

Jonathan Rasmusson
(256 pages) ISBN: 9781680501834. $29
https://pragprog.com/book/jrtest

Explore It!

Uncover surprises, risks, and potentially serious bugs with exploratory testing. Rather than designing all tests in advance, explorers design and execute small, rapid experiments, using what they learned from the last little experiment to inform the next. Learn essential skills of a senior explorer, including how to analyze software to discover key points of vulnerability, how to design experiments on the fly, how to hone your observation skills, and how to focus your efforts.

Elisabeth Hendrickson
(186 pages) ISBN: 9781937785024. $29
https://pragprog.com/book/ehxta

The Pragmatic Bookshelf

The Pragmatic Bookshelf features books written by professional developers for professional developers. The titles continue the well-known Pragmatic Programmer style and continue to garner awards and rave reviews. As development gets more and more difficult, the Pragmatic Programmers will be there with more titles and products to help you stay on top of your game.

Visit Us Online

This Book's Home Page
https://pragprog.com/book/ksrtc
Source code from this book, errata, and other resources. Come give us feedback, too!

Keep Up-to-Date
https://pragprog.com
Join our announcement mailing list (low volume) or follow us on Twitter @pragprog for new titles, sales, coupons, hot tips, and more.

New and Noteworthy
https://pragprog.com/news
Check out the latest Pragmatic developments, new titles, and other offerings.

Save on the ebook

Save on the ebook versions of this title. Owning the paper version of this book entitles you to purchase the electronic versions at a terrific discount.

PDFs are great for carrying around on your laptop—they are hyperlinked, have color, and are fully searchable. Most titles are also available for the iPhone and iPod touch, Amazon Kindle, and other popular e-book readers.

Send a copy of your receipt to support@pragprog.com and we'll provide you with a discount coupon.

Contact Us

Online Orders:	*https://pragprog.com/catalog*
Customer Service:	*support@pragprog.com*
International Rights:	*translations@pragprog.com*
Academic Use:	*academic@pragprog.com*
Write for Us:	*http://write-for-us.pragprog.com*